高职高专国际贸易专业（含金融方向）系列规划教材

国际贸易单证制作

GUOJIMAOYIDANZHENGZHIZUO

主　编　陈卫华　王红梅
副主编　姚晴霞　徐林　张英杰

西安交通大学出版社
XI'AN JIAOTONG UNIVERSITY PRESS
国家一级出版社
全国百佳图书出版单位

内 容 提 要

本教材以信用证结算方式为例，根据国际贸易单证工作流程，以任务为单元组织内容。

全书分三大篇：第一篇为国际贸易单证制作准备篇；第二篇为国际贸易单证制作基础篇，包括制作开证申请书、审证和改证、制作发票和装箱单、制作海运托运单和提单、制作报检单、制作原产地证书、制作出口收汇核销单和出口报关单、制作投保单和保险单、制作附属单据、制作汇票和审核出口单据，共十一个工作任务，每个工作任务包括学习目标、任务设计、任务描述、操作示范、必备知识、拓展知识和技能训练七个部分；第三篇为国际贸易单证制作综合实训篇，包括汇付、托收和信用证三大结算方式下的制单综合实训。

本教材既可作为高职高专院校国际经济与贸易、国际商务等专业的教材，也可作为外贸职员和其他涉外机构商务人员的业务参考书。

前 言

国际货物贸易本质上是一种单据贸易。进出口双方履行合同义务,必定涉及单据的交接。据报道,中国外贸标准化不足每年损失超万亿,这其中很大一部分是因为单据问题造成的。此外,在进出口贸易履约过程的每一环节,几乎都涉及单据的流转。任何环节单据出现差错,都会不同程度地影响到货物的进出口贸易,给进出口双方带来不便或损失。因此,单据工作对我国的进出口贸易至关重要。

国内现有的60多万家进出口企业,其中大多数是中小企业,出于节约人力资本的考虑,他们希望招聘能熟练、准确制作单据的大中专毕业生担任单证员。

鉴于上述原因,培养合格的单证员十分迫切。尽管合格单证员的培养,涉及诸多因素,但是一本好的单证制作教材是必不可少的。编者在吸取国内众多单证教材优点的基础上,以涉及单证较为全面的信用证结算方式为例,基本按照进出口贸易顺序(以出口为主),以工作任务为单元的模式进行编写。考虑到进口贸易和出口贸易中诸多单据的共性,鉴于篇幅的原因,进口单据本教材基本未涉及。读者在学好制作出口单据的基础上,即可掌握对进口单据的制作方法。此外,出于完整性的考虑,本教材在第三篇设计了汇付和托收结算方式下单据制作实训。

本教材共三大篇:第一篇为国际贸易单证制作准备篇,独立成章;第二篇为国际贸易单证制作基础篇,包括制作开证申请书、审证和改证、制作发票和装箱单、制作海运托运单和提单、制作报检单、制作原产地证书、制作出口收汇核销单和出口报关单、制作投保单和保险单、制作附属单据、制作汇票和审核出口单据,共11个工作任务;第三篇为国际贸易单证制作综合实训篇,包括汇付、托收和信用证三大结算方式下的单证制作训练。

本教材的核心部分是第二篇。每个工作任务包括学习目标、任务设计、任务描述、操作示范、必备知识、拓展知识和技能训练七个部分。通过完成"任务设计"中的任务,可以基本达到"学习目标"。完成任务时,需要注意事项在"任务描述"中有精炼的提示。至于如何完成任务,"操作示范"会娓娓道来,引导学生一步步完成任务。学生通过完成"技能训练"中的任务,可以巩固学习目标,达到举一反三之效。七个部分一环环紧紧相扣,浑然一体。

为了充分反映进出口贸易实际,本教材中的合同、单证一般都仿照真实文件的外观样式,涉及的当事人、交易内容等也均经过一定的处理。如所述内容同现实情况雷同,应属巧合,谨此说明。

南通纺织职业技术学院陈卫华担任本教材的主编,负责教材框架的制定、统稿和全书的校核工作,南京信息职业技术学院王红梅担任第二主编,苏州农业职业技术学院姚晴霞担任第一副主编,常州工程职业技术学院徐林担任第二副主编,秦皇岛职业技术学院张英杰担任第三副主编。本书编写的具体分工为:陈卫华(第一篇,第二篇的任务一、任务二、任务八、任务十一,第三篇的部分内容)、王红梅(第二篇的任务九,第三篇的部分内容)、姚晴霞(第二篇的任务三、任务十)、徐林(第二篇的任务五)、张英杰(第二篇的任务七)、郭静(第二篇的任务六)、梁磊(第二篇的任务四)。

在编写过程中,编者参考了众多国内外论著的研究成果,除注明出处的部分外,限于篇幅未能一一说明,在此一并向有关专家、学者、作者致以衷心的感谢。

编者水平有限,本教材在内容、编排和格式等方面难免有不妥之处,真诚欢迎同行和广大读者指正,以便再版时予以修正。

编　者
2011年7月于南通

目录

第一篇 国际贸易单证制作准备篇 / 1

第二篇 国际贸易单证制作基础篇——信用证下国际贸易单证制作 / 13

13	任务一	制作开证申请书
28	任务二	审核信用证和修改信用证
44	任务三	制作发票和装箱单
63	任务四	制作海运托运单和提单
85	任务五	制作报检单
105	任务六	制作原产地证
121	任务七	制作出口收汇核销单和出口货物报关单
144	任务八	制作投保单和保险单据
162	任务九	制作附属单据
173	任务十	制作汇票
181	任务十一	审核出口单据

第三篇　国际贸易单证制作综合实训篇 / 203

203	综合实训一　汇付（电汇）方式下单据制作
209	综合实训二　托收方式下单据制作
210	综合实训三　信用证方式下单据制作

参考文献 / 223

第一篇
国际贸易单证制作准备篇

在国内贸易活动中,贸易合同的履行,一般是通过商品与货币的交换来实现的。但在国际贸易活动中,买卖双方分处不同的国家或地区,距离遥远,在绝大多数情况下,商品与货币不能进行简单的交换,而是以国际贸易单证作为交换的手段,即出口方通过向进口方提交同出口货物有关的合格单据,来履行交货的合同义务,而进口方则必须在履行完付款或承兑义务后,才能获取出口方提供的同货物有关的合格单据,进而凭单据提取货物。因此,从某种意义上讲,国际货物贸易本质上是一种单据交易。

国际货物贸易中涉及的各个流转环节,都伴有相关单证的流转。各种单证都有自己特定的属性与功能,它们的签发、组合、流转、交换与应用,反映了合同的履行进程,也反映了买卖双方权利、责任、义务的发生、转移和终止。因此,为了顺利履行合同,每一个外贸人,都应当重视国际贸易单证工作,掌握单证制作的基本要求,正确、完整、及时、简洁、清晰地制作出各种合格单据。

一、国际贸易单证工作的作用和单证制作的基本要求

从贸易合同签订开始,直至货物装运、保险、检验检疫、保管、货款的支付以及进口方提货的整个过程,每个环节都需要相应的单证缮制、处理、交接和传递,以满足企业、运输、银行、保险、检验检疫、海关以及政府机关管理对外贸易等多方面的需要。因此,单证工作涉及面广、工作量大、时间性强,不仅需要涉外企业各部门之间相互协调配合,还需与众多管理部门发生联系,环环相扣。

(一)国际贸易单证工作的作用

1. 履行合同义务的必要环节

正如上文所言,国际货物贸易本质上是一种单据交易。因此,在国际货物贸易合同的履行中,出口方除了要按时、保质保量地提供满足合同要求的货物外,还需通过银行或径直向进口方提供合同或信用证要求的合格单据;对进口方而言,接受出口方提供的合格单据是其必须履行的合同义务,而且只有取得了单据,才有可能提取相应的货物。目前国际贸易中常用的三种贸易合同(FOB合同、CFR合同、CIF合同),均是以出口方提交与货物有关的单证作为其对交货义务履行的证明,而进口方的付款责任均是以收到出口方提交的合格单证为前提。

此外,对进出口双方而言,为了顺利履行合同,还必须准备合同或信用证要求以外的在各自国内流转的相关单证。根据进出口国家的对外贸易政策和合同的性质,进出口双方可能需要制作的单据包括托运单、投保单、报检单和进、出口报关单等。

2. 经营管理的重要环节

进出口企业的经营管理涉及方方面面,单证工作是其中的一个重要环节。从进出口签约开始,直至货款的收付,甚至贸易争端的解决等诸多业务管理上的问题,最后都会在单证工作上集

中反映出来。因此,单证工作是进出口企业经营管理中的一个十分重要的环节。

单证工作贯穿贸易的全过程,它不仅仅是单证的缮制和组合,还是妥善处理各种问题,解决好各种矛盾,从而确保安全、及时、足额收汇,使企业的经营成果得到可靠的保证。

3. 政策性很强的涉外工作

国际贸易单证工作是一项政策性很强的涉外工作。它一方面要体现国家的对外政策,遵守国家有关外贸的各项法律、法规;另一方面还要符合国际惯例,如信用证业务中单据的制作应符合《跟单信用证统一惯例(1993年修订本)》(以下简称 UCP600)和《国际标准银行实务》(以下简称 ISBP681)的相关规定,跟单托收项下单据的制作应符合《托收统一规则》(以下简称 URC522)的规定。

4. 展示企业形象、体现企业实力的窗口

一般而言,不管是国内贸易还是国际贸易,企业都愿意同形象好、实力强的对手进行交易。由于国际贸易中的交易双方分处两个不同的国家或地区,相互间的了解将更多地通过国际贸易单据作为媒介。规范、整洁、清晰的单证,能展现企业高品位的业务质量,为企业塑造良好的形象,有利于业务的开展。

5. 国际结算的依据

UCP600 第 5 款规定:"银行处理的是单据,而不是单据可能涉及的货物、服务或履约行为。"第 7 款关于开证行的责任,则规定:"只要规定的单据提交指定银行或开证行,并且构成相符交单,则开证行必须承付。"在信用证结算方式下,开证行或出口方凭以向进口方收取货款的,不是实际货物而是符合信用证要求的单据。汇付中的货到付款和托收结算方式下,出口方也是凭符合合同要求的单据收款。

国际贸易的发展,使得国际贸易货物"单据化",即可以把对货物的相关要求,通过提交相关的单据来体现。海运事业的发展,使得部分海运单证已从一般的货物收据,变为可以转让的货物所有权凭证,如海运提单的转让即意味着提单代表的货物所有权的转让。卖方交单意味着交付了货物;而买方付款后取得单据,则代表着买到了商品。"商品单据化、单据商品化"已成为现代国际货物贸易的特点。买卖双方的货款收付不再以货物为依据,而是以单据为依据。

(二)国际贸易单证制作的基本要求

国际贸易中几乎所有环节的具体操作都与单证密切相关,单证的质量如何直接决定了合同是否能顺利履行,同时也从侧面反映出外贸企业的形象及从业人员的素质。特别是结汇单据的缮制质量,关系到卖方能否安全迅速收汇和买方能否及时收货。结汇单证制作技术性强,不能随意缮制,必须符合相关的单据制作依据,同时符合商业习惯和实际需要。各种结汇单证的制作,原则上应该满足"五要求",即"正确、完整、及时、简明、整洁"。

1. 结汇单据缮制的依据

制作和审核出口结汇单据的主要依据是贸易合同、信用证、有关商品的原始资料、国际贸易惯例和国内管理规定等。在实际业务中,要根据支付方式注意以下问题:

(1)在信用证支付方式下,制单和审单的主要依据是信用证、有关商品的原始资料、UCP600、ISBP681 和国内相关规定。信用证取代贸易合同成为制单和审单的首要依据。

(2)在托收结算方式下,制单和审单的主要依据是贸易合同、有关商品的原始资料、URC522 和国内相关规定。其中贸易合同是制单和审单的首要依据。

(3)在汇付结算方式下,制单和审单的主要依据是贸易合同、有关商品的原始资料和国内相关规定。其中贸易合同是制单和审单的首要依据。

有关商品的原始资料,一般为生产单位提供的交货单、货物出厂装箱单等单据,包括货物具体数量、重量、规格、尺码等。

(4)符合进口国对单据或进口货物的特殊规定。目前,有不少国家对进口的单据都有特殊的规定。如果制作单据时,疏忽进口国的这些规定,就很有可能遭到进口国当局的拒绝接受。

2.单据制作的基本要求

(1)正确。单证的制作必须正确,这是进出口业务各环节顺利进行和安全收汇的前提。单证如果不正确,就会影响业务的顺利进行。比如,单证与货物不符,会影响货物按时清关,进而影响其他业务环节的正常进行。另外,无论是托收还是信用证结算方式,买方和银行都要严格审核单据,如果单据不正确,即使卖方提交的货物合格,买方和银行都有拒付货款的权利。因此,在制单工作的各项要求中,正确是最重要的一条。

正确制作单据,必须满足两方面的要求:一是要求各种单据必须做到"三相符",即"单证相符"、"单单相符"和"单货相符";二是要求符合相关的国际惯例和进口国对单据或进口货物的特殊规定,这一点在前面已经提及,以下仅对"三相符"原则做一下具体阐述。

①"单证相符"是指单据的缮制必须严格按照信用证的要求办理:一是单据的有关规定与信用证不应矛盾;二是所有单据与信用证表面一致。贯彻"单证相符"的原则,并不意味着必须按照信用证的原文制作,而是要正确理解信用证的条款,按照信用证条款的文意制作,具体的制作要求,将在以下各个章节中具体阐述。

②"单单相符"是指同一个信用证项下要求提供的各种单据之间的相关内容彼此不矛盾,尤其是各种单据的签发日期既要符合国际惯例,又要符合贸易实际。

③"单货相符"是指单据上记载的内容必须与实际货物内容相符。一方面,在信用证业务中,尽管银行仅凭单据付款,而不管货物的实际交付情况,但信用证是依据贸易合同开立的,单货不一致,极易造成所交货物与合同不相符合,从而导致违约情况的发生。另一方面,单货不一致也会在检验、报关时遇到麻烦。

(2)完整。单据制作的完整性要求包括三个方面,即单据的种类要齐全、单证的内容要完整、单据的份数要完整。

①单据的种类要齐全。出口方应按照合同或信用证要求的单证种类,提供齐全的单证,不能有遗漏,否则将影响出口方的及时收汇和进口方的利益。比如,FOB或CFR贸易术语项下,出口方应及时提供装船通知,以便于进口方及时投保。对可以享受普惠制的出口产品,即使合同和信用证未要求提交普惠制产地证,出口方也应该提供该种产地证,否则,进口国海关不给予关税的减免。

②单证的内容要完整。任何单证都有它的特定作用,这种作用是通过单证本身的特定内容即格式、项目、文字、签章等来体现的。如果格式使用不当、项目遗漏、文理不通、签章不全,就不能构成有效文件,也就不能为银行接受。商业汇票、提单、保险单、产地证等,必须签署后才有效,否则将是无效的单据,银行或进口方可以拒绝接受。某些有抬头的提单和保险单,只有经过背书后才能实现货物所有权和索赔权的转移,如果遗漏背书,在汇付结算方式下(托收或信用证项下,有银行对单据把关),将给进口方的及时提货或向保险公司的索赔造成麻烦。

③单证份数要完整。各类单证的份数应当齐备,不可短缺。信用证要求提供的一式多份的发票、装箱单等单据,必须至少提供一份正本,其余的可提供副本。而对于非信用证结算的出口合同中要求提供的一式多份的发票、装箱单等单据,最好进一步明确一式多份的含义,避免在实

际提供单据时,因理解不同引发争议。此外,产地证、提单、保险单等单据,不同的出证机构出具的份数,可能有差异,在实务中,应结合信用证或合同的要求,选择满足份数要求的机构签发。

(3)及时。单证工作的时间性很强,各种单据均有一个合理的出单日期。单证制作的及时性包括以下两方面的要求:

①及时制单。国际货物贸易的流转环节,伴随着相关单据的流转,单证是在各个不同的环节缮制的,单证制作的及时性直接影响到货物托运工作的顺利进展和各个相关部门的有效衔接。因此,一笔业务的整套单据中,各种单据的出单日期必须合理、有序,即每一种单据的出单日期必须既符合国际贸易惯例、商业习惯和要求,又不能超出信用证或合同规定的有效期。通常提单日期是确定各种单据日期的关键。一般情况下,各种单据的出具日期的先后顺序,可以按以下原则掌握:

a. 发票日期应在各单据日期之首;

b. 装箱单、重量单的签发日期应等于或迟于发票日期,但必须在提单日之前;

c. 提单日期不得晚于信用证或合同规定的最迟装运期,但也不应该早于规定的最早装运期;

d. 保险单的签发日期应早于或等于提单日期,但也不能早于发票日期;

e. 产地证的签发日期不早于发票日期,也不迟于提单日期;

f. 商检证日期不晚于提单日期,但也不能过分早于提单日期,尤其是鲜货、容易变质的商品,以免买方因检验时间太早而怀疑商品质量与检验结果不符;

g. 受益人证明、装船通知日期等于或晚于提单日期;

h. 船公司证明应早于或等于提单日期;

i. 汇票日期应晚于提单、发票等其他单据,但不能晚于信用证规定的效期和交单期,实务中通常以按提单日或晚于提单日一、两天作为汇票的出票日。

②及时交单。不管是汇付、托收还是信用证结算方式,出口方都应当养成及时交单的习惯。货到付款、托收方式下的及时交单,便于出口方尽早收回货款。信用证项下的及时交单是指向银行交单的日期不能超过信用证规定的交单有效期。有些信用证除了规定有效期外,还另外规定了交单期。因此,出口方的交单期必须同时满足信用证有效期和交单期的规定,否则银行将拒付货款。如果信用证只规定了有效期,未规定交单期,按 UCP600 第 14 条 C 款规定:"……则须由受益人或其代表在不迟于本惯例所指的发运日之后的 21 个日历日内交单,但是在任何情况下都不得迟于信用证的截止日"。

(4)简明。单证的简明要求单证的内容应力求简化,力戒繁琐,各项内容布局要合理,层次分明,重点项目突出。

(5)整洁。单据的整洁一方面要求单据的表面清洁、美观、大方,单据中的各项内容清楚、易认,各项内容的记载简洁、明了;另一方面要求单证格式的设计和缮制,力求标准化和规范化,单证内容的排列要行次整齐、字迹清晰,重点项目要突出显目。因此,在实际制作单据时,应当谨慎细致,尽量减少甚至不出现差错涂改现象。出现涂改的,应加盖校对章;有些单据的栏目不允许涂改,缮制时应特别注意。

二、国际贸易单证流转的一般程序

(一)出口单证流转的一般程序

一个完整的出口交易过程,包括出口前的准备工作、交易磋商、签订合同及履行合同。出口方履约的过程也是出口单证流转的过程,其程序如图 1-1 所示。不同的贸易条件、不同的结算

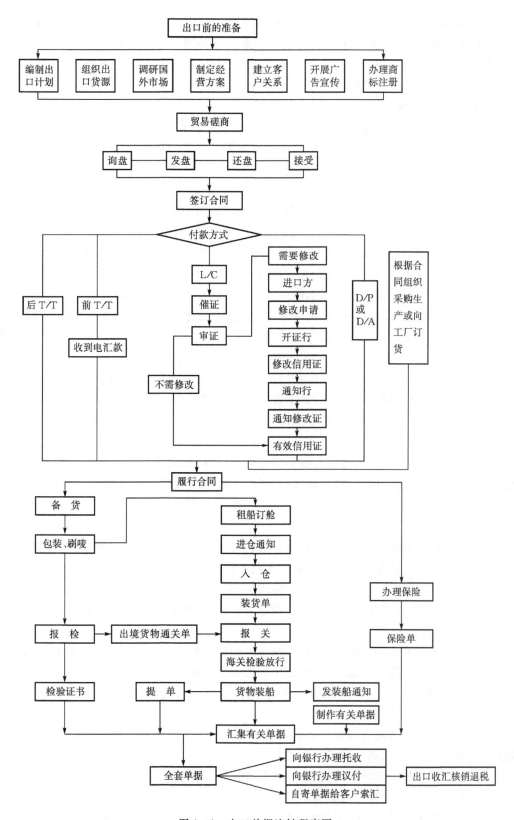

图1-1　出口单据流转程序图

方式,出口合同履行过程中包括的工作环节和手续是不一样的。对出口方而言,采用 CIF 贸易术语和信用证结算方式时,履行的义务是较多的,相应地流转的单证也较多,而采用其他贸易术语和结算方式时,义务相对较少,流转的单证也较少。以下结合三种常用的结算方式,分析履行出口合同过程中单据的流转情况。

1. 交易磋商和合同签订

出口方通过和目标客户交易磋商,就合同条款达成一致意见后,签订书面合同。合同通常一式两份,出口方签署后将合同寄给进口方,进口方签署后回寄一份给出口方,这样进出口双方各执一份有双方签字的合同,履行各自的合同义务。

2. 催证、审证和改证

对于汇付和托收结算方式,出口方在合同签订后,应当按照合同的要求组织采购、生产或向国内工厂订货;而对于信用证结算方式,则还可能涉及催证、审证和改证工作。

催开信用证是指出口方催促进口方及时办理开立信用证手续并将信用证送达出口方,以便出口方及时装运货物出口,履行合同义务。在信用证结算方式下,按时开证是进口方履行合同应尽的义务。但是在实际业务中经常遇到国外进口方拖延开证或者在市场行情发生变化或资金发生短缺的情况时,故意不开证。因此,出口方应催促进口方迅速依照合同办理开证手续,必要时,可请驻外机构或有关银行协助代为催证。如经催证,进口方仍不开证,可向进口方提出"保留索赔权"的声明;反之,如不及时催证,进口方到时可借此推卸责任。

经催证出口方收到信用证后,应和通知行一起,根据出口合同和 UCP600 等贸易惯例,审查信用证是否存在与合同不符的条款,以及不能接受或难以办到的条款。通知行着重审核信用证的真实性,以及开证行的政治背景、资信能力、付款能力和索汇等方面的内容;出口方着重审核信用证的性质和内容是否与出口合同一致。

信用证经过审核之后,发现确实存在不符合当地政策、影响合同履行和安全收汇等问题时,必须及时要求进口方通过开证行进行修改,并坚持在收到修改信用证通知并经确认无误后才能发货,以免造成损失。

3. 备货与报检

为了按时、保质、保量交付约定的货物,在订立合同或收到有效信用证后,出口方必须及时落实货源,备妥应交的货物,并做好出口货物的报检工作。

(1)备货。备货工作主要包括按合同或信用证的要求安排生产加工或仓储部门组织货源和催交货物,核实货物的加工、整理、包装或刷唛情况,对应交的货物进行验收和清点。在备货工作中,应注意以下事项:

①发运货物的时间。为了保证按时交货,应根据合同和信用证对装运期的规定,并结合船期安排,做好供货工作,使船货衔接好,以防止出现船等货或货等船的情况。

②货物的品质或规格。交付货物的品质或规格,必须符合合同的要求,如果不符,应进行筛选、加工和整理,直至符合合同的要求。

③货物的数量。必须按合同数量备货,且应留有余地,以备必要时作为调换之用,如合同和信用证允许溢短装,应考虑溢短装部分的需要。

④货物的包装。按约定的条件包装,核实包装是否适合长途运输和保护商品的要求,如发现包装不良或有破损,应及时修整或调换。

⑤在包装的明显部位,应按约定的唛头式样刷制唛头,同时应注意包装上的其他标志是否符合要求。

(2)报检。凡国家规定必须办理法定检验的出口货物和按约定条件必须向商检机构办理检验的,在备妥货物后,应向商品检验检疫机构申报检验检疫。当货物经检验合格后,商检机构签发出境货物通关单或其他检验合格证,凭出境货物通关单,海关放行出口货物。

申请报检时,应提供的单证包括出境货物报检单和随附单证,其中随附单证包括合同、发票、装箱单和其他单证。出口企业应当在检验证规定的有效期内,将货物装运出口,如在规定的有效期内不能装运出口,应向商检机构申请展期,并由商检机构进行复检,复检合格后,才准予出口。

4. 租船订舱

合同采用 CIF、CFR 贸易术语,出口方必须负责与承运人订立运输合同。在实际业务中,出口方一般委托专业性较强的货运代理公司办理出口货物运输事宜。托运时,托运人填写出口货物托运单委托货代公司代为订舱。出口货物托运单又称订舱委托书(booking note),是出口企业向货代公司提供的托运货物的必要文件,也是货代公司向船公司订舱配载的依据。托运单一式数份,其中包括后续出口报关时必须提交的装货单。货代公司签发装货单并退还给出口方,出口方凭装货单到海关办理出口报关手续。

5. 办理保险

合同采用 CIF 贸易术语,出口方一般要在装运前作为投保人向保险公司办理货物运输险。出口方填写投保单,并提交发票和合同(信用证),保险公司据此缮制和签发保险单。作为保险凭证的保险单据的出单日期不应迟于装运日期。

6. 出口报关

所有进出国境的货物,必须经由设立海关的港口、车站、国际航空站进出。进出口货物收发货人或其代理人向海关申报货物的进出口,经海关查验放行后,货物才可以提取或装运出口。出口货物应在运输工具离境的 24 小时前办理出口报关手续,需要的报关单证有:出口货物报关单、发票、箱单、装货单、出口收汇核销单。其他单据,如各类许可证件、出境货物通关单、代理报关委托书(自理报关不需要)、加工贸易登记手册(仅对加工贸易)等则根据具体情况提交。海关检查各种出口报关单据和货物后,在装货单上加盖海关"放行章",出口货物发货人凭此通知承运人装船。

7. 货物装运

出口方将盖有海关"放行章"的装货单交承运人,承运人凭此将出口货物装运。装船完毕,船长或大副根据装货实际情况签发大副收据(mate's receipt),交出口方。出口方凭此向船公司或其代理换取海运提单。海运提单既是物权凭证,又是出口结汇单据,出口方必须仔细检查各项目是否符合合同或信用证的要求。货物装运后,出口方应根据合同或信用证的规定,及时给进口方发送装运通知(shipping advice),以便进口方准备付款、赎单,办理进口报关和接货手续。如为CFR、FOB 合同,由买方自办保险,则及时发出装运通知尤为重要。

8. 制作并汇集结汇单据,办理结汇

出口货物装运后,出口方汇集发票、装箱单、检验证明、保险单、提单等结汇单据,并制作合同或信用证要求的其他结汇单据,根据不同的结算方式,进行后续的处理:汇付结算方式下,则自寄单据给进口方;托收结算方式下,则将全套单据送托收行办理托收;信用证结算方式下,则将全套单据送议付行议付。

9. 出口收汇核销和出口退税

出口收汇核销制度是国家加强出口收汇管理,确保国家外汇收入,防止外汇流失的一项重要措施。出口单位应事先从外汇管理部门领取有顺序编号的核销单如实填写。在出口报关时,海关在审核出口报关单和核销单的内容和核销编号完全一致后,海关在专为出口核销用的报关单和核销单上盖"验讫"章。出口企业结汇后,凭核销单和银行提供的出口收汇核销专用联的结汇水单或收账通知及其他规定的单据,到国家外汇管理部门办理核销手续。国家外汇管理部门按规定办理核销后,在核销单上加盖"已核销"章,并将其中的出口退税专用联退给出口企业。

符合国家规定范围的出口货物结汇以后,出口企业可以向主管退税业务的税务机关办理出口货物在生产、加工、出口等环节上的增值税、消费税的免征或退还。办理出口退税的主要单证是出口货物报关单(出口退税专用联)、出口收汇核销单(出口退税专用联)、增值税专用发票、出口发票。

10. 单证保管

出口方在交单结汇后,应将一套完整的副本单据进行归档备查。

(二)进口单证流转的一般程序

不同的结算方式和不同的贸易术语,进口流程稍有差异,相应地,单证的流转也同出口贸易有所不同,其程序图见图1-2。总体来说,在国际贸易中,进口方制作单据的工作量比出口方小。

1. 申请开证或预付货款

进口合同签好后,进口方应根据合同中确定的结算方式,履行相应的合同义务。若是预付货款结算方式,则应按照合同中约定的汇款时间,向往来银行申请汇款;若是信用证结算方式,则应根据合同制作"开立信用证申请书",并备好开证必需的其他单证,及时向往来银行申请开证。信用证的内容以合同为依据,对于品质、数量、包装、价格、运输和保险等条件及各种所需单证等项目,要与合同条款一致。经开证行开出的信用证,如由于各种原因需要修改,则还需通过原来的开证行及时进行修改,以便出口方根据有效的信用证及时出货制单。

2. 安排运输

进口方是否需要安排运输,取决于贸易术语。按FOB成交的合同,应由进口方负责安排运输。租船订舱工作应按合同或信用证的规定及时办理,进口方可委托货运代理公司办理,也可直接向经营远洋运输的公司或其他运输机构办理。办妥运输手续后,进口方应按规定的期限及时将船名及船期通知出口方,以方便出口方备货装运。如某些情况下,进口方租船订舱存在困难,可委托出口方代办。

3. 办理保险

按FOB、CFR成交的合同,由进口方办理货物运输保险。进口方在收到出口方的装运通知后,应根据船名、提单号、开船日期、货物数量、装运港、目的港等内容,填写投保单,随附发票和合同(信用证)送交保险公司,办理保险手续。为了简化手续,防止货物在装运后因信息传递不及时而发生漏保或来不及投保的情况,进口方也可以事先与保险公司签订"预约保险合同",对承保货物的范围、险别、费率、责任、适用条款以及赔付办法等,做出具体规定。这样,预约保险合同的每批进口商品一经起运,保险公司即自动按预约保险合同所订立的条件承保。但进口方应及时将收到的国外装运通知送交保险公司,并按约定办法缴纳保险费。

4. 付款赎单

出口方的单据送达后,应根据不同的结算方式,进行不同的处理。在信用证结算方式下,开证行收到出口方通过出口地银行提交的全套出口单据后,审单以确定付款责任。若"单证一致"、"单单一致",即对外付款或承兑,同时,通知进口方前来付款赎单或承兑赎单。但目前在我国银行的贸易实务中,开证行收到信用证项下的单据后,首先应征求进口方对单据的审核意见,在进

第一篇 国际贸易单证制作准备篇

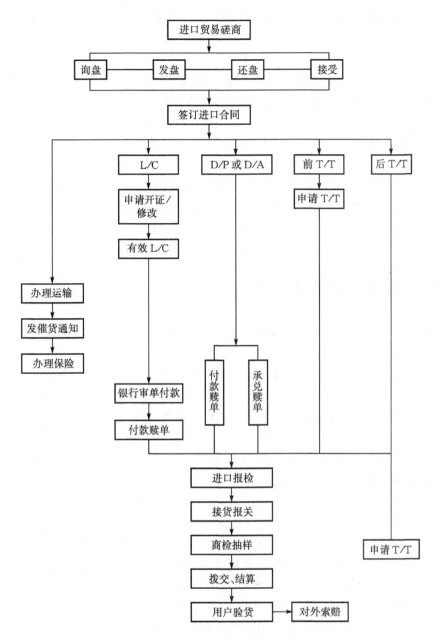

图 1-2 进口单据流转程序图

口方同意付款后,再对外付款。若经审单,发现单证不符或单单不符的情况,开证行可以通过发出拒付电文来解除自己的付款义务。随后,进口方可同出口方进行磋商,作出其他适当的处理。

托收结算方式下,进口方收到代收行的付款或承兑赎单通知后,应及时对合格单据付款后赎单;货到付款结算方式下,进口方收到单据后,应按合同规定的付款时间,及时申请汇款。

5. 报检

需要报检的进口货物包括法定检验的进口货物和合同约定的进口货物。法定检验检疫的进口货物到货后,进口方必须向卸货口岸或到达站的国家出入境检验检疫局分支机构办理登记。国家出入境检验检疫局在报关单据上加盖"已接受登记"的印章,海关凭此验放。

凡不属于法定检验的进口货物,买卖合同规定由检验检疫机构检验检疫的,依照法定检验商品办理。

6.报关

货物到进口港后,进口方或其代理人填写进口货物报关单,并随附商业发票、装箱单、提货单及其他视具体情况可能需要提交的单证,如进口许可证、入境货物通关单、原产地证等单据,向海关报关。海关接受申报后进行货、证查验,并核定进口税额,进口方付清关税,以及进口海关代征的增值税、消费税后,即可持盖有海关放行章的提货单提取货物。

7.验收和索赔

进口货物都要认真验收,如发现品质、数量、包装等有问题应及时取得有效的检验证书,以便向有关责任方提出索赔或采取其他救济措施。对外索赔时,进口方应加强同国家出入境检验检疫机构的配合,认真检验,鉴定货损情况,查明原因,分清责任。一般根据造成损失原因的不同,进口索赔的对象有出口方、承运人或保险公司。

三、国际贸易单证员的岗位要求

国际贸易单证员是指在进出口贸易履约过程中,主要从事审证、订舱、报检、报关、投保、结汇等业务环节的单证办理和制作工作的操作型国际贸易从业人员。

国际贸易单证工作是国际贸易从业人员必须掌握的基础性工作,是开展国际贸易业务工作的基础。在国际贸易企业中,国际贸易单证员对企业顺利实现收付汇起到举足轻重的作用。

一名合格的国际贸易单证员应当具有较高的职业素质、较强的职业能力和较广的专业知识。

1.国际贸易单证员的职业素质要求

国际贸易单证员应当具备守法意识、诚信品质、责任意识、敬业精神、团队精神等职业素质,如图1-3所示。

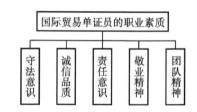

图1-3 国际贸易单证员的职业素质要求

在国际贸易单证工作中,国际贸易单证员应当树立严守法律的意识,这是最重要的和最首要的职业素质,应将严格遵守《中华人民共和国对外贸易法》及其他相关法律、法规作为日常的行为规范。此外,在实际工作中,不管对国内客户还是对国外客户,都应当诚实守信、实事求是地处理相关业务。单证工作几乎涉及国际贸易的每一个流转环节,单证质量直接关系到出口方是否能安全收汇。因此,国际贸易单证员应具有极强的责任感,工作一丝不苟,关注每一个细节,保质保量地制好每一份单据。同时国际贸易单证员应当培养良好的团队合作意识,与同事之间精诚合作。单证工作量大任务重,且时间要求较高,因此单证员应当具备敬业精神,吃苦耐劳。

2.国际贸易单证员的职业能力要求

国际贸易单证员应具备英语读写能力、开证审证能力、单证制作能力、单证审核能力、人际沟通能力,见图1-4。

(1)英语读写能力。进出口贸易合同、信用证、结汇单证等的制作等,除了极个别情况外,都需要用英语。因此,单证员必须具有较好的英语基础和较高的英语读写能力。

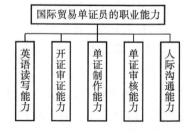

图1-4 国际贸易单证员的职业能力要求

(2)开证审证能力。在信用证结算方式下,国际贸易单证员应能够根据进出口合同正确制作开证申请书,熟练审核信用证。在汇付和托收结算方式下,应能准确制作汇款申请书和托收申请书。

(3)单证制作能力。国际货物贸易本质上是一种单据交易,交易的每一个环节都伴随着单据的流转,正确、及时制作相关单据,是国际贸易单证员必备的最基本的职业能力。相关单证包括信用证、汇付、托收结算方式下的订舱单证、报检单证、报关单证、投保单证和结汇单证等。

(4)单证审核能力。国际贸易单证员应能根据信用证或合同的要求准确地审核订舱单证、报检单证、报关单证和结汇单证等。

(5)人际沟通能力。国际贸易业务涉及的部门多,单证员一方面需要同企业本身的相关部门进行沟通,另一方面可能还要同货代公司、商检机构、外经委、保险公司、外汇银行、外汇管理局、海关、税务机关等进行沟通。因此,建立好同这些单位的相关人员的业务关系,将有助于高效地办理单证业务。

3.国际贸易单证员的专业知识要求

(1)国际贸易基础知识。国际贸易单证员应熟悉进、出口业务流程,掌握商品品质规定、国际货物包装、价格术语、运输、保险、结算方式、检验、索赔、不可抗力和仲裁等国际贸易相关基础知识。

(2)国际结算知识。国际贸易单证员应熟悉汇票、本票、支票等结算工具,掌握信用证、汇付和托收的操作流程。

(3)国际结算单证知识。国际贸易单证员应熟悉国际贸易单证工作流程,掌握订舱单证、报检单证、报关单证、投保单证和结汇单证等的基础知识、制作要点和办理流程,掌握国际贸易单证审核原则、方法和技巧。

(4)国际贸易惯例。国际贸易单证员应了解《联合国国际货物销售合同公约》,熟悉《托收统一规则》(URC522)和《国际贸易术语解释通则》(INCOTERMS 2010)的条款,掌握《跟单信用证统一惯例》(UCP600)和《国际标准银行实务》(ISBP681)的条款。

(5)外贸法规政策。国际贸易单证员应了解我国《对外贸易法》、进出口贸易政策、《进出口货物原产地条例》等,熟悉《海关法》、《进出口商品检验法》等。

必备知识

一、国际贸易单证的概念

国际贸易单证是国际结算中应用的单据、文件与证书,凭借它们来处理国际货物的商检、报关、保险、运输、交付和结汇等。狭义的单证是指单据和信用证,广义的单证是指各种文件和凭证。

二、国际贸易单证的种类

在国际贸易中,从不同的角度,单证可以分为以下几大类。

1.根据单证的性质划分

(1)金融单证。金融单证是指汇票、本票、支票或其他用于取得款项的类似凭证。

(2)商业单证。商业单证是指发票、运输单证、物权单证或其他类似单证,或者一切不属于金融单证的其他单证。

2. 根据单证的用途划分

(1)资金单证。资金单证是指汇票、本票、支票等结算工具。

(2)商业单证。商业单证是指商业发票、形式发票、装箱单、重量单、规格单等由出口商出具的单证。

(3)货运单证。货运单证是指各种运输方式单据的统称。UCP600将货运单据分为七大类,分别是:海运提单,不可转让海运单,租船合约提单,空运单,公路、铁路或内陆水运单据,快递收据,邮政收据或投邮证明。此外,还包括托运单、报检单、报关单等。

(4)保险单证。保险单证是指投保单、保险单、预保单、保险证明等。

(5)公务单证。公务单证是指海关发票、领事发票、原产地证明书、检验检疫证、配额证明、许可证等由官方机构出具的单证和证明。

(6)附属单证。附属单证是指寄单证明、寄样证明、装运通知、船公司证明等。

3. 根据商品的流向划分

(1)进口单证。进口单证是指进口许可证、进口配额证、进口付汇核销单、信用证、进口报关单、进口商品检验证明等进口国的企业及有关部门涉及的单证。

(2)出口单证。出口单证是指出口许可证、出口报关单、出口配额证、包装单证、运输单证、商业发票、汇票、商检证书、出口原产地证书等出口国的企业及有关部门出口时涉及的单证。

4. 根据单证签发的单位划分

(1)出口方自制的单证。出口方自制的单证是指汇票、商业发票、装箱单、重量单等。

(2)协作单位签发的单证。协作单位签发的单证是指运输单证、保险单证等由买卖双方之外的其他当事人签发的单证。

(3)政府机构、社会团体签发的单证。政府机构、社会团体签发的单证是指许可证书、商检证书、产地证书等由与外贸相关的政府部门或专业性机构签发的单证。

5. 根据是否用于结汇划分

(1)结汇单证。结汇单证是指信用证或合同中要求寄送给进口方、出口方凭以收汇的单证,如商业汇票、装箱单、海运提单、保险单、检验证书、原产地证书、受益人证明、装船通知等。

(2)非结汇单证。非结汇单证是指不需要寄送给进口方用于收汇,但在货物进出口环节中在国内流转的单证,如托运单、报检单、投保单、进出口货物报关单、进出口许可证、进出口配额证、出口收汇核销单、进口付汇核销单、提货单等。

第二篇
国际贸易单证制作基础篇
——信用证下国际贸易单证制作

任务一 制作开证申请书

学习目标

能力目标

1. 能读懂外贸合同和开证申请书的各项内容
2. 能根据外贸合同,正确熟练地制作开证申请书并办理开证手续

知识目标

熟悉开证申请书的格式,掌握开证申请书的制作要求

任务设计

2010年4月5日南通器械进出口公司同日本的T.C公司签订了一份出口手工工具的出口合同,合同内容如下:

SALES CONTRACT

CONTRACT NO.：NT201004005
DATE：　　　　　APR.5,2010
SIGNED AT：　　NANTONG,CHINA

THE SELLER：NANTONG TOOL IMPORT & EXPORT CO.,LTD.
ADDRESS：　58 HAONAN ROAD NANTONG, JIANGSU CHINA

THE BUYER：TKAMLA CORPORATION
ADDRESS：6-7,KAWARA MACH TOKYO,JAPAN

THIS CONTRACT IS MADE BY AND BETWEEN THE SELLER AND THE BUYER, WHEREBY THE SELLER AGREES TO SELL AND THE BUYER AGREES TO BUY THE UNDER-MENTIONED GOODS ACCORDING TO THE CONDITIONS STIPULATED BELOW：

(1) Name of Commodity and Specification	(2) Quantity	(3) Unit Price	(4) Amount
HAND TOOLS ①9pc Extra Long Hex Key Set ②8pc Double Offset Ring Spanner ③12pc Double Offset Ring Spanner ④12pc Combination Spanner ⑤10pc Combination Spanner AS PER PROFORMA INVOICE NO. NT2010004 DATED MAR. 1, 2010	1 200 SETS 1 200 SETS 800 SETES 1 200 STES 1 000 SETS	FOB NANTONG USD1.76 USD3.10 USD7.50 USD3.35 USD5.80	USD2 112.00 USD3 720.00 USD6 000.00 USD4 260.00 USD5 800.00
Total	5 400SETS	USD21 892.00	
MORE OR LESS 10% OF THE QUANTITY AND THE AMOUNT ALLOWED.			

(5) **Packing**: ①8pc double offset ring spanner packed in 1 plastic carton of 16 sets each;
　　　　　　②9pc extra long hex key set, 12pc combination spanner, 10pc combination spanner packed in 1 plastic carton of 10sets each;
　　　　　　③12pc double offset ring spanner packed in 1 plastic corton of 8 sets each.
　　　　　Packed in THREE 40'CONTAINER
(6) **Delivery**: From <u>NANTONG, CHINA</u> to <u>TOKYO, JAPAN</u>
(7) **Shipping Marks**: <u>　　　T.C</u>
　　　　　　　　　　　TOKYO
　　　　　　　　　　C/NO. 1−UP

(8) **Time of Shipment**: Latest date of shipment JUN. 10, 2010
(9) **Partical Shipment**: Not allowed
(10) **Transshipment**: Allowed
(11) **Terms of Payment**: By 100% confirmed irrevocable and transferable negotiable letter of credit to be available at 30 days after sight draft to be opened by the sellers.
　　　　　　　　　　L/C must mention this contract number. L/C advised by BANK OF CHINA NANTONG BRANCH. All banking charges outside JAPAN are for account of beneficiary.
(12) **Documents**: +Signed commercial invoice in triplicate.
　　　　　　　　+Packing list in triplicate.
　　　　　　　　+Certificate of orgin GSP FORM A, issued by the Chamber of Commerce or other authority duly entitled for this purpose.
　　　　　　　　+Full set of B/L, clean on board, marked "freight collect", consigned to order and notify the applicant.
　　　　　　　　+Certificate of Quality issued by the Entry-Exit Inspection and Quarantine Bureau at the port of NANTONG.

　　　　＋Certificate of Quantity issued by the Entry-Exit Inspection and Quarantine Bureau at the port of NANTONG.
　　　　＋Beneficiary's certified copy of fax send to the applicant within 24 hours after shipment advising L/C No., name of vessel, date of shipment, name, quantity, weight and value of goods.

(13) **Inspection**: The Inspection Certificate of Quality and Quantity issued by the Entry-Exit Inspection and Quarantine Bureau at the port of NANTONG shall be part of the documents to be presented for negotiation under the L/C. The buyer shall have the right to reinspect the quality and quantity of the cargo. The reinspection fee shall be borne by the buyer.

(14) **Claims**: Any claims by the buyer regarding the goods shall be filed within 45 days after arrival of the cargo at the port of destination specified in the relative B/L and supported by survey report issued by a recognized surveyor approved by the seller.

(15) **Force Majeure**: If the shipment of the contracted goods is prevented or delayed in whole or in part by reason of war, earthquake or other causes of Force Majeure, the Sellere shall not be liable. However, the Seller shall notify the Buyer immediately and furnish the latter by registered airmail with a certificate issued by the China Council for the Promotion of International Trade attesting such event or events.

(16) **Arbitration**: Any dispute arising from the execution of or in connection with this contract shall be settled amicably through negotiation. In case no settlement can be reached through negotiation, the case shall then be submitted to China International Economic & Trade Arbitration Commmision in Shanghai(or in Beijing) for arbitration in accordance with its arbitration rules. The arbitration award is final and binding upon both parties. The fee for arbitration shall be borne by losing party unless otherwise awarded.

The Seller:　　　　　　　　　　　　　　　　**The Buyer**:
NANTONG TOOL IMPORT & EXPORT CO., LTD.　　TKAMLA CORPORATION
　　汤丽丽　　　　　　　　　　　　　　　　　　TOM

合同签完后,进口方 TKAMLA CORPORATION 应根据合同制作开证申请书,及时向往来银行申请开证。TKAMLA CORPORATION 的业务员从 TKAMLA CORPORATION 的往来银行东京三菱银行领回了开证申请书,开证申请书如下：

IRREVOCABLE DOCUMENTARY CREDIT APPLICATION

To:　　　　　　　　　　　　　　　　　　　Date:

( ) Issued by airmail ( ) Issue by teletransmission 　　( ) SWIFT 　　( ) TLX 　　( ) CABLE	Credit No. Date and place of expiry of credit
Applicant	Beneficiary
Advising Bank	Amount(both in figures and words)

Partial shipment ( )allowed ( )not allowed	Transshipment ( )allowed ( )not allowed	Credit available with _____ By ( )sight payment ( )acceptance ( )negotiation ( ) deferred payment at against the documents detailed herein ( )and beneficiary's draft for _____ ____ of invoice value at _____sight
Loading on board/dispatch/taking in charge at/ from _____ Not later than _____ For transportation to _____		
( )FOB ( )CFR ( )CIF other terms _____		

Description of goods:

Documents required:(marked with ×)
1. (   )signed commercial invoice in _____ copies indicating L/C No.
2. (   )Packing list/Weight memo in _____ copies indicating quantity,gross and net weights of each package.
3. (   )Full set of clean on boardocean bills of lading made out to order and blank endorsed, marked "freight (   )to collect/(   )prepaid"notifying _____ .
    (   )Airway bills/cargo receipt/copy of railway bills issued by _____ showing "freight (   ) to collect/(   )prepaid" (   )indicating freight amount and consigned to _____ .
4. (   )Insurance Policy/Certificate in _____ for _____ of the invoice value showing ciaims payabe in China in the same currency of the draft,blank endorsed,covering _____ .
5. (   )Certificate of Quality in ____ copies issued by _____ .
6. (   )Certificate of _____ Origin in _____ copies issued by _____ .
7. (   )Beneficiary's certified copy of fax send to the applicant within _____ days after shipment advising L/C No. , name of vessel,date of shipment,name ,quantity,weight and value of goods.
    (   )Other documents,if any.

Additional instructions:
1. (   )All banking charges outside the opening bank are for beneficiary's account.
2. (   )Documents must be presented within ____ days after date of shipment but within the validity of this credit.
3. (   )Both quantity and credit amount _____ percent more or less are allowed.
    (   )Other terms,if any.

Signature:

任务分解

1. 读懂合同条款和空白开证申请书
2. 根据合同,正确制作开证申请书

任务描述

根据进出口贸易合同条款,及时准确制作开证申请书,是单证员必备的一项基本技能。开证申请书缮制得准确与否,直接决定了信用证的质量和受益人是否需要修改信用证的问题,开证申请书是决定交易能否顺利进行的首要条件。因此,单证员务必在读懂合同条款和空白开证申请书的基础上,严格按合同条款,缮制开证申请书,确保开证申请书内容和合同条款的一致性。

操作示范

第一步:读懂合同条款和空白开证申请书

认真仔细地阅读贸易合同和空白开证申请书,弄清合同条款的要求和申请书各个项目的含义,为准确缮制开证申请书做好准备。

第二步:根据合同,正确制作开证申请书

开证申请书空白格式由开证行提供,分正反两面:正面是一些需要根据合同条款填写的项目;反面是申请人对开证行的申明,用以明确双方责任。进口方根据银行规定的开证申请书格式,一般填写一式三份,一份留业务部门,一份留财务部门,一份交银行。填写开证申请书,必须按合同条款的具体规定,写明对信用证的各项要求,内容要明确、完整、无词意不清的记载。

1. **开证申请书抬头(to)**

开证申请书的抬头应填写开证行。本案中,开证行是"BANK OF TOKYO-MITSUBISHI UFJ LTD,TOKYO JAPAN"。

2. **申请日期(date)**

本栏填写进口方向开证行申请开立信用证的日期,通常以将开证申请书送往开证行的日期作为申请日期。本案中,填写 APR.10,2010。

3. **信用证的开立方式**

信用证的开立方式主要有信开和电开两种。所谓信开方式,是指开证行根据开证申请书,在信用证模板上进行选择和添加某些条款并由有权签字人签字、通过快邮方式发出的信用证。这种方式开出的信用证,通知行需要核对印鉴以判断信用证的真伪,目前这种方式已很少使用。所谓电开,是指开证行通过电讯方式开出信用证,包括通过电报开证、电传开证和 SWIFT 开证。进行电报和电传开证,开证行在开证时要加密押,通知行要核对密押以核实信用证的真伪;而通过 SWIFT 系统开证,不需要加押和核押,较为便捷。目前,已加入 SWIFT 系统的银行,大都通过该系统开证。本案中,选择"Issued by SWIFT"。

4. **信用证的效期和交单地点(date and place of expiry of credit)**

任何信用证都必须规定有效期和交单地点,有效期是针对交单地点而言的。一般情况下,交单地点规定在受益人所在国,信用证有效期一般根据最迟装运期加交单期确定。本案例填写:jun.25,2010 in China。

5. 开证申请人（applicant）

本栏目填写开证申请人，即合同买方的名称和地址：Tkamla Corporation ,6－7,Kawara Mach Tokyo, Japan。

6. 受益人（beneficiary）

本栏目填写受益人，即合同卖方的名称和地址：Nantong Tool Import & Export Co.,Ltd,58 Hao Nan Road Nantong, Jiangsu China。

7. 通知行（advising bank）

本栏目填写通知行的名称、地址和swift代码。通知行通常由卖方提供，一般是卖方的往来银行。如果卖方未提供，则由开证行指定。一般情况下，开证行指定出口方所在地的海外分行作为通知行，在没有海外分行时，则选择代理行。本案中，填写：Bank of China Nantong Branch, China Bic Code：BKCHCNBJ95GX, No.98, Middle Road of Renmin, Nantong, Jiangsu China。

8. 金额（amount）

本栏根据合同金额，以大小写同时填写，两者必须一致。本案中，填写 USD21 892.00（SAY U.S. Dollars twenty one thousand eight hundred and ninety two only.）。

9. 分批装运（partial shipment）

根据合同规定进行选择。本案合同不允许分批装运，因此选择 not allowed。

10. 转运（transshipment）

根据合同规定进行选择。本案合同允许转运，因此选择 allowed。

11. 装运港（loading on board）

根据合同规定进行填写。本案中填写：Nantong China。

12. 目的港（for transportation to）

根据合同规定进行填写。本案中填写：Tokyo Japan。

在有转运港的情况下，则应在目的港后显示转运港的信息。如经香港转运纽约，则目的港应填写为："New York, USD via Hong Kong"。

13. 最迟装运期（latest date of shipment）

根据合同规定进行填写。本案中填写：Jun.10,2010。

14. 贸易术语（terms of delivery）

根据合同规定进行选择。本栏选择：FOB。如果合同使用的是 FOB、CFR、CIF 以外的贸易术语，则在"other terms"处填写合同规定的贸易术语。如合同使用的是 FCA 贸易术语，则如此表示：（×）other terms：FCA。

15. 指定银行和付款方式

在"credit available with"后填写指定银行，并选择对应的结算方式。通常以通知行作为指定银行，本案中，在"credit available with"后填写 Bank of China Nantong Branch，并选择"negotiation"。

16. 汇票条款

若需要提交汇票，则在该栏填写汇票金额和期限。至于付款人，则由开证行确定，无需在开证申请书中填写。本案中填写：beneficiary's draft for 100% of invoice value at 30 days after sight。

17. 单据条款（documents required）

根据合同条款选择需要提供的单据。本案中，合同需要的发票、装箱单、FORMA 产地证、提单、质量证明和受益人证明，在空白申请书中均有，直接选择后再根据合同进行正确填写即可，同时补充未列出的数量证明。

18. 货物描述（description of goods）

根据合同规定填写。

19. 特殊条款（additional instructions）

特殊条款通常包含两种情况：一种是合同中未提及但是必须要交代的，如费用条款和交单期限条款；另一种是合同中要求的，但是在以上各栏目中无法体现的。本案中，费用条款和单据提交的期限条款，直接选择后根据实际要求填写即可，另外还需添加唛头条款和要求信用证加具保兑和提及合同号码的条款。

20. 签章（signature）

正确填写好以上各项内容后，分别在开证申请书的正面和反面盖章、签名。

制作好的开证申请书如下：

IRREVOCABLE DOCUMENTARY CREDIT APPLICATION

To: BANK OF TOKYO-MITSUBISHI UFJ LTD
TOKYO JAPAN   DATE: APR. 10, 2010 JAPAN

( ) Issued by airmail
(×) Issue by teletransmission
  (×) SWIFT
  ( ) TLX
  ( ) CABLE
	Credit No.
	
	Date and place of expiry of credit:
	JUN. 25, 2010 IN CHINA

Applicant: TKAMLA CORPORATION 6-7, KAWARA MACH TOKYO, JAPAN	Beneficiary NANTONG TOOL IMPORT & EXPORT CO., LTD. 58 HAONAN ROAD NANTONG, JIANGSU CHINA
Advising Bank: BANK OF CHINA NANTONG BRANCH, CHINA BIC CODE: BKCHCNBJ95GX No. 98, MIDDLE ROAD OF RENMIN, NANTONG, JIANGSU CHINA	Amount (both in figures and words) USD21 892.00 (SAY U.S. DOLLARS TWENTY ONE THOUSAND EIGHT HUNDRED AND NINETY TWO ONLY.)

Partial shipment	Transshipment	Credit available with BANK OF CHINA, NANTONG BRANCH
( ) allowed (×) not allowed	(×) allowed ( ) not allowed	By ( ) sight payment ( ) acceptance (×) negotiation

Loading on board/dispatch/taking in charge at/from NATONG, CHINA Not later than JUN. 10, 2010 For transportation to TOKYO, JAPAN	( ) deferred payment at against the documents detailed herein (×) and beneficiary's draft for <u>100</u> of invoice value at <u>30 days</u> after sight
(×) FOB ( ) CFR ( ) CIF other terms _____	
Description of goods:	

Name of Commodity and specification	Quantity	Unit Price	Amount
HAND TOOLS ①9pc Extra Long Hex Key Set ②8pc Double Offset Ring Spanner ③12pc Double Offset Ring Spanner ④12pc Combination Spanner ⑤10pc Combination Spanner AS PER PROFORMA INVOICE NO. NT2010004 DATED MAR. 1,2010	1 200 SETS 1 200 SETS 800 SETES 1 200 STES 1 000 SETS	FOB NANTONG USD1.76 USD3.10 USD7.50 USD3.35 USD5.80	USD2 112.00 USD3 720.00 USD6 000.00 USD4 260.00 USD5 800.00
Total Amount	5 400SETS	USD21 892.00	
MORE OR LESS 10% OF THE QUANTITY AND THE AMOUNT ALLOWED.			

Documents required:(marked with ×)
1. (×)Signed commercial invoice in THREE copies indicating L/C No..
2. (×)Packing list in THREE copies indicating quantity, gross and net weights of each package.
3. (×)Full set of clean on board ocean bills of lading made out to order and blank endorsed, marked "freight (×)to collect/( )prepaid"notifying THE APPLICANT.
( )Airway bills/cargo receipt/copy of railway bills issued by _____ showing "freight ( )to collect/( )prepaid" ( )indicating freight amount and consigned to _____.
4. ( )Insurance Policy/Certificate in ____ for ____ of the invoice value showing claims payable in China in the same currency of the draft, blank endorsed, covering _____.
5. (×)Certificate of Quality in THREE copies issued by the Entry-Exit Inspection and Quarantine Bureau at the port of NANTONG.
6. (×)Certificate of FORM A Origin in TWO copies issued by the Chamber of Commerce or other authority duly entitled for this purpose.
7. (×)Beneficiary's certified copy of fax send to the applicant within 24 hours after shipment advising L/C NO., name of vessel, date of shipment, name, quantity, weight and value of goods.
( )Other documents, if any.
8. (×) Certificate of Quantity issued by the Entry-Exit Inspection and Quarantine Bureau at the port of NANTONG.

Additional instructions:
1. (×)All banking charges outside the opening bank are for beneficiary's account.
2. (×)Documents must be presented within 15 days after date of shipment but within the validity of this credit.
3. (×)Both quantity and credit amount 10 percent more or less are allowed.
( )Other terms, if any.
4. Shipping mark: T.C
     TOKYO
      C/NO. 1－UP
5. The L/C is confirmed and transferable and L/C must mention this contract number.
6. Packed in 40' container.

            NANTONG TOOL IMPORT & EXPORT CO., LTD.
            Signature:汤丽丽

必备知识

一、信用证的含义和特点

1. 信用证的含义

根据国际商会第 600 号出版物《跟单信用证统一惯例》(UCP600) ARTICLE 2 的规定:"信用证指一项不可撤销的安排,无论其名称或描述如何,该项安排构成开证行对相符交单予以承付的确定承诺。"(Credit measns any arrangement, however named or discribed, that is irrevocable and thereby constitutes a definite undertaking of the issuing bank to honour a complying presentation.)

定义中提到的承付和相符交单在 UCP600 的 ARTICLE 2 中也有定义。承付是指:如果信用证为即期付款信用证,则即期付款;如果信用证为延期付款信用证,则承诺延期付款并在承诺到期日付款;如果信用证为承兑信用证,则承兑受益人开出的汇票并在汇票到期日付款。而相符交单是指与信用证条款、UCP600 的相关适用条款以及 ISBP681 一致的交单。

2. 信用证的特点

(1) 开证行承担第一性付款责任。信用证是银行开立的有条件的承诺付款的书面文件。只要受益人在信用证规定的期限内提交符合规定的单据,开证银行就必须保证付款,而不论开证申请人拒付还是倒闭。因此,开证行付款承诺是一项独立的责任。

(2) 信用证是一份自足的文件。信用证是根据贸易双方签订的合同开立的,信用证一经开出,就成为独立于合同以外的文件。信用证各当事人权利和义务完全以信用证中所列条款为依据,不受贸易合同的约束,开证行及其他参与信用证业务的当事人只能根据信用证规定办事,不受贸易合同的约束。

(3) 信用证业务是纯单据业务。在信用证业务中,各有关方面处理的是单据,而不是与单据有关的货物或服务。银行在处理信用证业务时,只审查受益人所提交的单据是否与信用证条款相符,以决定是否履行其付款责任。只要受益人提交符合信用证条款的单据,开证行就应承担付款责任,申请人也应接受单据并向开证行付款赎单。如果申请人付款后发现货物有缺陷,则可凭单据向有关责任方提出损害赔偿要求,而与银行无关。因此,作为受益人,应确保相符交单,才能从开证行处顺利收汇。

二、信用证结算方式的业务流程

在国际贸易结算中使用的跟单信用证有不同的类型,其业务程序也各有特点,但都要经过申请开证、开证、通知、交单、索偿、赎单这几个环节。现以最常见的议付信用证为例,说明其业务程序(见图 2-1)。

进出口双方签署的贸易合同中规定以信用证方式支付货款,具体流转程序如下:

① 申请开证。开证申请人按合同规定的期限,提交

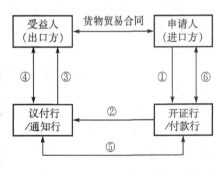

图 2-1 议付信用证流转程序图

开证所需资料和一定比例的押金或其他担保品向所在地银行申请开证。

②开证行开立信用证。开证行严格审核开证所需的相关资料,确保手续齐备,资料表面合法后,接受申请人的开证申请,将信用证开给出口方所在地的分行或代理行并请他们通知受益人。

③通知行通知信用证。通知行核对签字印鉴或密押无误将信用证通知受益人。

④受益人交单,指定银行议付。受益人收到信用证后,审证并根据情况要求修改并确认修改后,即备货装运,同时备齐信用证要求的全套议付单据,在有效期内送指定银行交单议付,指定银行议付。

⑤寄单索偿。议付行议付后,将全套议付单据寄给开证行或指定银行请求偿付货款,开证行或指定行审单无误后,偿付给议付行。

⑥申请人付款赎单。开证行通知申请人付款赎单,开证申请人应到开证行审核单据,若单据无误,即应付清全部货款与有关费用;若单据和信用证不符,开证申请人有权拒付。开证申请人付款后,即可从开证行取得全套单据。

 **拓展知识**

一、信用证的当事人

(1)开证申请人(applicant),又称开证人(opener),是指向银行提出申请开立信用证的一方,一般为进口方,即贸易合同的买方。

(2)开证行(opening bank;issuing bank),是指接受开证人委托、开立信用证的银行,一般是进口地的银行。开证人与开证行的权利和义务以开证申请书为依据。信用证一经开出,按信用证规定的条款,开证行负有承担第一性付款的责任。

(3)受益人(beneficiary),是指信用证上所指定的有权使用该信用证的人,一般为出口方,也就是贸易合同的卖方。它有按时交货、提交符合信用证要求的单据的义务和索取货款的权利。

(4)通知行(advising bank;notifying bank),是指受开证行的委托,将信用证通知(或转递)给受益人的银行。通知行一般是出口方所在地的银行,而且通常是开证行的代理行。通知行的主要义务是审核信用证的表面真实性。

(5)议付行(negotiating bank),是指对受益人交来的汇票及/或单据办理议付的银行。

(6)付款行(paying bank;drawee bank),是指开证行授权进行信用证项下付款或承兑并支付受益人出具的汇票的银行。开证行通常为付款行,付款行也可以是接受开证行委托的代为付款的第三家银行。付款行的付款是终局性的付款,付款后,不可再向受益人追索。

(7)偿付行(reimbursing bank),又称信用证清算银行(clearing bank),是指受开证行的指示或授权,对有关代付行或议付行的索偿予以照付的银行。偿付行是开证行的付款代理,它只凭代付行或议付行的索偿付款,不审查单据,不负单证不符之责,因此它的付款并不是终局性的付款,一旦开证行随后发现单据不符合信用证的规定,开证行可以向代付行或议付行追索已由偿付行支付的款项。

(8)保兑行(confirming bank),是指应开证行或受益人的请求在信用证上加具承担保证兑付责任的银行,它和开证行处于相同的地位,即对于汇票及/或单据承担不可撤销的付款责任,保兑行有必须议付或代付的责任。在已经议付或代付之后,不论开证行发生什么变化,都不得向受益人追索。因此,保兑行的付款也是终局性的付款。

(9)转让行(transferring bank),是指应受益人(在转让信用证时又称第一受益人)的委托,将可转让信用证转让给信用证的受让人(第二受益人)的银行。转让行一般为通知行,可以是议付行、付款行或保兑行或开证行。

二、信用证的类型

1. 保兑信用证和非保兑信用证

保兑信用证(confirmed L/C),是指另一家银行即保兑行应开证行请求,对其所开信用证加以保证兑付的信用证。非保兑信用证(unconfirmed L/C)是指未经除开证行以外的其他银行保兑的信用证,即一般的不可撤销信用证。

2. 即期付款信用证、延期付款信用证、承兑信用证和议付信用证

(1)即期付款信用证(sight payment L/C),是指规定受益人开立即期汇票随附单据,或不需要汇票仅凭单据向指定银行提示,请求付款的信用证。即期付款信用证是否需要汇票,完全取决于具体的信用证的规定。

(2)延期付款信用证(deferred payment L/C),又称迟期付款信用证,或称无承兑远期信用证,是指仅凭受益人提交的单据,经审核单证相符确定银行承担延期付款责任起,至付款到期日付款的信用证。这种信用证的特点是受益人不必开具汇票,开证行也不存在承兑汇票的问题。由于这种信用证不使用汇票,不作承兑,因此也不能贴现。在实践中大多使用于金额较大的资本货物的交易。

(3)承兑信用证(acceptance L/C),是指被信用证指定的付款行在收到符合信用证规定的远期汇票和单据时,先在汇票上履行承兑手续,等汇票到期日再行付款的信用证。

(4)议付信用证(negotiation L/C),是指开证行在信用证中,邀请其他银行买入汇票及/或单据的信用证,即允许受益人向某一指定银行或任何银行交单议付的信用证。议付信用证按是否限定议付行,又可分为公开议付信用证和限制议付信用证两种。前者是指任何银行均可办理议付,后者则是指仅由被指定的一家银行办理议付。

3. 即期信用证和远期信用证、假远期信用证和预支信用证

(1)即期信用证(sight L/C),是指开证行或其指定的付款行在收到符合信用证条款的跟单汇票及/或装运单据后,立即履行付款义务的信用证。

(2)远期信用证(time L/C;usance L/C),是指开证行或其指定的付款行在收到符合信用证条款的汇票及/或单据后,在规定的期限内保证付款的信用证。其主要作用是便利进口方资金融通。承兑信用证、延期付款信用证和远期议付信用证都是远期信用证。

(3)假远期信用证(usance L/C payable at sight),是指贸易双方达成即期交易,但进口方出于某种目的和需要,在信用证中要求受益人以即期价格报价,开立远期汇票,由进口方负担贴现息及有关费用,而受益人按规定即期收汇的一种信用证。

(4)预支信用证(anticipatory L/C),是指允许受益人在货物装运交单前预支货款的信用证,有全部预支和部分预支两种。

4. 可转让信用证和不可转让信用证

(1)可转让信用证(transferable L/C),是指受益人(第一受益人)有权将信用证的全部或部分金额转让给"第三者"(第二受益人)使用的信用证。

(2)不可转让信用证(untransferable L/C),是指受益人无权将使用信用证的权利转让给其他人使用的信用证。凡信用证中未注明"transferable"的信用证,均为不可转让信用证。

5. 循环信用证

循环信用证(revolving L/C),是指受益人在一定时间内使用了规定金额,能够重新恢复信用证原金额并再度使用,直至达到该证规定次数或累计总金额用完为止的信用证。

6. 对开信用证

对开信用证(reciprocal L/C),是指两张信用证的开证申请人互以对方为受益人而开立的信用证。其特点是第一张信用证的受益人和开证申请人分别是第二张信用证的开证申请人和受益人。这种信用证通常用于易货贸易、来料或来件加工装配业务中。

7. 对背信用证

对背信用证(back to back L/C),是指原证受益人要求原证的通知行或其他银行以原证为基础和担保,另行开立的一张内容相似的新信用证给实际供货人,这另开的信用证即为对背信用证。

8. 备用信用证

备用信用证(standby L/C),又称担保信用证(guarantee L/C),是指开证行开给受益人的一种有条件的保证付款的书面文件。其主要内容是在信用证中规定,在开证申请人未能按时偿还贷款或货款,未能履行投标人的职责时,开证行负责为其支付。如开证申请人履行了信用证中规定的上述某项义务,则该信用证就不起作用,所以其被称作备用信用证。

三、开证申请与 ISBP681 条款

ISBP681 中有关"信用证的申请和开立"有三个条款,需要申请人在申请开立信用证前加以关注。

(1)信用证条款独立于基础交易,即使信用证明确提及了基础交易。但是,为避免在审单时发生不必要的费用、延误和争议,开证申请人和受益人应当仔细考虑要求何种单据、单据由谁出具和提交单据的期限。

(2)开证申请人承担其有关开立或修改信用证的指示不明确所导致的风险。除非另有明确规定,开立或修改信用证的申请即意味着授权开证行以必要或适宜的方式补充或细化信用证条款,以使信用证得以使用。

(3)开证申请人应当注意,UCP600 的许多条文,诸如第 3 条、第 14 条、第 21 条、第 23 条、第 24 条、第 28 条(i)、第 30 条和第 31 条,其对术语的界定可能导致出乎意料的结果,除非开证申请人对这些规定充分熟悉。例如,在多数情况下,要求提交提单而且禁止转运的信用证必须排除 UCP600 第 20 条(c)款的适用,才能使禁止转运发生效力。

技能训练

(一)训练资料

SALES CONTRACT

NO. SC2009001
DATE: AUG. 5, 2009
SIGNED AT: NANTONG, CHINA

BUYER: JAE&SONS PAPERS COMPANY
　　　　203 LODIA HOTE OFFICE 1546, DONG-DU,
　　　　BUSAN, KOREA
SELLER: NANTONG PRIEMARY ECONOMIC TRADE CO., LTD.
　　　　ZHAXI INDUSTRY AREA NANTONG JIANGSU

　　This contract is made by the Seller; whereby the Buyer agrees to buy and the Seller agrees to sell the under-mentioned commodity according to the terms and conditions stipulated below:

1. COMMODITY: UNBLEACHED KRAET LINEBOARD.
   UNIT PRICE: USD390.00/PER METRIC TON, CFR BUSAN KOREA
   TOTAL QUANTITY: 100 METRIC TONS, MORE OR LESS 10% ARE ALLOWED
   PAYMENT TERM: BY IRREVOCABLE L/C 90 DAYS AFTER B/L DATE
2. TOTAL VALUE: USD39 000.00 (SAY U.S. DOLLARS THIRTY NINE THOUSAND ONLY.***** MORE OR LESS 10% ALLOWED.)
3. PACKING: TO BE PACKED IN STRONG WOODEN CASE(S), SUITABLE FOR LONG DISTANCE OCEAN TRANSPORTATION.
4. SHIPPING MARK: THE SELLER SHALL MARK EACH PACKAGE WITH FADELESS PAINT THE PACKAGE NUMBER, GROSS WEIGHT, MEASUREMENT AND THE WORDING: "KEEP AWAY FROM MOISTURE", "HANDLE WITH CARE", ETC. AND THE SHIPPING MARK: SC2009001
   BUSANKOREA
5. TIME OF SHIPMENT: BEFORE OCTOBER 2, 2009
6. PORT OF SHIPMENT: MAIN PORTS OF CHINA
7. PORT OF DESTINATION: BUSAN, KOREA
8. INSURANCE: TO BE COVERED BY THE BUYER AFTER SHIPMENT
9. DOCUMENTS REQUIRED:
   + SIGNED INVOICEIN TRIPLICATE INDICATING L/C NO. AND CONTRACT NO..
   +FULL SET(3/3) OF CLEAN ON BOARD OCEAN BILL OF LADING MARKED "FREIGHT PREPAID" MADE OUT TO ORDER BLANK ENDORSED NOTIFYINGTHE APPLICANT.
   +PACKING LIST /WEIGHT LISTIN TRIPLLCATE INDICATING QUANTITY/GROSS AND NET WEIGHT.
   +CERTIFICATE OF ORIGIN.
   +NO SOLID WOOD PACKING CERTIFICATE ISSUED BY MANUFACTURER.
10. OTHER CONDITIONS REQD IN L/C:
    +ALL BANKING CHARGES OUTSIDE THE OPENING BANK ARE FOR BENEFICIARY'S A/C.
    +DO NOT MENTION ANY SHIPPING MARKS IN YOUR L/C.
    +PARTIAL AND TRANSSHIPMENT ALLOWED.
11. REMARKS: THE LAST DATE OF L/C OPENING: AUG. 20, 2009

The Seller:	The Buyer:
NANTONG PRIEMARY ECONOMIC TRADE CO., LTD.	AE&SONS PAPERS COMPANY
ZHAXI INDUSTRY AREA	203 LODIA HOTE OFFICE
NANTONG JIANGSU	1546, DONG-DU, BUSAN, KOREA
魏成功	JACK

(二)制作开证申请书

IRREVOCABLE DOCUMENTARY CREDIT APPLICATION

To: Date:

( )Issued by airmail ( )Issue by teletransmission 　　　　( )SWIFT 　　　　( )TLX 　　　　( )CABLE		Credit No. Date and place of expiry of credit
Applicant		Beneficiary
Advising Bank		Amount(both in figures and words)
Partial shipment ( )allowed ( )not allowed	Transshipment ( )allowed ( )not allowed	Credit available with _____ By ( )sight payment 　　( )acceptance 　　( )negotiation 　　( )deferred payment at against the documents detailed herein 　　( )and beneficiary's draft for ____ 　　____ of invoice value at ____ sight
Loading on board/dispatch/taking in charge at/from _____ Not later than _____ For transportation to _____ ( )FOB ( )CFR ( )CIF other terms _____		
Description of goods:		
Documents required:(marked with ×) 1. ( )signedcommercial invoice in _____ copies indicating L/C No.. 2. ( )Packing list/Weight memo in _____ copies indicating quantity,gross and net weights of each package. 3. ( )Full set of clean on boardocean bills of lading made out to order and blank endorsed,marked "freight ( )to collect/( )prepaid"notifying _____. 　( ) Airway bills/cargo receipt/copy of railway bills issued by _____ showing "freight ( )to collect/( )prepaid" ( )indicating freight amount and consigned to _____. 4. ( )Insurance Policy/Certificate in ____ for ____ of the invoice value showing ciaims payabe in China in the same currency of the draft,blank endorsed,covering _____. 5. ( )Certificate of Quality in ____ copies issued by ____. 6. ( )Certificate of _____ Origin in ____ copies issued by ____ . 7. ( )Beneficiary's certified copy of fax send to the applicant within _____ days after shipment advising L/C No. ,name of vessel,date of shipment,name,quantity,weight and value of goods. 　( )Other documents,if any. 8. ( )Certificate on origin. 9. ( )No solid wood packing certificate issued by manufacturer.		

Additional instructions:
1. (　)All banking charges outside the opening bank are for beneficiary's account.
2. (　)Documents must be presented within _____ days after date of shipment but within the validity of this credit.
3. (　)Both quantity and credit amount _____ percent more or less are allowed.
   (　)Other terms, if any.
4. (　)Packing: to be packed in strong wooden cases, suitable for long distance ocean transportation.
5. (　)The seller shall mark each package with fadeless paint the package number, gross weight, measurement and the wording: "Keep away from moisture", "Handle with care", etc.

Signature:

任务二　审核信用证和修改信用证

学习目标

能力目标
1. 能根据进出口贸易合同,熟练查找信用证中的问题条款
2. 能根据审证结果,正确缮制信用证修改函电

知识目标
1. 掌握审证的方法和审证注意点
2. 掌握改证的原则和程序

任务设计

在任务一中,南通器械进出口公司和日本东京的 TKAMLA CORPORATION 在 2010 年 4 月 5 日签订了号码为 NT201004005 的合同。2010 年 4 月 13 日,南通器械进出口公司外贸单证员吴琳琳收到了中国银行南通分行国际业务部的信用证通知函,告知 TKAMLA CORPORATION 已通过东京三菱银行开来信用证。信用证通知书和信用证内容如下:

信用证通知书

BANK OF CHINA　NANTONG BRANCH
ADDRESS:98 REN MIN ZHONG ROAD,
　　　　　NANTONG, JIANGSU CHINA

CABLE:CHUNGKUO
TLX:8365100BOCNT CN
SWIFT:BKCHCNBJ95G
FAX:0513-85527796

信用证通知书
NOTIFICATION OF DOCUMENTARY CREDIT

2010/04/13

TO:
NANTONG TOOL IMPORT & EXPORT CO.,LTD.
58, HAONAN ROAD NANTONG, JIANGSU CHINA

WHEN CORREDPONDING

PLEASE QUOTE OUR REF NO.

AD95G10100801

ISSUING BANK BANK OF TOKYO MITSUBISHI UFJ LTD. 1-5-2 HONGOKU-CHO NIHONBASHI CHUO-KU TOKYO 103-0021 JAPAN		TRANSMITTED TO US THROUGH 转递行 REF NO.	
L/C NO. 信用证号 NT31173	DATED 开证日期 2010/04/12	AMOUNT 金额 EUR21 892.00	EXPIRY PLACE LOCAL
EXPIRY DATE 有效期 2010/06/25	TENOR 期限 DAYS: AT SIGHT	CHARGE 未付费用 RMB0.00	CHARGE BY 费用承担人 BENE
RECEIVED VIA 来证方式 SWIFT	AVAILABLE 是否生效 VALID	TEST/SIGN 印押是否相符 YES	CONFIRM 我行是否保兑 NO

DEAR SIRS, 敬启者：

　　WE HAVE PLEASURE IN ADVISING YOU THAT WE HAVE RECEIVED FROM THE A/M BANK A(N) LETTER OF CREDIT. CONTENTS OF WHICH ARE AS PER ATTACHED SHEET(S).

THIS ADVICE AND THE ATTACHED SHEET(S) MUST ACCOMPANY THE RELATIVE DOCUMENTS WHEN PRESENTED FOR NEGOTIATION.

兹通知贵司：我行收自上述银行信用证一份，现随附通知，贵司交单时，请将本通知书及信用证一并提示。

REMARK 备注：

　　PLEASE NOTE THAT THIS ADVICE DOES NOT CONSTITUTE OUR CONFIRMATION OF THE ABOVE L/C NOR DOES IT CONVEY ANY ENGAGEMENT OR OBLIGATION ON OUR PART.

THIS L/C CONSISTS OF SHEET(S), INCLUDING THE COVERING LETER AND ATACHMENT(S).
本信用证连同面函及附件共　　页。

IF YOU FIND ANY TERMS AND CONDITIONS IN THE L/C WHICH YOU ARE UNABLE TO COMPLY WITH AND OR ANY ERROR(S). IT IS SUGGESTED THAT YOU CONTACT APPLICANT DIRECTLY FOR NECESSARY AMENDMENT(S) SO AS TO AVOID ANY DIFFICULTIES WHICH MAY ARISE WHEN DOCUMENTS ARE PRESENTED.

如本信用证中有无法办到的条款/或错误,请与开证申请人联系,进行必要的修改,以排除交单时可能发生的问题。

THIS L/C ADVISED SUBJECT TO ICC UCP PUBLICATION NO.600

本信用证之通知系遵循 UCP600 办理。

此证如有任何问题及疑虑,请与国际结算部出口科联络,电话:0513－85527796

信用证

MT S700		ISSUE OF A DOCUMENTARY CREDIT
SEQUENCE OF TOTAL	*27:	1/1
FORM OF DOC. CREDIT	*40A:	IREVOCABLE AND NOT TRANSFERABLE
DOC. CREDIT NUMBER	*20:	NT31173
DATE OF ISSUE	31C:	100412
APPLICABE RULES	*40E:	UCP LATEST VERESION
EXPIRY	*31D:	DATE 100625 PLACE CHINA
APPLICANT BANK	*51A:	
		*BANK OF TOKYO－MITSUBISHI UFJ LTD
		*TOKYO JAPAN
APPLICANT	*50:	TKAMLA CORPORATION
		6－7,KAWARA MACH TOKYO, JAPAN
BENEFICIARY	*59:	NANTONG TOOL IMPORT & EXPORT CO.,LTD.
		58 HAONAN ROAD NANTONG, JIANGSU CHINA
AMOUNT	*32B:	CURRENCY EUR AMOUNT 21 892.00
AVAILABLE WITH/BY	*41D:	ANY BANK IN CHINA
		BY NEGOTIATION
DRAFTS AT…	42C:	AT SIGHT
DRAWEE	42D:	BANK OF TOKYO－MITSUBISHI UFJ LTD
		1－5－2 HONGOKU－CHO NIHONBASHI CHUO－KU
		TOKYO 103－0021 JAPAN
PARTIAL SHIPMENTS	43P:	ALLOWED
TRANSSHIPMENT	43T:	NOT ALLOWED
PORT OF LOADING	44A:	NANTONG
FOR TRANSPORTATION TO	44B:	TOKYO JAPAN
LATEST DATEE OF SHIPMENT	44C:	100610
DESCRIPT OF GOODS	45A:	HAND TOOLS
		AS PER PROFORMA INVOICE
		NT201004 DATED MAR.1,2010
		FOB TOKYO
DOCUMENTS REQUIRED	46A:	+SIGNED COMMERCIAL INVOICE IN TRIPCATE.
		+PACKING LIST IN TRIPLICATE.
		+CERTIFICATE OF ORIGIN GSP FORM A,ISSUED BY
		THE CHAMBER OF COMMERCE OR OTHER AUTH-

		ORITY DULY ENTITLED FOR THIS PURPOSE.
		+FULL SET OF B/L, CLEAN ON BOARD, MARKED "FREIGHT COLLECT", CONSIGNED TO : TKAMLA CORPORATION, 6-7, KAWARA MACH TOKYO, JAPAN, NOTIFY APPLICANT.
		+INSURANCE POLICY/CERTIFICATE IN DUPLICATE ENDORSED IN BLANK FOR 110% INVOICE VALUE, COVERING ALL RISKS OF CIC OF PICC (1/1/1981).
		+CERTIFICATE OF QUANTITY ISSUED BY THE ENTRY-EXIT INSPECTION AND QUARANTINE BUREAU AT THE PORT OF NANTONG.
		+BENEFICIARY'S CERTIFIED COPY OF FAX SENT TO THE APPLICANT WITHIN 24 HOURS AFTER SHIPMENT ADVISING L/C NO. NAME OF VESSEL, DATE OF SHIPMENT, NAME, QUANTITY, WEIGHT AND VALUE OF GOODS.
		+SIGNED APPLICANT'S CERTIFICATE CERTIFYING THAT THE QUALITY OF GOODS CONFIRMED WITH THE TERMS AND CONDITIONS OF THE CONTRACT NT201004005.
ADDITIONAL CONDITION.	47A：	+ A DISCREPANCY HANDLING FEE OF USD50.00 WILL BE ASSESSED BY THE BANK OF TOKYO-MITSUBISHI UFJ LTD, TOKYO BRANCH ON EACH PRESENTATION OF DOCUMENTS NOT IN STRICT COMPLIANCEWITH THE TERMS AND CONDITIONS OF THE CREDIT. THIS FEE IS FOR THE ACCOUNT OF THE BENEFICIARY AND WILL BE DEDUCTED FROM THE PROCEEDS WHEN PAYMENT IS EFFECTED.
		+ DRAFT MUST INDICATE THE NUMBER AND DATE OF THIS CREDIT.
CHAGREGS	71B：	ALL BANKING CHARGE ARE FOR ACCOUNT OF BENEFICIARY.
PRESENTATIONPERIOD	48：	DOCUMENTS MUST BE PRESENTED WIHTIN 15 DAYS AFTER THE DATE OF SHIPMENT BUT WITHIN THE VALIDITY OF THE CREDIT.
CONFIRMATION	*49：	WITHOUT
"ADVISE THROUGH"	57D：	BANK OF CHINA, NANTONG CITY CHONG CHUN SUB-BRANCH NO. 98 RENMIN MIDDLE ROAD, NANTONG, JIANGSU CHINA

任务分解

1. 读懂合同 NT201004005 条款和信用证 NT31173 条款

2. 根据合同，审核出口来证，找出问题条款
3. 分析找出的信用证问题条款，提出修改意见并撰写修改电文

任务描述

根据出口合同审核出口来证，是受益人收到信用证后首先要处理的事项。单证员通过认真研读合同条款和信用证，查找信用证和合同不一致的条款以及影响受益人安全收汇的"软条款"，在确认需要修改的内容后，制作修改函电，联系进口方通过开证行修改。准确理解合同和信用证条款，是做好审证工作的前提条件。

操作示范

第一步：读懂合同 NT201004005 条款和信用证 NT31173 条款

认真研读合同和信用证，特别注意金额、装运条款、信用证的类型、信用证的有效期、交单地点、交单期和单据要求等细节。

第二步：根据合同，审核出口来证，找出问题条款

审证中查找的问题条款包括三个方面的条款，即与合同不一致的条款、信用证漏开的合同条款和影响受益人收汇的"软条款"。

首先，查找信用证与合同不一致的条款。对照合同条款，逐条审核信用证条款后，发现如下不符：

(1)信用证类型不符。信用证为"NOT TRANSFERABLE"（不可转让），而合同要求为"TRANSFERABLE"（可转让）。

(2)形式发票号码不符。信用证中为"NT201004005"而合同中为"NT20100405"。

(3)分批装运规定不符。信用证中规定"PARTIAL SHIPMENT：ALLOWED"（分批装运允许），而合同中规定"PARTIAL SHIPMENT：NOT ALLOWED"（分批装运不允许）。

(4)转运条款规定不符。信用证中规定"TRANSSHIPMENT：NOT ALLOWED"，而合同中规定"TRANSSHIPMENT：ALLOWED"。

(5)货币类型不同。信用证中为"EUR"（欧元），而合同中为"USD"（美元）。

(6)汇票期限规定不同。信用证中为"AT SIGHT"（即期汇票），而合同要求"at 30 days after sight draft"（见票以后30天）。

(7)价格条款不符。信用证中为"FOB TOKYO"，而合同为"FOB NANOTNG"。

(8)提单抬头不符。信用证要求记名提单抬头："CONSIGNED TO：TKAMLA CORPORATION, 6-7, KAWARA MACH TOKYO, JAPAN"，而合同要求空白抬头"CONSIGNED TO ORDER"。

(9)要求提交保险单不符。信用证要求提交保险单，而合同采用的是 FOB 贸易术语，由进口方自办保险，不需要受益人提交保险单。

(10)费用条款规定不符。信用证规定"ALL BANKING CHARGE ARE FOR ACCOUNT OF BENEFICIARY"（所有银行费用由受益人承担），而合同规定"All banking charges outside JAPAN are for account of beneficiary"（日本以外的所有银行费用由受益人承担）。

(11)信用证显示为不保兑信用证与合同要求不符，合同要求为保兑信用证。

其次，查找信用证漏开的合同条款。

(12)信用证中未提及溢短装条款。经过审证发现，合同中要求的溢短装条款"MORE OR

LESS 10% OF THE QUANTITYI AND THE AMOUNT ALLOWED"在信用证未提及。

(13)信用证中未提及合同号。

最后,审核查找影响受益人收汇的"软条款"。

(14)信用证存在一个影响受益人收汇的"软条款"。"SIGNED APPLICANT'S CERTIFICATE CERTIFYING THAT THE QUALITY OF GOODS CONFIRMED WITH THE TERMS AND CONDITIONS OF THE CONTRACT NT201004005"(提交申请人签名的证明货物质量满足合同要求的证明)。

第三步:分析找出的信用证问题条款,提出修改意见并撰写修改电文

对于查找出的信用证中存在的与合同不一致的条款,必须具体分析后,再确定是否需要修改。一般而言,以下情况可以不改:对我方有利,又不影响对方利益;对我方不利,但是在不增加成本或仅增加很少成本的情况下,经过努力可以完成。以下情况必须修改:对我方有利,但是严重影响对方利益;对我方不利,必须增加较大成本才可以完成或完全无法完成。

根据这个原则,以上找出的13个不符点条款中:

对我方有利,又不影响对方利益的是:"(3)分批装运规定不符。信用证中规定"PARTIAL SHIPMENT:ALLOWED"(分批装运允许),而合同中规定"PARTIAL SHIPMENT:NOT ALLOWED"(分批装运不允许)。"因为信用证允许分批装运,且没有对如何分批作进一步的规定,受益人可以根据货物的市场行情作出分批与否的具体安排,有了更大的自主权。

对我方有利,但是严重影响对方利益的是:"(5)货币类型不同。信用证中为'EUR'(欧元),而合同中为'USD'(美元)。"因为欧元的价值比美元大,因此以欧元替代美元,进口方有较大的损失。

对我方不利,必须增加较大成本才可以完成或完全无法完成的是其余的11个条款。

因此,通过以上分析,需要修改的是除了(3)以外的13个条款,吴琳琳给TKAMLA CORPORATION的经理TOM发送了如下改证电文:

Dear sirs,

We are pleasure to receive your L/C No. NT31173 issued by BANK OF TOKYO-MITSUBISHI UFJ LTDTOKYO JAPAN. But we find it contains some discrepancies with S/C No. NT201004005. Please instruct the issuing bank to amend the L/C A.S.A.P. The L/C should be amended as follows:

(1) Under field 40A, form of doc. credit amends to "irrevocable and transferable".

(2) Under field 45A, the correct number of proform invoice No. is NT2010004, the correct terms of price is FOB NANTONG instead of FOB TOKYO.

(3) Under field 43T, transshipment is allowed instead of not allowed.

(4) Under field 32B, the correct currency is USD instead of EUR.

(5) Under field 42C, the tenor of draft is "at 30 days after sight" instead of "at sight".

(6) Under field 46A, the consignee of B/L should be "TO ORDER" instead of "TKAMLA CORPORATION, 6-7, KAWARA MACH TOKYO, JAPAN"; cancel the clause of "INSURANCE POLICY/CERTIFICATE IN DUPLICATE ENDORSED IN BLANK FOR 110% INVOICE VALUE, COVERING ALL RISKS OF CIC OF PICC (1/1/1981)"; cancel the clause "SIGNED APPLICANT'S CERTIFICATE CERTIFYING THAT THE QUALITY OF GOODS CONFIRMED WITH THE TERMS AND CONDITIONS OF THE CONTRACT NT201004005".

(7) Under field 71B, the charge clause amends to "All banking charges outside JAPAN are for account of beneficiary."
(8) Under field 49, "a named bank" should be indicated instead of "WITHOUT".
(9) Under field 47A, to insert the clause "MORE OR LESS 10% OF THE QUANTITYI AND THE A-MOUNT ALLOWED" and "THE CONTRACT NO IS NT201004005".

必备知识

一、审核信用证

1. 审证的含义

广义的审证包括银行(通知行)审证和受益人审证,狭义的审证即受益人审证。实务中,银行审证包括审核开证行的资信、付款责任、索汇路线及信用证的真伪等,而出口方着重审核信用证的条款是否与贸易合同规定相一致。由于信用证业务中,出口方只有提交了满足信用证要求的单据,才可能从开证行或其他行获得付款。因此认真审核信用证,找出与合同不一致的信用证条款,并根据实际情况联系进口方通过开证行修改,对出口方的安全及时收汇十分重要。下面仅对出口方审证作相关讨论。

2. 审证的依据

(1)贸易合同。进口方根据贸易合同缮制开证申请书,开证行依据开证申请书开立信用证,因此本质上信用证是依据贸易合同开立的,其条款应当与贸易合同条款相符。出口方若不能履行信用证条款,就无法凭信用证取得货款。因此,审查信用证条款与贸易合同是否相符,是出口方收到信用证后首先要做的工作。

在审证的过程中,应正确理解"相符",它并非指信用证与合同条款表面的严格一致,信用证条款"宽于"合同,对受益人有利,或即使在"严于"合同条款时受益人出于某种考虑愿意作出某种"让步",均可认为信用证与合同条款一致。

(2)UCP600。UCP600是信用证业务中最重要的国际惯例之一,目前已被世界上大多数国家和地区的银行采用。受益人在审证时应按照UCP600的规定来确定是否可以接受信用证的某些条款。

(3)实际业务情况。审核贸易合同中未提及或无法援引UCP600的某些信用证条款,应当结合实际业务考虑是否接受。

3. 审证的内容

信用证内容涉及信用证本身的条款、合同条款、汇票、单据要求、银行之间的寄单指示和款项划拨指示六个方面,前面四项内容由受益人审核,审核的要点包括:

(1)对信用证性质和类型的审核。UCP600第3条规定:"A CREDIT IS IRREVOCABLE EVEN IF THERE IS NO INDICATION TO THAT EFFECT"(信用证是不可撤销的,即使未如此表明)。因此,审证时要特别关注信用证的40A场,如果该场显示有"REVOCABLE"字样,则必须修改信用证。关于信用证的种类,在SWIFT信用证中有两处从不同的角度表明,一处是第41场,另一处是第49场。第41场显示的按兑用方式进行的分类。UCP600第6条b款规定:"A CREDIT MUST STATE WHETHER IT IS AVAILABLE BY SIHGT PAYNMENT,

DEFERRED PAYMENT,ACCEPTANCE OR NEGOTIATION "(信用证必须规定其是以即期付款、延期付款、承兑还是以议付的方式兑用)。第 49 场显示信用证的保兑性质。另外,信用证是即期还是远期往往通过汇票的付款期限反映。

(2)对信用证金额与币别的审核。信用证的总金额与币别是否与合同一致。若信用证列有商品数量和单价时,应计算总值是否正确。需要特别注意的是:当数量允许"溢短装"时,信用证金额是否有相应的机动幅度。通常情况下,数量和金额规定有相同的机动幅度,但在某些情况下,只规定数量的机动幅度,而没有金额的机动幅度。

(3)对汇票条款的审核。UCP600 第 6 条 c 款规定:"A CREDIT MUST NOT BE ISSUED AVAILABLE BY A DRAFT DRAWN ON THE APPLICANT."(信用证不得开成以申请人为付款人的汇票兑用)。信用证汇票的付款人必须是开证行或其指定行,如果是以开证申请人为付款人的,应要求修改。汇票付款期限的规定必须与合同规定相一致。

(4)对货物描述的审核。信用证规定的装运货物是受益人装运货物和制作单据的依据。因此,接到来证后,必须依照合同对信用证内规定的品名、牌号、规格、数量、包装、单价等项目仔细核对。

(5)信用证的截止日和交单地点的审核。UCP600 第 6 条 d 款规定:"信用证必须规定一个交单的截止日。规定的承付或议付的截止日将被视为交单的截止日。"通常信用证在规定截止日的同时,也规定交单地点,它包括出口地、进口地和第三国三种情况。出口地交单对出口方最有利,进口地交单和第三国交单对出口方不利,因为交单地点在国外,出口方将承担邮递迟延、邮件遗失等风险。因此,出口方应尽可能争取在出口地交单。

(6)装运期。装运期是出口方将货物装上运往目的地的运输工具或交付给承运人的日期,原则上应与合同相一致。信用证的截止日和装运期之间应有一定的合理间隔,一般为 10—15 天,以便出口方在货物装运后有足够的时间制单、审单、办理议付手续。如果信用证未规定装运期,则最迟装运期与信用证有效期为同一天,即通常所称的"双到期"。这种规定方法不太合理,出口方应视具体情况提请进口方修改。

(7)交单期。信用证的交单期是指运输单据出单日期后必须提交符合信用证条款的单据的特定期限。交单期不得迟于信用证的截止日。如果未规定该期限,按 UCP600 第 14 条 c 款的规定,银行将不接受迟于装运日后 21 天提交的单据。

(8)对运输条款的审核。装运条款通常包括装运地(港)、目的地(港)、装运期、分批装运和转运等信息。装运地(港)、目的地(港)应与合同一致,交货地必须与价格条款一致。若信用证中未注明可否分批及/或转运,按 UCP600 第 31 条 a 款规定:"PARTIAL DRAWINGS OR SHIPMENTS ARE ALLOWED"(允许部分支款或部分发运),则视为允许分批及/或转运。

(9)对保险条款的审核。首先根据价格条款确认是否应该由出口方办理保险,确认后检查投保险别、投保加成等是否与合同一致。若要求的投保险别或投保金额超出了贸易合同的规定,除非信用证上表明由此而产生的超保费由开证申请人承担并允许在信用证项下支付,否则应予以修改。若保险加成过高,还需征得保险公司的同意,否则应予以修改。

(10)对单据条款的审核。信用证要求提交的单据的种类、名称、份数、内容、出单人等规定应当明确,如有不利于出口方顺利履行、安全收汇的条款,应要求申请人进行修改。如来证要求提供领事发票,如果装运地没有该国领事馆,接受这种单据条款必然影响出口方及时收汇,因此要求对方删除这一条款,或要求申请人改为由贸促会或商会认证。

(11)对附加条款的审核。对信用证中加列的一些合同中未规定的特殊条款,应认真审核,如办不到的,应要求修改。

(12)对"软条款"的审核。"软条款"是指信用证中所有无法由受益人自主控制的条款,这些条款通常置受益人于不利地位,它们通常以不同形式隐匿于信用证条款中,一旦受益人对此认识不清或处理不当,将会引发收汇风险。因此,受益人要提高对此类条款的敏感度,加强防范意识,把好审证环节,及时通知改证以消除隐患。

二、修改信用证

1. 含义

修改信用证是对已开立的信用证中的某些条款进行修改的操作。

信用证的修改可以由开证申请人提出,也可以由受益人提出。由于修改信用证的条款涉及到各个当事人的权利和义务,因而不可撤销信用证在其有效期内的任何修改,都必须征得各有关当事人的同意。

2. 修改程序

若修改由受益人提出,在征得申请人同意后,按图3-1所示的程序操作。

若修改由申请人提出,则在征得受益人的同意后,按图3-1所示的程序进行。

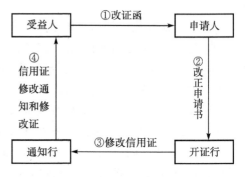

图3-1 修改信用证的流程

3. 修改信用证应注意的问题

(1)非改不可的一定要改,可改可不改的酌情处理。通过对信用证的全面审核,如发现问题,应分别情况及时处理。对于影响安全收汇,难以接受或做到的信用证条款,必须要求进口方修改。

(2)一次性修改。在同一信用证上,若有多处需要修改的,原则上应一次性提出。

(3)对于修改内容接受的规定。UCP600第10条e款规定:"对同一修改的内容不允许部分接受,部分接受将被视为拒绝修改的通知。"

(4)接受或拒绝修改的方式。UCP600第10条c款规定:"……受益人应提供接受或拒绝修改的通知。如果受益人未能给予通知,当交单与信用证与尚未表示接受的修改的要求一致时,即视为受益人已作出接受修改的通知并且从此时起,该信用证被修改。"

(5)修改费用的承担。最好在修改中明确修改费用由谁承担,一般按照责任归属来确定修改费用由谁承担。

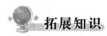 **拓展知识**

信用证 SWIFT 报文的内容

目前,大多数银行都加入了 SWIFT 系统,因此通过该系统开立的信用证在贸易实务中最为常见。在 SWIFT 系统中传送关于信用证的信息都使用 MT7 开头的报文类型,开立跟单信用证使用 MT700 报文。以下就 MT700 报文的内容作一下介绍,见下表。

MT700 报文的内容

M/O	项目编号	项目名称	容量	说明和要求
M	27	Sequence of total	1n/1n	合计次序。如果跟单信用证条款能够容纳在该 MT700 报文中,则该栏填 1/1;如该信用证由一份 MT700 和一份 MT701 报文组成,那么在 MT700 报文的该项目填入"1/2",在 MT701 报文的该项目中填入"2/2",依次类推。
M	40A	Form of documentary credit	24x	跟单信用证类别。由于 UCP600 中规定信用证是不可撤销的,因此该项目有以下几种填法:IRREVOCABLE,不可撤销跟单信用证;IRREVOCABLE TRANSFERABLE,不可撤销可转让跟单信用证;IRREVOCABLE STANDBY,不可撤销备用信用证。
M	20	Documentary credit number	16x	信用证号码。信用证的号码实际上即为开证行的业务编号,进出口双方和银行在相互业务联系中必须引用该编号。信用证号码必须清楚,没有变字等错误,如果信用证号码在信用证中前后出现多次,应注意其相互是否一致,否则应电洽其修改。
O	23	Reference to pre-advice	16x	预通知的编号
O	31C	Date of issue	6n	开证日期。如电文中没有此项目,那么开证日期就是开证行的发电日期。信用证的开证日期应明晰、完整。开证日期表明进口方是否根据商务合同规定的开证期限开立信用证。同时,在需要使用开证日期计算其他时间或根据开证日期来判断所提示单据的出单日期是否在开证日之后等情况时尤为重要。
O	40E	Applicable rules	4*35x	适用的惯例。这是 UCP600 新增的项目。一般用"UCP LATEST VERSION"表示适用最新版本,目前也就是 UCP600。
M	31D	Date and place of expiry	4*35x	到期日及地点。信用证的有效期是受益人向银行提交单据的最后日期,受益人必须在有效日期到期前或当天向银行提交单据,办理付款、承兑或议付手续。逾期交单,银行可以以信用证过期为由,解除所承担的义务。信用证的到期地点是受益人在有效期内向银行提交单据的地点,一般在出口国家,以便受益人办理交单。

续表

M/O	项目编号	项目名称	容量	说明和要求	
O	51a	Applicant bank	A or D	申请人的银行,一般指开证行	
M	50	Applicant	4*35x	申请人	
M	56	Beneficiary	[/34x]	受益人	
M	32B	Currency code,amount	3a15n	货币代号、金额	
O	39A	Percentage credit amount tolerance	2n/2n	信用证金额加减百分率,金额允许有10%的溢短装就用10/10。斜杠前数字表示溢装比例,斜杠后数字表示短装比例。	
O	39B	Maximum credit amount	13x	最高信用证金额	
O	39C	Additional amountscoverd	4*35x	可附加金额	
M	41a	Available with...By...	A or D	在……银行使用有效,使用方式为……当项目代号为"41A"时,银行用SWIFT代码表示;当项目代号为"41D"时,银行用行名地址表示;如果信用证为自由议付信用证,该项目代号为"41D",银行用"ANY BANK IN...(地点/国名)"表示;如果信用证为自由议付信用证,且对议付地点也无限制时,该项目代号应为"41D",银行用"ANY BANK"表示。	
O	42C	Drafts at…	3*35x	汇票期限	若信用证下需要开立汇票,则需要填写
O	42a	Drawee	A or D	付款人	
O	42M	Mixed payment details	4*35x	混合付款指示	
O	42P	Deferred payment details	4*35x	延迟付款指示	
O	43P	Partial shipments	1*35x	分批装运	
O	43T	Transshipment	1*35x	转船	

续表

M/O	项目编号	项目名称	容量		说明和要求
O	44A	Place of taking in charge at/of receipt	1*65x	接管地/接收地	这四项是 UCP600 中的新内容。把原来的 44A 和 44B 拆成这四个项目。原来的 44A 填写所有运输方式下的装运地,现在 44A 只能填写非海运和空运方式下的装运地,而 44E 则仅填写海运和空运下的装运地;原来的 44B 填写所有运输方式下的目的地,现在 44B 只能填写非海运和空运方式下的目的地,而 44F 则仅填写海运和空运下的卸货港/目的港。
O	44E	Port of loading / Airport of disparture	1*65x	装运港/始发港	
O	44F	Port of discharge/Airport of destination	1*65x	卸货港/目的港	
O	44B	Place of final destination/of delivery	1*65x	最终目的地/交货地	
O	44C	Latest date of shipment	6n	最后装船日	
O	44D	Shipment period	6*65x	装运期间	
O	45A	Description of goods and/or services	50*65x	货物描述/各种服务	当一份信用证由一份 MT700 报文和 1~3 份 MT701 报文组成时,项目 "45a""46a"、"47a"的内容只能完整地出现在某一份报文中(即在 MT700 或某一份 MT701 报文中),不能被分割成几部分,分别出现在几个报文中。在 MT700 报文中,"45a""46a"、"47a"三个项目代号应分别为"45A""46A"、"47A",在报文 MT701 中,这三个项目的代号应分别为"45B"、"46B"、"47B"。
O	46A	Documents required	50*65x	应提交的单据	
O	47A	Additional conditions	50*65x	附加条件	
O	71B	Charges	6*35x		费用。该项目的出现只表示费用由受益人负担。若报文无此项目,则表示除议付费、转让费外,其他费用均由开证申请人负担。

续表

M/O	项目编号	项目名称	容量	说明和要求
O	48	Period for presentation	6*35x	提示期间
M	49	Confirmation instructions	7x	保兑指示。该项目内容可能出现下列某一代码。 ①CONFIRM:要求收报行保兑该信用证。 ②MAY ADD:收报行可以对该信用证加具保兑。 ③WITHOUT:不要求收报行保兑该信用证。 要注意的是,即使这里显示"CONFIRM",也还需要有收报行的确认,即明确表示对该信用证保兑,保兑才生效。
O	53a	Reimbursement bank	A or D	偿付行
O	78	Instructions to the paying / accepting /negotion bank	12*65x	对付款/承兑/议付行的指示
O	57a	"advise through"bank	A,B or D	通过××银行通知
O	72	Sender to receiver information	6*35x	银行间的指示

若信用证内容超出MT700报文的容量,则同时需要开MT701报文。

M/O	项目编号	项目名称	容量
M	27	Sequence of total	1n/1n
M	20	Documentary credit number	
O	45B	Description of goods and / or services	100*65x
O	46B	Documents required	100*65x
O	47B	Additions conditional	100*65x

技能训练

(一)训练资料

2009年12月1日,南通里诺公司(NANTONG LINUO COMMERCE LTD.)同西班牙的

SUCONTESA TEXTIL 公司签订了出口女士泳衣的合同。进口方根据合同开来了信用证。合同和信用证的具体内容如下：

1. 合同

SALES CONTRACT

NO.:PMY－091201
DATE:NOV.15,2009
SIGNED AT:NANTONG,CHINA

THE SELLER: NANTONG LINUO COMMERCE LTD.　　THE BUYER: SUCONTESA TEXTIL,SA
　　　　　ROOM 1808 RUNYOU BUILDING　　　　　　　　　　　CL PROGRES 164
　　　　　NO.71 RENMIN MIDDLE ROAD　　　　　　　　　　　BARSALONA SPAIN
　　　　　NANTONG, JIANGSU CHINA

　　THIS CONTRACT IS MADE BY AND BETWEEN THE SELLER AND THE BUYER, WHEREBY THE SELLER AGREES TO SELL AND THE BUYER AGREES TO BUY THE UNDER－MENTIONED GOODS ACCORDING TO THE CONDITIONS STIPULATED BELOW:

Commodity & specification	Quantity	Price terms	
		Unit price	Amount
LADIES SWIMWEAR FABRIC CONSTRUCTION KNIT　BLACK　BROWN	5 000PCS 8 000PCS	FOB NANTONG USD1.50/PCS USD1.60/PCS	USD7 500.00 USD12 800.00 USD20 300.00
TOTAL AMOUNT: U.S. DOLLARS TWENTY THOUSAND THREE HUNDRED ONLY.			

PACKING:1PC/PLOYBAG,500PCS/CTN
TIME OF SHIPMENT:DURING JAN, 2010 BY SEA
LOADING OF PORT AND DESTINATION:FROM NANTONG TO BARCELONA
PARTIAL SHIPMENT AND TRANSSHIPMEN:ALLOWED
SHIPING MARK:　S T
　　　　　　　　BARCELONA
　　　　　　　　NOS.1－26
INSURANCE:　TO BE EFFECTED BY THE BUYER
TERMS OF PAYMENT:THE BUYER SHALL OPEN THROUGH A BANK ACCEPTABLE TO THE SELLER AN IRREVOCABLE SIGHT LETTER OF CREDIT TO REACH THE SELLER 30 DAYS BEFORE THE MONTH OF SHIPMENT AND TO REMIAN VALID FOR NEGOTIATION IN CHINA UNTIL 15TH　DAY AFTER THE FORESAID TIME OF SHIPMENT.

2. 信用证

ISSUE OF A DOCUMENTARY CREDIT

SEQUENCE OF TOTAL	*27:	1/1
FORM OF DOC. CREDIT	*40A:	REVOCABLE
DOC. CREDIT NUMBER	*20:	LC091201
DATE OF ISSUE	31C:	091215
APPLICABLE RULES	*40E:	UCP LATEST VERESION
EXPIRY	*31D:	DATE 100202 PLACE IN SPAIN
APPLICANT BANK	*51A:	CECAESMM059
		*CAIXA D'ESTALVIS DE SABADELL
		*SABADELL(BARCELONA)
APPLICANT	*50:	SUCONTESA TEXTIL,SA
		CL PROGRES 164 BADALONA SPAIN
BENEFICIARY	*59:	NANTONG LINUO COMMERCE LTD
		ROOM 1808 RUNYOU BUILDING
		NO.71 RENMING MIDDLE RD NANTONG
AMOUNT	*32B:	CURRENCY EUR AMOUNT 20 300.00
AVAILABLE WITH/BY	*41A:	ANY BANK IN CHINA
		BY NEGOTIATION
DRAFTS AT...	42C:	30 DAYS AFTER SIGHT
DRAWEE	42A:	SUCONTESA TEXTIL,SA
PARTIAL SHIPMENTS	43P:	NOT ALLOWED
TRANSSHIPMENT	43T:	NOT ALLOWED
PORT OF LOADING	44E:	ANYCHINES PORT
FOR TRANSPORTATION TO	44F:	SABADELL,SPAIN
LATEST DATE OF SHIPMENT	44C:	100115
DESCRIPT OF GOODS	45A:	GOODS AS PER S/C NO. PMY-091201 DATED ON NOV.15,2009
		LADIES SWIMWEAR
		FABRIC CONSTRUCTION KNIT
		BLACK CLOUR/5 000PCS AT USD1.50/PC FOBNANTONG
		BROWN CLOUR/8 000PCS AT USD1.60/PC FOBNANTONG
		PACKING:200PCS/CTN
DOCUMENTS REQUIRED	46A:	
		+ SIGNED COMMERCIAL INVOICE IN TRIPICATE.
		+ PACKING LIST IN TRIPLICATE.
		+ CERTIFICATE OF ORIGIN GSP FORM A, ISSUED BY OFFICIAL AUTHORITIES OF COMMERCE OR OTHER AUTHORITY DULY ENTITLED FOR THIS PURPOSE.

ADDITIONAL CONDITION.	47A:	+FULL SET OF CLEAN ON BOARD B/L MADE OUT TO ORDER, MARKED "FREIGHT PREPAID" NOTIFY APPLICANT. + INSURANCE POLICY/CERTIFICATE IN DUPLICATE ENDORSED IN BLANK FOR 110% INVOICE VALUE, COVERING ALL RISKS OF CIC OF PICC (1/1/1981). + A DISCREPANCY HANDLING FEE OF USD50.00 WILL BE ASSESSED BY CAIXA D'ESTALVIS DE SABADELL ON EACH PRESENTATION OF DOCUMENTS NOT IN STRICT COMPLIANCE WITH THE TERMS AND CONDITIONS OF THE CREDIT. THIS FEE IS FOR THE ACCOUNT OF THE BENEFICIARY AND WILL BE DEDUCTED FROM THE PROCEEDS WHEN PAYMENT IS EFFECTED. + DRAFT MUST INDICATE THE NUMBER AND DATE OF THIS CREDIT.
CHAGREGS	71B:	ALL BANKING CHARGE ARE FOR ACCOUNT OF BENEFICIARY
PRESENTATION PERIOD	48:	DOCUMENTS MUST BE PRESENTED WIHTIN 5 DAYS AFTER THE DATE OF SHIPMENT BUT WITHIN THE VALIDITY OF THE CREDIT.
CONFIRMATION	*49:	WITHOUT
"ADVISE THROUGH"	57D:	BANK OF CHINA, NANTONG CITY CHONG CHUN SUB-BR NO. 98 RENMIN MIDDLE ROAD, NANTONG, JIANGSU CHINA

(二)根据以上资料,完成如下任务

(1)根据 PMY－091201 合同,审核信用证 LC091201,找出问题条款。

(2)分析找出的信用证 LC091201 的问题条款,提出修改意见并撰写修改电文。

任务三 制作发票和装箱单

学习目标

能力目标

能够根据信用证和相关出货资料,正确缮制发票和装箱单

知识目标

1. 掌握发票的作用
2. 熟悉发票和装箱单的种类
3. 熟悉 UCP600 和 ISBP681 中关于发票的条款

任务设计

2009年7月1日,苏州泰山箱包有限公司与美国 ORTAI 有限公司签订了一份拉杆箱出口的销售合同,具体内容如下:

SALES CONTRACT

CONTRACT NO.:TSSC081005
DATE: JUL.1,2009

THE SELLER: SUZHOU TAISHAN SUITCASE & BAG CO.,LTD.
ADDRESS: 66,ZHONGSHAN ROAD SUZHOU, JIANGSU CHINA
TEL: 0086-0512-84524788   FAX:0086-0512-84524788
THE BUYER: ORTAI CO., LTD.
ADDRESS: 30 EAST 40TH STREET,NEW YORK,U.S.A
TEL: 001-212-992-9789   FAX:001-212-992-9789

THIS CONTRACT IS MADE BY AND BETWEEN THE SELLER AND THE BUYER,WHEREBY THE SELLER AGREES TO SELL AND THE BUYER AGREES TO BUY THE UNDER-MENTIONED GOODS ACCORDING TO THE CONDITIONS STIPULATED BELOW:

(1) Name of Commodity and Specification	(2) Quantity	(3) Unit Price	(4) Amount
Trolley Cases		CIF NEW YORK	
Art no. TS503	1 104PCS	USD6.50	USD7 176.00
Art no. TS504	1 149PCS	USD6.00	USD6 894.00
Art no. TS505	1 440PCS	USD5.80	USD8 352.00
Total	3 693PCS	USD22 422.00	

(5) **Packing**: 1 pc in 1 PE bag; 3 pcs/CTN each.
　　　　　　　Packed in THREE 40'CONTAINER
(6) **Delivery**: From <u>SHANGHAI, CHINA</u> to <u>NEW YORK, U.S.A</u>
(7) **Shipping Marks**:　　ORTAI
　　　　　　　　　　　　TSI0601005
　　　　　　　　　　　　NEW YORK
　　　　　　　　　　　　C/NO. 1—1231
(8) **Time of Shipment**: Latest Date of Shipment Aug. 25, 2009
(9) **Partial Shipment**: Not Allowed
(10) **Transshipment**: Not Allowed
(11) **Terms of Payment**: By irrevocable sight letter of credit, reaching the Seller not later than Jul. 25, 2009 and remaining valid for negotiation in China for further 15 days after the effected shipment. In case of late arrival of L/C, the Seller shall not be liable for any delay in shipment and shall have the right to rescind the contract and/or claim for damages.
(12) **Documents**:
  ＋Signed commercial invoice in 2 copies, indicating L/C No. and contract No. certifying the contents in this invoice are true and correct.
  ＋Packing list in 2 copies.
  ＋Original GSP FORM A certificate of origin on official form issued by a trade authority or government body.
  ＋Full set of clean on board marine bill of lading made out to order, endorsed in blank, marked freight prepaid and notify applicant.
  ＋Insurance policies or certificates in duplicate, endorsed in blank for 110 percent of invoice value covering ICC CLAUSES(A).
  ＋Manufacturer's quality certifying the commodity is in good order.
  ＋Beneficiary's certificate certifying that one set of copies of shipping documents has been sent to applicant within 5 days after shipment.
(13) **Inspection**: The Inspection Certificate of Quality and Quantity issued by the Entry-Exit Inspection and Quarantine Bureau shall be taken as the basis of delivery.
(14) **Claims**: Any claims by the buyer regarding the goods shall be filed within 45 days after arrival of the cargo at the port of destination specified in the relative B/L and supported by survey report issued by a recognized surveyor approved by the seller.
(15) **Force Majeure**: If the shipment of the contracted goods is prevented or delayed in whole or in part by reason of war, earthquake or other causes of Force Majeure, the Seller shall not be liable. However, the Seller shall notify the Buyer immediately and furnish the letter by registered airmail with a certificate issued by the China Council for the Promotion of International Trade attesting such event or events.
(16) **Arbitration**: Any dispute arising from the execution of or in connection with this contract shall be settled amicably by negotiation. In case no settlement can be reached, the case shall then be submitted to China International Economic & Trade Arbitration Commission in Shanghai(or in Beijing) for arbitration in accordance with its arbitration rules. The arbitration award is final and binding upon both parties. The fee for arbitration shall be borne by losing party unless otherwise awarded.

The Seller:　　　　　　　　　　　　　　　　The Buyer:
SUZHOU TAISHAN SUITCASE & BAG CO., LTD.　　ORTAI CO., LTD.
　张奇　　　　　　　　　　　　　　　　　　　Jack Smith

2009年7月15日,苏州泰山箱包有限公司外贸单证员李芳收到了中国银行苏州分行国际业务部的信用证通知函,告知美国ORTAI有限公司已经通过花旗银行纽约分行开来信用证。信用证内容如下:

MT700		ISSUE OF A DOCUMENTARY CREDIT
SENDER		CITY NATIONAL BANK NEW YORK, U.S.A
RECEIVER		BANK OF CHINA, SUZHOU BRANCH
Sequence of Total	27:	1/1
Form of Documentary Credit	40A:	IRREVOCABLE
Documentary Credit Number	20:	N5632405TH11808
Date of Issue	31C:	090715
Date and Place of Expiry	31D:	090909 CHINA
Applicant Bank	51D:	CITY NATIONAL BANK 133 MORNINGSIDE AVE NEW YORK, NY 10027 Tel:001-212-865-4763
Applicant	50:	ORTAI CO., LTD. 30 EAST 40TH STREET, NEW YORK, NY 10016 TEL:001-212-992-9788 FAX:001-212-992-9789
Beneficiary	59:	SUZHOU TAISHAN SUITCASE & BAG CO., LTD. 66 ZHONGSHAN ROAD SUZHOU 116001, CHINA TEL:0086-0512-84524788
Currency Code Amount	32B:	USD 22 422.00
Available with/by	41D:	ANY BANK IN CHINA BY NEGOTIATION
Drafts at	42C:	SIGHT
Drawee	42D:	ISSUING BANK
Partial Shipment	43P:	NOT ALLOWED
Transshipment	43T:	NOT ALLOWED
Port of Loading	44E:	SHANGHAI, CHINA
Port of Discharge	44F:	NEW YORK, U.S.A
Latest Date of Shipment	44C:	090825
Description of Goods and/or Services	45A:	CIF NEWYORK TROLLEY CASES AS PER SC NO. TSSC0801005
Documents Required	46A:	+MANUALLY SIGNED COMMERCIAL INVOICE IN 2 COPYES INDICATING L/C NO. AND CONTRACT NO. CERTIFYING THE CONTENTS IN THIS INVOICE ARE TRUE AND CORRECT. +FULL SET OF ORIGINAL CLEAN ON BOARD MARINE BILLS OF LADING MADE OUT TO ORDER, ENDORSED IN BANK MARKED FREIGHT PREPAID. AND NOYIFY APPLICANT. +PACKING LIST IN 2 COPYES ISSUED BY THE BENEFICIARY. +ORIGINAL GSP FORM A CERTIFICATE OF ORIGIN ON OFFICIAL FORM ISSUED BY A TRADE AUTHORITY OR GOVERNMENT BODY.

		+INSURANCE POLICIES OR CERTIFICATES IN DUPLICATE, ENDORSED IN BLANK FOR 110 PERCENT OF INVOICE VALUE COVERING ICC CLAUSES(A).
		+MANUFACTURER'S QUALITY CERTIFICATE CERTIFYING THE COMMODITY IS IN GOOD ORDER.
		+BENEFICIARY'S CERTIFICATE CERTIFYING THAT ONE SET OF COPIES OF SHIPPING DOCUMENTS HAS BEEN SENT TO APPLICANT WHTHIN 5 DAYS AFTER SHIPMENT.
Additional Conditions	47A:	+UNLESS OTHERWISE EXPRESSLY STATED, ALL DOCUMENTS MUST BE IN ENGLISH.
		+ANY PROCEEDS OF PRESENTATIONS UNDER THIS DC WILL BE SETTLED BY TELETRANSMISSION AND A CHARGE OF USD 50.00 (OR CURRENCY EQUIVALENT) WILL BE DEDUCTED.
		+SHIPPING MARKS:ORTAI TSI0601005 NEWYORK C/NO. 1-1231
Confirmation Instructions	49:	WITHOUT
Advise Through Bank	57D:	BANK OF CHINA SUZHOU BRANCH
Sender to Receiver Information:	72:	DOCUMENTS TO BE DESPATCHED BY COURIER SERVICE IN ONE LOT TO CITY NATIONAL BANK

2009年8月5日,苏州泰山箱包有限公司实际出运的拉杆箱信息如下:

品名	Trolley Cases		商标	TAISHAN
装箱率	3只/纸箱			
货号	Art No. TS503:1 104只	纸箱重量	净重4公斤/箱,毛重4.6公斤/箱	
		纸箱尺寸	53.5×37×79.5cm	
		集装箱容量	40'FCL:368CTNS	
	Art No. TS504:1 149只	纸箱重量	净重3.5公斤/箱,毛重4公斤/箱	
		纸箱尺寸	53.5×34.5×82cm	
		集装箱容量	40'FCL:383CTNS	
	Art No. TS505:1 440只	纸箱重量	净重3公斤/箱,毛重3.5公斤/箱	
		纸箱尺寸	48×32.5×78.5cm	
		集装箱容量	40'FCL:480CTNS	

任务分解

1. 制作商业发票
2. 制作装箱单

任务描述

在出口业务中,商业发票是全套单据的核心,装箱单及其他单据均是以商业发票为中心来缮制的。因此,在信用证支付方式下,我们制作的第一个结汇单据就是商业发票,而商业发票的缮制必须以信用证的要求为依据,以保证单证相符而顺利结汇。

操作示范

第一步:读懂合同条款和信用证条款

认真仔细地阅读贸易合同和信用证条款,弄清合同条款的要求和信用证各条款的含义,为准确缮制单据做好准备。

第二步:制作商业发票

商业发票由出口企业自行拟制,无统一格式,但其基本内容大致相同,以下是苏州泰山箱包有限公司商业发票的格式。

SUZHOU TAISHAN SUITCASE & BAG CO., LTD.
66 ZHONGSHAN ROAD SUZHOU, JIANGSU CHINA
TEL:0086－0512－84524788   FAX:0086－0512－84524788

COMMERCIAL INVOICE

TO:		Invoice No.:	
		Invoice Date:	
		S/C No.:	
		L/C No.:	

Transport Details:		FROM		TO
Marks and Numbers	Description of Goods	Quantity	Unit Price	Amount
	TOTAL:			

TOTAL VALUE IN WORDS:

SUZHOU TAISHAN SUITCASE & BAG CO., LTD.

张奇

1. 发票名称

根据 ISBP681 的规定,若信用证只要求发票而未做进一步定义,则提交"发票(invoice)"、"商业发票(commercial invoice)"、"海关发票(customs invoice)"、"税务发票(tax invoice)"、"领事发票(consular invoice)"等形式的发票都可以接受,但是"临时发票(provisional invoice)"、"形式发票(pro-forma invoice)"或类似的发票不可接受,除非信用证另有授权;当信用证要求提交商业发票时,标为"发票"和"商业发票"的单据都是可以接受的。

本案中,由于信用证中发票条款要求的单据名称是"COMMERCIAL INVOICE",所以发票名称可以是 COMMERCIAL INVOICE,也可以是 INVOICE。

2. 出单人名称和地址

根据 UCP600 的规定,若信用证无另外规定,商业发票的出单人为受益人。发票的顶端往往要有醒目的出单人名称、详细地址。通常出口企业在印刷空白发票时就印刷上这些内容。

本案中,在商业发票的顶端填写出单人名称、地址及联系方式:

SUZHOU TAISHAN SUITCASE & BAG CO., LTD.
66,ZHONGSHAN ROAD SUZHOU, JIANGSU CHINA
TEL:0086-0512-84524788   FAX:0086-0512-84524788

3. 受单人或抬头名称和地址

根据 UCP600 的规定,若信用证无另外规定,商业发票的受单人或抬头为开证申请人。

本案中,应填写:ORTAI CO., LTD.
30 EAST 40TH STREET, NEW YORK, NY 10016

4. 发票号码、发票日期、信用证号码、合同号码等参考信息

发票号码由出口方统一编制,一般采用顺序号,便于查对。

发票日期应早于提单日期,不能迟于信用证有效期。根据 UCP600 的规定,如果信用证没有特殊规定,银行可以接受签发日期早于开证日的发票。

信用证号码参照信用证缮制。

合同号应与信用证上列明的一致,一笔交易有几份合同的,都应打在发票上。

本案的填写:
Invoice No.:TSI0801005
Invoice Date:AUG.5,2009
S/C No.:TSSC0801005
L/C No.:N5632405TH11808

5. 起运地和目的地

该栏目为非必需栏目,可以省略。如不省略,起运地和目的地均应明确具体,不能笼统,如果需要转运,应将转运港名称表示出来,例如:货物从上海经鹿特丹转船至英国伦敦。这一栏目填写如下:From Shanghai to London, U.K. with transshipment(W/T) at Rotterdam.

本案的填写:FROM SHANGHAI TO NEW YORK U.S.A BY SEA.

6. 唛头(shipping marks and numbers)

一般由卖方自行设计,但若合同或信用证规定了唛头,则须按规定。若无唛头,可打上 N/M (No Mark)。

本案的填写:ORTAI
　　　　　TSI0601005

NEW YORK
C/NO.1-1231

7. 货物描述(description of goods)

发票中的货物描述必须与信用证规定一致,但并不要求如同镜子反射那样完全相同。货物细节可以在发票中的若干地方表示,当合并在一起与信用证规定一致即可。在其他一切单据中,货物描述可使用与信用证中货物描述无矛盾的统称。由此可见,信用证对发票描述的要求高于其他单据。

发票中的货物描述必须反映实际装运的货物。例如,信用证的货物描述显示两种货物,如9辆卡车和9辆摩托车,如果信用证不禁止分批装运,而发票表明只装运了5辆摩托车,是可以接受的。当然,列明信用证规定的全部货物描述,然后注明实际装运货物的发票也是可以接受的。

本案的填写:Trolley Cases
    TS503
    TS504
    TS505

8. 数量、单价和金额

凡"约"、"大概"、"大约"或类似的词语,用于信用证数量、单价和金额时,应理解为有关数量、单价和金额不超过10%的增减幅度。值得注意的是,商品数量单位一定要与单价中的数量单位一致。

单价由计价货币、单位数额、计量单位和价格术语等四部份组成。如果信用证中写明了贸易术语的来源,则发票必须表明相同的来源。如信用证条款规定,"CIF SINGAPORE INCOTERMS 2000",那么"CIF SINGAPORE"和"CIF SINGAPORE INCOTERMS"都不符合信用证的要求,只有"CIF SINGAPORE INCOTERMS 2000"符合信用证的要求。发票必须显示信用证要求的折扣或扣减,发票还可显示信用证未规定的与预付款或折扣等有关的扣减额。

金额必须准确计算,正确缮打,并认真复核,特别要注意小数点的位置是否正确,金额和数量的横乘、竖加是否有矛盾。

发票金额一般不应超过信用证金额,但当采用部分金额信用证方式支付、部分金额其他付款方式支付时(例如,90%合同金额采用即期信用证支付和10%合同金额采用前T/T支付),开具发票金额就可能超过信用证规定的金额。根据UCP600的规定,按指定行事的指定银行、保兑行(如有的话)或开证行可以接受金额大于信用证允许金额的商业发票,其决定对有关各方均有约束力,只要该银行对超过信用证允许金额的部分未作承付或者议付。

本案的填写:

Quantity	Unit Price	Amount
	CIF NEW YORK	
1 104PCS	USD6.50/PC	USD7 176.00
1 149PCS	USD6.00/PC	USD6 894.00
1 440PCS	USD5.80/PC	USD8 352.00
3 693PCS		USD 22 422.00

9. 发票上加各种证明

国外来证有时要求在发票上加注各种费用金额、特定号码、有关证明句,一般可将这些内容打在发票商品栏以下的空白处,大致有以下几种:

(1)加注运费、保险费和FOB金额。

(2)注明特定号码。如进口证号、配额许可证号码等。

(3)缮打证明句。如出口澳大利亚享受GSP待遇,往往要求加注"发展中国家声明";又如,有些来证要求加注非木质包装证明句等。

(4)但也有来证要求过分苛刻,如来证要求卖方在列出一系列详细费用包括成本、海洋运费、内陆运费以后,再给出CFR价的总额。对如此要求应根据实际情况考虑是否接受,如果难以办到,就应及时要求对方修改条款。

本案的填写:

WE HEREBY CERTIFY THAT THE CONTENTS IN THIS INVOICE ARE TRUE AND CORRECT.

10. 出单人签名(signature)

商业发票只能由信用证中规定的受益人出具。UCP600规定商业发票可不必签字,但有时来证规定发票需要签字的,还是要签字,如"SIGNED COMMERCIAL INVOICE..."。在无手签要求的情况下,可以使用印鉴,但若来证要求"MANUALLY SIGNED"或"HAND SIGNED",则必须手签。

本案的填写:

SUZHOU TAISHAN SUITCASE & BAG CO., LTD.

张奇

11. 发票份数

发票有正副本之分,发票正副本份数的确定方法包括:①若信用证规定"发票若干份Invoice in × copies"时,如发票三份,则提交至少一份正本发票;②若信用证规定"一份发票One invoice"或"发票一份Invoice in one copy"时,则需提交一份正本发票;③若信用证规定"发票的一份One copy of invoice"时,则提一份副本发票即为符合要求,当然也可提交一份正本发票。

本案操作:至少出具一份正本,共两份。

制作好的商业发票如下:

SUZHOU TAISHAN SUITCASE & BAG CO., LTD.				
66,ZHONGSHAN ROAD SUZHOU, JIANGSU CHINA				
TEL: 0086-0512-84524788 FAX: 0086-0512-84524788				
COMMERCIAL INVOICE				
TO:	ORTAI CO., LTD. 30 EAST 40TH STREET, NEW YORK, NY 10016	Invoice No.:	TSI0801005	
		Invoice Date:	AUG. 5,2009	
		S/C No.:	TSSC0801005	
		L/C No.:	N5632405TH11808	
Transport Details:	FROM SHANGHAI CHINA TO NEW YORK U.S.A BY SEA			
Marks and Numbers	Description of Goods	Quantity	Unit Price	Amount

ORTAI	Trolley Cases		CIF NEW YORK	
TSI0601005	TS503	1 104PCS	USD6.50/PC	USD7 176.00
NEW YORK	TS504	1 149PCS	USD6.00/PC	USD6 894.00
C/NO.1-1231	TS505	1 440PCS	USD5.80/PC	USD8 352.00
	TOTAL:	3 693PCS		USD 22 422.00
TOTAL VALUE IN WORDS:	SAY U.S. DOLLARS TWENTY TWO THOUSAND FOUR HUNDRED AND TWENTY TWO ONLY.			
WE HEREBY CERTIFY THAT THE CONTENTS IN THIS INVOICE ARE TRUE AND CORRECT. SUZHOU TAISHAN SUITCASE & BAG CO., LTD. 张奇				

第三步：制作装箱单

根据信用证、货物实际出运信息和已制作的商业发票，制作符合信用证要求的装箱单。商业发票由出口企业自行拟制，无统一格式，但其基本内容大致相同，以下苏州泰山箱包有限公司的装箱单的格式。

SUZHOU TAISHAN SUITCASE & BAG CO., LTD
66,ZHONGSHAN ROAD SUZHOU, JIANGSU CHINA
TEL: 0086－0512－84524788 FAX: 0086－0512－84524788
PACKING LIST

TO:		Invoice No.:	
		Invoice Date:	
		S/C No.:	
		L/C No.:	

Transport Details:

Marks and Numbers	Number and Kind of Package Description of Goods	Packages	Quantity	G.W (KGS)	N.W (KGS)	MEAS. (CBM)
	Total:					
TOTAL PACKAGES IN WORDS:						

SUZHOU TAISHAN SUITCASE & BAG CO., LTD.
张奇

装箱单缮制方法如下：

1. **单据名称**

单据名称最好符合信用证规定。如信用证要求提供重量单，则名称应写为"WEIGHT LIST"；如信用证要求提供尺码单，则名称应写为"MEASUREMENT LIST"。

本案的填写：PACKING LIST

2. **抬头**

填写受单方的名称与地址。多数情况下填写进口方的名称和地址，并与信用证的开证申请人的名称和地址一致。

本案的填写：ORTAI CO., LTD.
30 EAST 40TH STREET, NEW YORK, NY 10016

3. **号码和日期**

本栏目一般填发票号码和日期。

本案的填写：

Invoice No.： TSI0801005
Invoice Date： AUG.5,2009

4. **唛头**

填写唛头，且须与发票、信用证及实物印刷完全一致。

本案的填写：ORTAI
　　　　　　TSI0601005
　　　　　　NEW YORK
　　　　　　C/NO.1-1231

5. **包装种类和件数、货物描述**

填写货物及包装的详细资料，包括货物名称、规格、数量和包装说明等内容。涉及一票货物多个品种的，分别填写品名、包装情况及包装数量。

本案的填写：

Number and kind of package Description of goods	PACKAGES	Quantity
Trolley Cases TS503 TS504 TS505 PACKED IN 3 PCS/CTN, SHIPPED IN 3×40'FCL	368CTNS 383CTNS 480CTNS	1 104PCS 1 149PCS 1 440PCS

6. **货物的毛重、净重和体积**

按出运货物的实际情况填列，均应符合信用证的规定。涉及一票货物多个品种的，分别填写单件包装的毛重、净重和尺码以及对应品种的总毛重、总净重和总尺码。单件包装的毛重、净重及尺码前用"@"注明。本案的填写：

G.W (KGS)	N.W (KGS)	MEAS. (CBM)
5 078.4	4 416	57.886 4
4 596	4 021.5	57.833
5 040	4 320	58.8

7. 其他

根据信用证中关于装箱单的特殊要求条款,制作时应在装箱单上注明。如"所有单据注明信用证号码、开证日期和开证行名称"等。

本案中无需填写。

8. 签署

当信用证没有规定装箱单签名时,可以不盖章签名,当然也可以盖章签名。

本案的填写:

SUZHOU TAISHAN SUITCASE & BAG CO., LTD.

　　　　张奇

制作好的装箱单如下:

SUZHOU TAISHAN SUITCASE & BAG CO., LTD.
66,ZHONGSHAN ROAD SUZHOU, JIANGSU CHINA
TEL:0086-0512-84524788　FAX:0086-0512-84524788
PACKING LIST

TO:	ORTAI CO., LTD. 30 EAST 40TH STREET, NEW YORK, NY 10016	Invoice No.:	TSI0801005
		Invoice Date:	AUG.5,2009
		S/C No.:	TSSC0801005
		L/C No.:	N5632405TH11808

Transport Details: FROM SHANGHAI CHINA TO NEW YORK U.S.A BY SEA

Marks and Numbers	Number and Kind of Package Description of Goods	Packages	Quantity	G.W (KGS)	N.W (KGS)	MEAS. (CBM)
ORTAI TSI0601005 NEW YORK C/NO.1-1231	Trolley Cases TS503 TS504 TS505 Packed in 3PCS/CTN, SHIPPED IN 3 × 40'FCL	368CTNS 383CTNS 480CTNS	1 104PCS 1 149PCS 1 440PCS	5 078.4 4 596 5 040	4 416 4 021.5 4 320	57.886 4 57.833 58.8
	Total:	1 231CTNS	3 693PCS	14 714.4	12 757.5	174.519

TOTAL PACKAGES IN WORDS: SAY ONE THOUSAND TWO HUNDRED AND THIRTY ONE CARTONS ONLY.
SUZHOU TAISHAN SUITCASE & BAG CO., LTD. 张奇

必备知识

一、商业发票

1. 商业发票的含义

商业发票是卖方(出口方)向买方(进口方)开具的载有交易货物名称、数量、价格等内容的总清单,是装运货物的总说明。它虽不是物权凭证,但作为买卖双方交接货物、结算货款的主要单据,它对该笔交易作出详细的叙述,是贸易必不可缺的单据,也是信用证项下单据的中心单据。

2. 商业发票的作用

(1)交易的证明文件。发票是一笔交易的全面叙述,它详细列明了货物名称、数量、单价、总值、重量和规格等内容,它能使进口方识别所装的货物是否属于某笔订单,是否按照合同规定的内容和要求装运所需货物。所以发票是最重要的履约证明文件。

(2)记账的凭证。发票是销售货物的凭证,世界各国的企业都凭发票记账。对出口方来说,通过发票可以了解销售收入、核算盈亏、掌握经济效益。对进口方来说,同样根据发票逐笔记账,按时结算货款,履行合同义务。

(3)报关征税的依据。货物装运前,出口方需向海关递交商业发票等单据向海关报关,发票中载明的价值和有关货物的说明是计税和统计的依据。因此它是海关验关放行的重要凭证之一。国外进口方进口申报时同样需向当地海关当局呈送发货人的发票,海关凭以核算税金,并使进口方得以迅速清关提货。

(4)替代汇票。在信用证不要求使用跟单汇票时,开证行应根据发票金额付款,这时发票就代替了汇票。其他在不用汇票结汇的业务中(如汇款方式),也用发票替代汇票进行结算。

除以上几点外,发票还作为统计、投保、理赔、外汇核销、出口退税等业务的重要凭证。

3. 发票的种类

我国进出口贸易中使用的发票主要有商业发票(commercial invoice)、海关发票(customs invoice)、形式发票(pro-forma invoice)、领事发票(consular invoice)及厂商发票(manufacturer's invoice)。

4. UCP600中有关商业发票的条款

(1)UCP600第18条a款规定,商业发票必须看似由受益人出具(第38条规定的情形除外),必须出具成以申请人为抬头(第38条g款规定的情形除外),必须与信用证的货币相同,无需签字;b款规定,按指定行事的指定银行、保兑行(如有的话)或开证行可以接受金额大于信用证允许金额的商业发票,其决定对有关各方均有约束力,只要该银行对超过信用证允许金额的部分未作承付或者议付;c款规定,商业发票上的货物、服务或履约行为的描述必须与信用证中显示的内容相符。

(2) UCP600第17条a款规定,信用证中规定的各种单据必须至少提供一份正本。b款规定,除非单据本身表明其不是正本,银行将视任何单据表面上具有单据出具人正本签字、标志、图章或标签的单据为正本单据。c款规定,除非单据另有显示,银行将接受单据作为正本单据,如果该单据表面看来由单据出具人手工书写、打字、穿孔签字或盖章;或表面看来使用单据出具人的正本信笺;或声明单据为正本,除非该项声明表面看来与所提示的单据不符。d款规定,如果信用证要求提交副本单据,则提交正本单据或副本单据均可。e款规定,如果信用证使用诸如"一式两份""两张""两份"等术语要求提交多份单据,则可以提交至少一份正本,其余份数以副本来满足。但单据本身另有相反指示者除外。

(3) UCP600第30条a款规定,"约"或"大约"用于信用证金额或信用证规定的数量或单价时,应解释为允许有关金额或数量或单价有不超过10%的增减幅度。b款规定,在信用证未以包装单位件数或货物自身件数的方式规定货物数量时,货物数量允许有5%的增减幅度,只要总支取金额不超过信用证金额。c款规定,如果信用证规定了货物数量,而该数量已全部发运,及如果信用证规定了单价,而该单价又未降低,或当第30条b款不适用时,则即使不允许部分装运,也允许支取的金额有5%的减幅;若信用证规定有特定的增减幅度或使用第30条a款提到的用语限定数量,则该减幅不适用。

5. **ISBP681中有关商业发票的条款**

ISBP681中与发票相关的条款是57—67条,体现在两个方面:一是对发票的界定。如信用证要求"发票"而未作进一步界定,则提交任何形式的发票均可(如商业发票、海关发票、税务发票、最终发票、领事发票等)。但是,"临时发票""预开发票"或类似发票则不可接受。当信用证要求提交商业发票时,标为"发票"的单据可以接受。二是对货物、服务或履约行为的描述及其他有关发票的一般事项。

二、包装单据

包装单据是指一切记载或描述商品包装情况的单据,也是商业发票的补充单据,其主要种类如下:

1. **装箱单(packing list)**

装箱单又称包装单,是表明出口货物的包装形式、包装内容、数量、重量、体积或件数的单据。其主要用途是作为海关验货、公证行和进口方提货点数的凭证。装箱单还可作为商业发票补充文件,用以补充说明各种不同规格货物所装之箱号及各箱的重量、体积、尺寸等内容。

2. **重量单(weight list)**

重量单又称磅码单,是用于以重量计量、计价的商品清单。一般列明每件包装商品的毛重和净重、整批货物的总毛重和总净重;有的还须增列皮重;按公量计量、计价的商品,则须列明公量及计算公量的有关数据。凡提供重量单的商品,一般不需提供包装单。

3. **尺码单(measurement list)**

尺码单又称体积单,是着重记载货物的包装件的长、宽、高及总体积的清单。供买方及承运人了解货物的尺码,以便合理运输、储存及计算运费。

拓展知识

一、海关发票

1. 含义和作用

海关发票是进口国(地区)海关制定的一种专用于向该国(地区)出口的一种特别的发票格式。其主要目的和作用是证明商品的成本价值和商品的生产国家,以作为进口货物估价完税和实行差别税率的依据。目前,提供海关发票的主要国家(地区)有美国、加拿大、澳大利亚、新西兰、牙买加等。

2. 海关发票的主要内容与缮制方法

各国的海关发票都有其固定格式。在此,仅介绍我国对外贸易业务中使用较多的加拿大海关发票。

(1) Vendor(Name and Address):卖方(名称和地址)。本栏填卖方的全称和地址,信用证条件下即为受益人。

(2) Date of Direct Shipment to Canada:直接运往加拿大的装运日期。填实际装运日期。

(3) Other References (Include Purchaser's Order No.):其他参考项目(包括买方订单号)。根据信用证的要求填写有关合同号、订单号、发票号等。

(4) Consignee(Name and Address):收货人(名称和地址)。填入买方的全称和地址,信用证项下即为开证申请人。

(5) Purchaser's Name and Address(If Other than Consignee):买方名称和地址(如非收货人)。如买方不是收货人,此栏则填写买方名称。如买方与收货人系一个人,应填入"The same as No. 4,consignee"。

(6) Country of Transshipment:转运国家。将货物运至加拿大中途转运的国家或地区名称填入本栏。例如,"Transshipment at Singapore"。如为直运,则应填制"N/A"(即为 Not applicable 的缩写)。

(7) Country of Origin of Goods:货物原产地国。应填"China"。如该批货物有多个原产地国,可在"12栏"注明。

(8) Transportation(Give Mode and Place of Direct Shipment to Canada):运输说明(提供直运加拿大的运输方式和装运地点)。将运输方式和装运地填入此栏。

(9) Conditions of Sale and Terms of Payment (i. e. Sale, Consignment Shipment, Leased Goods, etc.):销售条件和支付方式(即销售、委托发运、租赁商品等)。按合同或信用证的规定填入价格术语和支付方式。

(10) Currency of Settlement:结算货币和名称。填入合同或信用证规定的支付货币的名称。

(11) No. of Packages:件数。应填写该批货物外包装的总件数和包装单位。

(12) Specification of Commodities(Kind of Packages, Marks and Numbers, General Description and Characteristics, i. e. Grade, Quality.):商品详细说明(包装种类、唛头、品名和品质)。填入该批货物的品名、包装、品质规格和唛头等各项内容,并须与发票相关内容一致。

(13) Quantity(State Unit):数量(表明单位)。应填写该批货物成交的数量。

(14) Unit Price:单价。单位价格应包括贸易术语、计价货币和数量单位,例如,CIF TOKYO USD 10.00 PER DOZEN。

(15) Total:总值。填入该批成交货物总金额,不同商品规格应分别列明,并累计出总额。

(16)Total Weight：总重量。应分别列出净重和毛重的总重量,并填入此栏。

(17)Invoice Total：发票总值。将"15栏"的总金额填入。

(18)If any of fields 1 to 17 are included on an attached commercial invoice, check this box：如第1至17栏的内容已在所附的商业发票中,在其方格内打上记号。

如果第1至第17栏的内容已记载在所附的发票中,在方格内填入"×"记号,并在末行横线上填明该项商业发票号码。

(19)Exporter's Name and Address(If other than Vendor)：出口方名称及地址(如并非卖方)。如果出口方名称与"第1栏"相同,则应填制"The same as No.1, vendor";如不是,则应填写实际出口商的全称和地址。

(20)Originator(Name and Address)：负责人(名称及地址)。填写出口方名称和地址,并由负责人手签。

(21)Departmental Ruling(If applicable)：主管当局现行条例(如适用者)。通常填N/A,即为不适用。

(22)If fields 23 to 25 are not applicable, check this box：如第23栏至第25栏不适用,则在方格内打上记号。如果该货物不适用(23)、(24)和(25)的内容,可在方格内打上"×"记号。

(23)If included in field 17 indicate amount。如第17栏已包括,则注明其金额。如果下列项目已注明在第17栏内,则列出下列要求的金额。

①Transportation charges, expenses and insurance from the place of direct shipment to Canada：直接运至加拿大的运费和保险费。应填入运费和保险费的总和,如不适用则填入N/A或Nill。

②Cost for construction, erection and assembly incurred after importation into Canada：货到加拿大后,因建造、安置和组装而产生的费用。按实际费用填入,如不适用,则用N/A或Nill。

③Export packing：出口包装费。注明实际出口包装费用,如不适用,应填写N/A或Nill。

(24)If not included in field 17 indicate amount：如果第17栏不包括,则注明金额。如果本栏下列①、②、③各项不包括在第17栏总金额内,则注明要求的金额。通常①、②和③三项填N/A或Nill。在FOB条件下,如果卖方代为买方租船订舱,该运费应货到支付,所以在①栏内填实际运费金额。

(25)Check(If applicable)：如适用在方格内打上记号。本栏属于加工贸易专用,如为其他贸易方式,则在方格内填入N/A。

二、形式发票

形式发票是出口方向进口方发出的有关货物名称、规格、单价等内容的非正式参考性发票,供进口方申请进口批汇之用,不能用于托收和议付。

三、领事发票

领事发票又称签证发票,是某些国家为了解进口货物的原产地、有无倾销行为等情况而规定的,以进口国驻出口国领事签证的发票,作为征收进口关税的前提。目前,已很少使用领事发票。

四、厂商发票

厂商发票是进口国为确定出口商有无倾销行为,以及为了海关估价、核税和征收反倾销税,而由出口货物的制造厂商所出具的,以本国货币计算的,用来证明出口国国内市场出厂价的发票。

技能训练

(一) 训练资料

1. 信用证

MT 700		ISSUE OF A DOCUMENTARY CREDIT
APPLICATION HEADER		RJHISARIA××× *ALRAJHI BANKING AND INVESTMENT *CORPORATION *RIYADH (HEAD OFFICE)
SEQUENCE OF TOTAL	27:	1/1
FORM OF DOC. CREDIT	40A:	IRREVOCABLE
DOC. CREDIT NUMBER	20:	LC123
DATE OF ISSUE	31C:	071015
DATE/PLACE OF EXPIRY	31D:	DATE 071225 PLACE IN CHINA
APPLICANT	50:	RED FLOWER TRADING CO. P.O. BOX 536, RIYADH 22766, KSA TEL: 00966-1-4659215 FAX: 00966-1-4659217
BENEFICIARY	59:	NANJING HUIHUANG FOODS CO., LTD. YUN MANSION RM3908 NO. 85 FUZI RD., NANJING 210005, CHINA TEL: 0086-25-4715000 FAX: 0086-25-4711111
AMOUNT	32B:	CURRENCY USD AMOUNT 13600.00
PERCENTAGE CREDIT AMOUNT TOLERANCE	39A:	10/10
AVAILABLE WITH/BY	41D:	ANY BANK IN CHINA, BY NEGOTIATION
DRAFTS AT ...	42C:	30 DAYS AFTER B/L DATE
DRAWEE	42A:	RJHISARI *ALRAJHI BANKING AND INVESTMENT *CORPORATION *RIYADH (HEAD OFFICE)
PARTIAL SHIPMENTS	43P:	NOT ALLOWED
TRANSSHIPMENT	43T:	NOT ALLOWED
PORT OF LOADING/ AIRPORT OF DEPARTURE	44E:	CHINA MAIN PORT, CHINA
PORT OF DISCHARGE	44F:	DAMMAM PORT, SAUDI ARABIA
LATEST DATE OF SHIPMENT	44C:	071215
GOODS DESCRIPTION	45A:	ABOUT 1700 CARTONS CANNED MUSRHOOM PIECES & STEMS 24 TINS × 220 GRAMS NET WEIGHT (G. W. 420 GRAMS) AT USD8.00 PERCARTON, ROSE BRAND, CIF DAMMAM PORT, SAUDI ARABIA, AS PER S/C NO. UY90, DATED SEP.19, 2007.

DOCUMENTS REQUIRED	46A: + SIGNED COMMERCIAL INVOICE MANUALLY IN TRIPLICATE AND MUST SHOW BREAK DOWN OF THE AMOUNT AS FOLLOWS: FOB VALUE, FREIGHT CHARGES, PREMIUM AND TOTAL AMOUNT CIF. + FULL SET CLEAN ON BOARD BILL OF LADING MADE OUT TO THE ORDER OF ALRAJHI BANKING AND INVESTMENT CORP, MARKED FREIGHT. PREPAID AND NOTIFY APPLICANT, INDICATING THE FULL NAME, ADDRESS AND TEL NO. OF THE CARRYING VESSEL'S AGENT AT THE PORT OF DISCHARGE. + PACKING LIST IN ONE ORIGINAL PLUS 5 COPIES, ALL OF WHICHMUST BE MANUALLY SIGNED. + INSPECTION (HEALTH) CERTIFICATE FROM C. I. Q. (ENTRY-EXIT INSPECTION AND QUARANTINE OF THE PEOPLE'S REPUBLIC. OF CHINA) STATING GOODS ARE FIT FOR HUMAN BEING. + CERTIFICATE OF ORIGIN DULY CERTIFIED BY CCPIT, STATING THE NAME OF THE MANUFACTURERS OR PRODUCERS AND THAT GOODS EXPORTED ARE WHOLLY OF CHINESE ORIGIN. + THE PRODUCTION DATE OF THE GOODS NOT TO BE EARLIER THAN HALF MONTH AT TIME OF SHIPMENT. BENEFICIARY MUST CERTIFY THE SAME.
ADDITIONAL CONDITIONS	47A: + A DISCREPANCY FEE OF USD50.00 WILL BE IMPOSED ON EACH SET OF DOCUMENTS PRESENTED FOR NEGOTIATION UNDER THIS L/C WITH DISCREPANCY. THE FEE WILL BE DEDUCTED FROM THE BILL AMOUNT.
CHARGES	71B: ALL CHARGES OUTSIDE KSA ON BENEFICIARIES' ACCOUNT INCLUDING REIMBURSING COMMISSION, DISCREPANCY FEE (IF ANY) AND COURIER CHARGES.
PERIOD FOR PRESENTATION	48: WITHIN 10 DAYS AFTER THE DATE OF SHIPMENT, BUT WITHIN THE VALIDITY OF THIS CREDIT.

CONFIRMATION INSTRUCTIONS	49：	WITHOUT
REIMBURSEMENT	53D：	ALRAJHI BANKING AND INVESTMENT CORP BANK RIYADH (HEAD OFFICE)
INSTRUCTIONS TO PAYING BANK	78：	DOCUMENTS TO BE DESPATCHED IN ONE LOT BY COURIER. ALL CORRESPONDENCE TO BE SENT TO ALRAJHI BANKING AND INVESTMENT. COPRORATION RIYADH (HEAD OFFICE)
SENDER TO RECCIVER	72：	REIMBURSEMENT IS SUBJECT TO ICC URR 525. INFORMATION.

2. 货物实际装运信息

(1)数量：1 750 纸箱

(2)纸箱尺寸：30 厘米×25 厘米×20 厘米

(3)商业发票号码：2007NHT098

(4)商业发票日期：2007 年 11 月 26 日

(5)SHIPPING MARKS：RFT
　　　　　　　　　ROSE BR AND
　　　　　　　　　RIYADH
　　　　　　　　　C/NO：1－UP

(6)装运港：上海港

(7)国外运费：1 000 美元

(8)国外保费：80 美元

(9)南京辉皇食品有限公司的法人代表：章胜

(二)根据以上资料，制作商业发票和装箱单

1. 商业发票

COMMERCIAL INVOICE				
TO：		Invoice No.：		
		Invoice Date：		
		S/C NO.：		
		L/C NO.：		
Transport Details：		FROM		TO
Marks and Numbers	Description of Goods	Quantity	Unit Price	Amount
TOTAL：				

TOTAL VALUE IN WORDS：	

2. 装箱单

PACKING LIST						
TO：			Invoice No.： Invoice Date： S/C No.： L/C No.：			
Transport Details：							
Marks and Numbers	Number and Kind of Package Description of Goods	Packages	Quantity	G. W (KGS)	N. W (KGS)	MEAS. (CBM)
	Total：					
TOTAL PACKAGES IN WORDS：							

任务四　制作海运托运单和提单

学习目标

能力目标

学会用英文准确、规范地缮制海运托运单和提单

知识目标

1. 掌握海运托运单和提单的含义、作用、缮制方法
2. 熟悉海运托运单和提单的填写规范

任务设计

根据提供的资料缮制海运托运单和提单。

1. 售货合同

GUANGDONG　BAOSHI　TOOLS　MANUFACTURE CO.,LTD.
ZHANQIAN ROAD, GUANGZHOU, CHINA

TEL: 020—22568741
FAX: 020—22682103　　　　　　　　　　S/C NO.: 20093321
　　　　　　　　　　　　　　　　　　DATE: MAR. 18,2009

SALES　CONTRACT

TO: ABC CORP. OF LONDON
　　66/66 ACOMMERCIAL STREET, LONDON

Dear Sirs,

We hereby confirm having sold to you the following goods on terms and conditions as specified belows:

SHIPPING MARK	DESCRIPTIONS OF GOODS	QTY (PCS)	UNIT PRICE (USD)	AMOUNT (USD)
N/M	TOOLS Double Open End Spanner 8×10MM 10×12MM	60 000 80 000	CIF LONDON 0.50 0.40	 30 000.00 32 000.00
	TOTAL:	140 000		62 000.00

(1) PRODUCT FINISHED TIME: MAR. 20, 2009
(2) TERMS OF PAYMENT: 30% T/T in advance, the others 70% T/T before Shipment.
(3) FROM: GUANGDONG, CHINA

(4)TO:LONDON,UK
(5)LATEST DATE OF SHIPMENT:MAY. 10,2009
OUR BANK INFORMATION IS AS FOLLOWS:
BENEFICIARY: SHANGHAI TIANYE TOOLS MANUFACTURE CO.,LTD.
BENEFICIARY ADDRESS: NO.3188,GANXIANG TOWN, JINSHAN DISTRCT,SHANGHAI,CHINA
BANK NAME: BANK OF CHINA SHANGHAI BRANCH JIN SHAN SUB BRANCH
ACCOUNT NO.: RMB80456861
BANK ADDRESS: NO.98,WEILING ROAD, SHIHUA,JINSHAN DISTRICT SHANGHAI, CHINA

THE BUYER: THE SELLER:
PT. HYCO LANGGENC   SHANGHAI TIANYE TOOLS MANUFCTURE CO., LTD.
PIFER   **HUA ZHANG**

2. 其他补充资料

补充资料
(1) INVOICE NO.: BS005   DATE: APR.10,2009
(2) PACKING   G.W   N.W   MEAS
Double Open End Spanner
8×10MM (MTM)   2KGS/CTN   1.8KGS/CTN   0.02M3/CTN
Packed in 1 carton of 100 pcs each
10×12MM(MTM)   2.5KGS/CTN   2.2KGS/CTN   0.01M3/CTN
Packed in 1 carton of 100 pcs each
(3) FREIGHT: USD2 400.00
(4) THE VESSEL NO.: B050588661
(5) S/S:JENNEY ;SHIPMENT DATE: MAY. 1, 2009
(6) 发货人账号:045686
(7) 外币账号:MY564321321
(8) 境内货源地:广州
(9) 生产厂家:广东宝石工具制造有限公司(3105226441)

任务分解

1. 读懂所给资料
2. 根据所给资料,制作海运托运单和提单

任务描述

根据合同、补充资料准确、规范地制作出口托运单是单证员必备的一项技能,在实际业务中,要确保托运单、海运提单与合同及其他单据的一致性。

操作示范

第一步：读懂所给的销售合同和其他补充资料

认真仔细地阅读所给资料，尤其要注意装运港、目的港、装运期等信息。

第二步：根据所给资料，缮制出口托运单

不同公司的出口托运单的格式可能有差异，但是基本栏目差不多，下面是一份托运单。

SHIPPING LETTER OF INSTRUCTION

DATE：　　年　　月　　日

托运人		合同号	
		发票号	
		信用证号	
收货人		运输方式	
		装运港	
		卸货港	
通知人		装运期	
		可否转运	
		可否分批	
		运费支付方式	
		正本提单	

标记及号码 Marks & Numbers	货名 Description of Goods	件数 Quantity	总重量 Weight Kilos		总尺码 Measurement
			净 Net	毛 Gross	

共计件数（大写） Total Number of Packages in Writing	

备注 Remarks：

以下对各栏目的填制作详细说明：

1. **托运人（shipper）**

填写托运人的全称、街名、城市、国家名称，并填写联系电话、传真号。托运人可以是：①货主；②货主的贸易代理人；③货主的货运代理人。在信用证结算方式下，托运人一般按信用证的受益人填写。

本案填写：

托运人(Shipper)	GUANGDONG BAOSHI TOOLS MANUFACTURE CO.，LTD.

2. 收货人（consignee）

填写收货人的全称、街名、城市、国家名称，并填写联系电话、传真号。

(1)收货人可以不记名，填写凭指示字样如"to order"、"to order of shipper"等；

(2)收货人可以记名，填写实际收货人，或货运代理人；

(3)实际业务中有两个或两个以上的收货人，托运单中该栏填写第一收货人，通知人栏填写第二收货人。

本案填写：

收货人(Consignee)	ABC CORP. OF LONDON 66/66 A COMMERCIAL STREET,LONDON

3. 通知人（notify）

填写货物到达目的港时船方发送到货通知的对象，由该通知人通知收货人货物已经到达目的港，有时被通知人即为进口方。

本案填写：

通知人(Notify)	ABC CORP. OF LONDON 66/66 A COMMERCIAL STREET,LONDON

4. 参考业务号

该栏目按照所给资料填写合同号、发票号。由于本案是汇付结算方式，所以信用证号留空不填。

本案填写：

合同号	20093321	发票号	BS005	信用证号	

5. 运输方式

填写海洋运输、航空运输、铁路运输等运输方式。

本案填写：BY SEA

6. 装运港（port of loading）

填写实际装船港口的具体名称，如"上海"、"大连"，不能填"中国港口"，必要时加上港口所在国（地区）的名称。

7. 卸货港（port of discharge）

填写实际货物被最后卸离船舶的港口全称，必要时加上港口所在国（地区）的名称。

本案6、7两栏的填写如下：

装运港(Port of loading)	GUANGDONG,CHINA
目的港(Port of discharge)	LONDON,UK

8. 装运期

该栏目按照合同或信用证规定填写装运期限，但同时要结合世界备货情况在"备注"栏目写明预定船只。

本案填写：

装运期	LATEST DATE OF SHIPMENT:MAY. 10,2009
备注	请订 2009 年 5 月 1 日船期

9. 转运和分批装运

若合同或信用证规定了转运港,则要标出转运港,否则只要标注是否允许转运即可;若信用证没有规定是否允许转运,则根据 UCP600 规定,允许转运。

关于分批装运,只要标注是否允许分批装运即可;若信用证没有规定是否允许分批装运,则根据 UCP600 规定,允许分批装运。

本案填写：

可否转运	NO	可否分批	NO

10. 运费支付方式

这一栏的填写取决于贸易术语。在 CFR 、CIF、CPT 、CIP 贸易术语下,运费预付(FREIGHT PREPAID),在 FOB、FAC 贸易术语下,运费到付(FREIGHT COLLECT/FREIGHT PAYABLE AT DESTINATION)。

本案填写：

运费支付方式	PREPAID

11. 正本提单份数

按照合同或信用证要求的正本提单份数填写。如来证要求"3 ORIGINAL BILL OF LADING"指 3 份正本提单;如来证要求"FULL SET OF BILL OF LADING",指全套提单,大多数承运人提供的全套提单为 3 份正本。

本案填写：

正本提单	3 COPIES

12. 运输标志（shipping marks）

如信用证有规定,按规定缮制(应与发票核对是否一致);信用证没有规定,可按发票上的运输标志缮制。

本案填写：N/M

13. 货名（description of goods）

一般只要列出货物的统称即可,不必详列商品的规格、成分等。

本案填写：

货名（Description of Goods）
TOOLS
Double Open End Spanner

14. 毛重（gross weight）和净重（net weight）

列出货物的毛重、净重总数,一般以千克为计量单位,应与其他单据上的重量一致,如报检单、通关单、报关单和提单等。

15. 尺码（measurement）

尺码即货物的体积,除信用证另有规定者外,一般以立方米为计算单位,要保留小数 2 位。

本案 14、15 栏的填写如下：

总重量(Weight Kilos)		总尺码(Measurement)
净重 Net	毛重 Gross	
2 840KG	3 200KG	20M3

16. 件数（quantity）

托运单中的件数是指最大包装的件数，一般以大、小同时表示。对于一批出口货物中含有不同包装种类的，则货物的总件数是各种包装件数相加。如托运 A 货 100 箱，B 货 50 包，则件数填写"150PKGS"。

本案填写：

件数 Quantity	1 400CTNS
共计件数（大写）Total Number of Packages in Writing	Say one thousand four hundred cartons only.

17．备注

合同或信用证中要求在提单中显示的相关内容，如信用证号、开证日、开证行等信息，于本栏显示；另外，在托运单无存放货物的仓库地址的专用栏目时，此栏填写存放货物的地址。

缮制好的海运托运单如下：

SHIPPING LETTER OF INSTRUCTION

DATE：2009 年 4 月 8 日

托运人	GUANGDONG BAOSHI TOOLS MANUFACTURE CO., LTD. ZHANQIAN ROAD, GUANGZHOU, CHINA	合同号	S/C NO.：20093321
		发票号	BS005
		信用证号	
收货人	ABC CORP. OF LONDON 66/66 ACOMMERCIAL STREET, LONDON	运输方式	BY SEA
		装运港	GUANGDONG,CHINA
		卸货港	LONDON,UK
通知人	ABC CORP. OF LONDON 66/66 ACOMMERCIAL STREET, LONDON	装运期	LATEST DATE OF SHIPMENT：MAY. 10,2009
		可否转运	NO
		可否分批	NO
		运费支付方式	PREPAID
		正本提单	3 COPIES

标记及号码 Marks & Nos	货名 Description of Goods	件数 Quantity	总重量 Weight Kilos		总尺码 Measurement
			净 Net	毛 Gross	
N/M	TOOLS Double Open End Spanner	1 400CTNS	2 840KG	3 200KG	20M3
共计件数（大写） Total Number of Packages in Writing		Say one thousand four hundred cartons only.			
备注 Remarks：					

第三步：根据出口托运单，缮制海运提单

海运提单的大多数栏目同托运单，这里仅就不同栏目的填制作一下说明：

(1)货物装船日期(shipped on board date)指货物装入船舱的日期。对于已装船提单，这一日期同提单的签发日；而收妥待运提单，指装船批注上的日期。

(2)船方的签名和印章。每张正本提单都必须有船方或其代理人的印章方始有效，同时注意信用证是否有提单必须手签的条款，如有此规定必须手签。

缮制好的海运提单如下：

Shipper		BILL OF LADING B/L No.：
GUANDONG BAOSHI TOOLS MANUFACTURE CO., LTD. CHINA		
Consignee		**COSCO**
ABC CORP. OF LONDON		
Notify Party		
ABC CORP. OF LONDON 66/66 ACOMMERCIAL STREET, LONDON		
Pre carriage by	Place of Receipt	CHINA OCEAN SHIPPING COMPANY
	GUANGZHOU, CHINA	
Ocean Vessel Voy. No.	Port of Loading	**ORIGINAL**
JENNEY	GUANGZHOU, CHINA	

Port of discharge	*Final destination	Freight payable at	Number original Bs/L
LONDON,UK	LONDON	LONDON	3
Marks and Numbers	Number and Kind of Packages; Description of Goods	Gross Weight (KGS)	Measurement (M3)
N/M	1 400CTN OF TOOLS Double Open End Spanner	3 200KG	20

Total Package(in words) PACKED IN ONE THOUSAND FOUR HUNDRED CTNS ONLY.

Freight and charges
FREIGHT PREPAID
LADEN ON BOARD DATE:MAY. 1, 2009

Place and date of issue
MAY.1,2009 AT GUANGZHOU

Signed for the Carrier
××××

*Applicable only when document used as a Through Bill of Loading

必备知识

一、运输单据的含义和种类

运输单据是承运人收到承运货物签发给出口方的证明文件,它是交接货物、处理索赔与理赔以及向银行结算货款或进行议付的重要单据。常用的有以下几种:

1. 海运提单(ocean bill of lading)

海运提单是承运人或其代理人收到货物后,签发给托运人的一种单证。海运提单是承运人或其代理人签发的货物收据,是货物所有权的凭证,是运输契约或其证明。

2. 海运单(seaway bill)

海运单的形式与作用同海运提单相似,其主要特点在于收货人已明确指定。收货人并不需要提交正本单据,而仅需证明自己是海运单载明的收货人即可提取货物。因此,海运单实质上是不可以转让的,它的应用范围比较窄,主要用于跨国公司成员之间的货物运输。

3. 铁路运单(railway bill)

铁路运单是由铁路运输承运人签发的货运单据,它是收、发货人同铁路之间的运输契约,其正本在签发后与货物同行,副本签发给托运人用于贸易双方结算货款。在货物发生损失时,还可以用于向铁路进行索赔。铁路运单不是物权凭证。

4. 空运单（airway bill）

空运单是由空运承运人或其代理人签发的货运单据，它是承运人收到货物的收据，也是托运人同承运人之间的运输契约，但不具有物权凭证的性质，因此空运单也是不可以转让的。

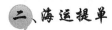海运提单

1. 海运提单的含义和作用

所谓海运提单，是指在海上运输方式下，船公司或其代理人签发的，确认已经收到或已装船某种货物，并且承诺将其运到指定地点交与提单持有人的一种具有法律效力的证明文件。海运提单也是托运人与船公司之间运输合同的证明，在托运人获得提单后，船公司有责任将托运人的货物安全、及时送达目的地，而托运人也有义务及时支付运费等相关费用。

海运提单的主要关系人是签订运输合同的双方：托运人和承运人。托运人即货方，承运人即船方。其他关系人有收货人和被通知人等。收货人通常是货物贸易合同中的买方；被通知人是承运人为了方便货主提货的通知对象，可能不是与货权有关的当事人。如果提单发生转让，则会出现受让人、持有人等提单关系人。

海运提单的性质和作用如下：

(1)海运提单是货物收据，表示提单签发人已经收到了提单所列货物。

(2)海运提单是物权凭证。提单的合法持有人有权提取或支配货物。在国际市场上，提单可以在载货船舶到达目的港之前转让，或是凭提单向银行办理抵押贷款。

(3)海运提单是承运人与托运人之间运输协议的证明，由于提单内列明了双方的权利和义务，所以是处理这类问题的主要依据。

2. 海运提单的分类

海运提单从不同角度可分为以下几种类型。

(1)按货物是否装船，海运提单分为已装船提单和备运提单。已装船提单(on board B/L，shipped on board B/L)是指货物已经装上指定船只的提单。提单内注有"Shipped On Board"字样，并注明装货船名和装船日期。除集装箱运输或多式联运所使用的运输单据外，必须提供已装船提单，才能凭以结汇和提货。备运提单(received for shipment B/L)是指表明货物已收妥但尚未装船的提单。提单内注有"…Received for Shipment…"字样，这种提单中只有签单日期没有装运日期，一般不能凭以结汇和提货。一旦货物装上船后，提单应加装船批注，从而构成已装船提单。

(2)按提单上有无不良批注，海运提单分为清洁提单和不清洁提单。清洁提单(clean B/L)是指货物装船时"表面状况良好"，提单签发时未被加注任何货损或包装不良之类批注的提单。结汇时如无特殊规定必须提供这种提单。不清洁提单(foul B/L，unclean B/L)是指提单上注有货物或包装缺陷的批注，如提单上注有"two carton are wet"即为不清洁提单。在进出口业务中，通常都要求卖方提供清洁提单。尤其是在信用证支付方式下，银行对运输单据的要求更为严格。UCP600第27条规定，银行只接受清洁运输单据。清洁运输单据是指未载有明确宣称货物或包装有缺陷的条文或批注的运输单据。

(3)按提单可否转让，海运提单分为记名提单、不记名提单和指示提单。记名提单(straight B/L)是指提单的"收货人"栏内具体写明了收货人名称的提单。由于这种提单只能由提单上指

定的收货人提取货物,不能转让给第三者,因此记名提单不能流通。不记名提单(blank B/L, open B/L, bearer B/L)是指提单的"收货人"栏内不写具体的收货人名称,而仅写"To Bearer"(交持单人)的提单。不记名提单是可转让的提单,转让手续简便,无需做任何背书,仅凭交付即可。但这种提单风险较大,一旦遗失或被盗,提单持有人即可凭手中的提单向船公司提取货物,所以这种提单在实务中应避免使用。指示提单(order B/L)是指提单的"收货人"栏内填上"To order of ×××"(凭×××人指示),或"To order"(凭指示)字样的提单。这种抬头的提单可以转让,但需要做背书手续。由谁背书,这就要根据发出指示的人的不同来决定。如为"To order of Shipper",转让时应由托运人背书;如为"To order of ×× Bank",转让时应由该指定的银行背书;如为"To order of Consignee",则由收货人背书。对于收货人栏为"To order",习惯上称为"空白抬头"的提单,虽然未列明具体的指示人,根据业务惯例,转让时一般由托运人背书。

(4)按提单内容的繁简,海运提单分为全式提单和简式提单。全式提单(long form B/L)除了提单正面记载有关托运人、收货人、装运港、目的港、货名、运费等事项外,还在提单的背面印有船方承运条款细则。简式提单(short form B/L)只有提单正面记载有关事项,背面为空白。简式提单一般在提单正面注明背面条款同本公司的全式提单或注明如有需要可向本公司索取。根据UCP600,除非信用证特别规定,银行一般不拒绝接受简式提单。

(5)其他提单。

①倒签提单(anti-dated B/L)是指承运人或其代理应托运人要求,在货物装船后签发提单,但提单上的签发日期较该批货物实际装船完毕日期为早,以符合信用证装运日期的规定。倒签提单具有欺骗性,应予以避免。

②顺签提单(post-date B/L)是指在货物装船完毕后,承运人或其代理人应托运人的要求而签发的提单,但是该提单上记载的签发日期晚于货物实际装船完毕的日期,即托运人从承运人处得到的以晚于该票货物实际装船完毕日期作为提单签发日期。由于顺填日期签发提单,因此称之为"顺签提单"。

③预借提单(advanced B/L)是指由于信用证规定的装运日期和交单结汇日期均已到期而货物因故未能及时装船,但已交到承运人管理之下,或已经开始装船但该批货尚未装毕,由托运人出具保函要求承运人或其代理签发已装船提单。按不少国家的法规和判例,承运人签发预借提单将丧失享受责任限制和免责的权利。

④过期提单(stale B/L):原来的概念是指晚于货物到达目的地的提单。按国际惯例,银行对过期提单是不接受的,但发货地与到货地航程较短的运输,例如我国沿海各港装往香港、日本、韩国的货物,航程仅2—3天,货运单据无论如何快速处理,也跟不上货物运输速度,因此如按以上过期提单的概念来掌握接受与否,不但不符情理,而且也缺乏可操作性,目前银行的掌握原则是根据UCP600规定:凡超过装运日期21天后提交的单据即为过期单据,但如信用证效期或信用证规定的交单期早于此限期,则以效期或规定的交单期为最后限期。

过期提单是商业习惯的一种提单,但它在运输合同下并不是无效提单,提单持有人仍可凭其要求承运人交付货物。

⑤交换提单(switch B/L)是指凭启运港签发的提单。在中途港由承运人的有关代理换发另一套提单,原启运港签发的提单称为"交换提单"。换发的一套提单或将装货人改为另一人,或以中途港作为装运港,这种做法主要是适应贸易需要,例如信用证开证人不愿将实际供货人泄露给其买户,以防今后跳过他直接发生买卖关系,或如进口地国家对启运地国家货物限制进口,因而

需以中途港为装运港。

⑥电子提单(electronic B/L)是指为适应 EDI 需要而设计的非书面化提单。承运人在接收发货人货物后给予发货人一个收到货物的电讯通知,通知内容中应包括一个日后传输电讯的密码,发货人必须向承运人确认该项收讯,根据该项确认,承运人承认发货人为提单的持有人,具有要求承运人放货或指定收货人或向另一方转让货物的权利,持有人在向承运人行使上述权利时须用含有密码的电讯通知。

电子提单转让时由原持有人向承运人发出通知,要求转让给指名的受让人,承运人据以向受让人发出电讯通知,如受让人电讯确认接受转让,承运人销毁原用密码,并向新持有人(受让人)发出一个新的密码,电子提单每经一次转让,都须调换一个新的密码。

电子提单的所有电讯都通过 EDI 程序处理,其电子数据效力等同于书写形式,但在承运人交货前的任何时间,持有人如有必要,有向承运人索要书面提单的选择权。电子提单须在国际法规的制约下有效地使用。

3. 海运提单的主要内容

(1)提单正面内容。提单正面主要包括提单名称、编号、托运人、收货人、船名和国籍、启运港、目的港、唛头、货名、件数、重量、体积、运费、提单份数、载货船公司名称、签发日期、地址、承运人或其代理人签字装船批注及一些其他特殊批注等。

提单正面还包括事先印妥的契约条文,内容大致是:

①装船条款(或确认条款),表明外表状况良好的货物已经装上船或已经收妥待运。

②内容不知悉条款,表明承运人对提单所列重量、数量、品质、内容、价值等不知悉,表示承运人对此不尽核对之责。

③承认接受条款,表明托运人、收货人、提单持有人接受本提单和背面所记载的一切规定的免责条款。

④签署条款,该条款是承运人或其代理人表明签发本提单(正本)的份数,各份提单具有相同效力,其中一份完成提货后其余各份均告失效和提取货物必须交出经背书的一份提单以换取货物或提货单的条款。

(2)提单背面内容。提单背面主要是发行提单的船公司根据《海牙规则》(The Hague Rules)与《汉堡规则》(Hamburg Rules)制订的承运人与货主之间权利义务的各项条款,是解决船、货双方纠纷的主要依据。这些条款可以归纳为下列内容:定义条款,首要条款,承运人责任条款,免责条款,包装与标志,运费条款,留置权,损失赔偿条款,转运或转船条款,卸货和交货条款,动植物及舱面货条款,危险品条款,共同海损和碰撞条款,战争、罢工、冰冻、检疫、港口拥挤条款,变更航线条款。

 **拓展知识**

一、航空托运单和航空运单

1. 航空托运单的含义、作用和缮制规范

根据《华沙公约》第 5 条第(1)和(5)款规定,货运单应由托运人填写,也可由承运人或其代理人代为填写;实际上,目前货运单均由承运人或其代理人填制,为此,作为填开货运单依据的托运书,应由托运人自己填写,而且托运人必须在上面签字。

航空托运单(shippers letter of instruction)是指托运人用于委托承运人或其代理人填开航

空货运单的一种表单,表单上列有填制货运单所需各项内容,并应印有授权于承运人或其代理人代其在货运单上签字的文字说明。

航空托运单包括下列主要内容:

(1) 托运人(shipper)。填写托运人的全称、街名、城市名称、国名,以及便于联系的电话号、电传号或传真号。

①集中托运时的托运人:货运代理人;直接托运方式时的托运人:货主。

②有时承运人要求托运人提供账号,以便在收货人拒付运费时向托运人索偿。

③在信用证结汇方式下,托运人一般按信用证的受益人内容填写。

④托运危险货物时,托运人必须填写实际托运人,航空公司不接受货运代理人托运。

(2) 收货人(consignee)。填写收货人的全称、街名、城市名称、国名(特别是在不同国家内有相同城市名称时,必须要填上国名)以及电话号、电传号或传真号。

①本栏不得填写"TO ORDER"或"TO ORDER OF SHIPPER"等字样,因为航空货运单不能转让。

②集中托运方式时收货人:货运代理人海外代理;直接托运时收货人:实际收货人。

③承运人一般不接受一票货物有两个或两个以上收货人。如果实际上有两个以上收货人,本栏填第一收货人,通知栏填第二收货人。

(3) 始发站机场(airport of departure)。

①填写始发站机场的全称。

②在对始发站机场的全称不清楚的情况下,允许填写始发站所在城市名称。

③与不同国家的其他城市同名的,还需要填写国家名称。

④ 同一城市的不同机场,需要填写机场名称。

(4) 目的地机场(airport of destination)。填目的地机场(不知道机场名称时,可填城市名称),如果某一城市名称用于一个以上国家时,应加上国名。例如:LONDON UK 伦敦,英国;LONDON KY US 伦敦,肯达基州,美国;LONDON TO CA 伦敦,安大略省,加拿大。

①按国际航空运输协会IATA(International Air Transport Association)规范的机场代码填报。

②机场名称不明确时,可填城市名称,并用城市名称。

③标签上的卸货港机场代码与托运单上目的地机场代码必须一致。

④如果有"转运路线"要求,可以填在专门栏目内。

(5) 要求的路线/申请定舱(requested routing/requseting booking)。本栏用于航空公司安排运输路线时使用,但如果托运人有特别要求时,也可填入本栏。

(6) 供运输用的声明价值(declared value for carriage)。填写供运输用的声明价值金额,该价值即为承运人负赔偿责任的限额。承运人按有关规定向托运人收取声明价值费。可在本栏内填入"NVD"(no value declared,未声明价值),如本栏空着未填写时,承运人或其代理人可视为货物未声明价值。

(7) 供海关用的声明价值(declared value for customs)。国际货物通常要受到目的站海关的检查,海关根据此栏所填数额征税。托运人若不办理此项声明价值,必须打上NCV字样 。

(8) 保险金额(insurance amount requested)。中国民航各空运企业暂未开展国际航空运输代保险业务,本栏可空着不填。

(9)处理事项(handling information)。填写附加的处理要求,例如,另请通知(also notify)。除填收货人之外,如托运人还希望在货物到达的同时通知他人,请另填写通知人的全名和地址。

(10)货运单所附文件(document to accompany airway bill)。填写随附在货运单上往目的地的文件,应填上所附文件的名称,例如,托运人的动物证明(shipper certification for live animals)。

(11)件数和包装方式(number and kind of packages)。填该批货物的总件数,并注明其包装方法,例如,包裹(package)、纸板盒(carton)、盒(case)、板条箱(crate)、袋(bag)、卷(roll)等,如货物没有包装时,就注明为散装(loose)。如货物运价种类不同时,应分别填写,并将总件数相加,包装种类用"packages"。

(12)实际毛重(actual gross weight)。本栏内的重量应由承运人或其代理人在称重后填入。如托运人已经填上重量,承运人或其代理人必须进行复核,用代码 K 表示千克。

①以公斤为单位时,保留小数后一位,并按 0.5 进位。

②多项货物时,在画线下方对应栏内打上毛重之和。

(13)运价种类。填所采用的货物运价种类的代号为:M——最低运价;N——45 公斤以下普通货物运价;Q——45 公斤以上普通货物运价;C——指定商品运价。

(14)计费重量(公斤)(charge able weight)(kg)。本栏内的计费重量应由承运人或其代理人在量过货物的尺寸(以厘米为单位)由承运人或其代理人算出计费重量后填入,如托运人已经填上时,承运人或其代理人必须进行复核。

①当货物是重货时,计费重量可以是货物的实际毛重。

②当货物是轻泡货时,计费重量可以是货物的体积重量。

③当货物临近重量分界点时,计费重量可以是较高重量、较低运价的分界点重量。

(15)费率(rate/charge)。填所适用的货物运价。

①使用最低运费时,填写与运价代号 m 相对应的最低运费。

②使用代号 n,q,c,s,r 运价时,填写相对应的运价。

(16)货物的品名及数量(包括体积及尺寸)[discription of goods(including dimensions or volume)]。填货物的品名和数量(包括尺寸或体积)。货物中的每一项均需分开填写,并尽量填写详细,本栏所属填写内容应与出口报关发票和进口许可证上所列明的相符。危险品应填写适用的准确名称及标贴的级别。

①不得填写表示货物类别的名称,应填写货物品名、数量、体积、产地等细节。

②危险品、鲜活易腐货,应分别填写其标准的学术名称。

③按货物外包装"最长×最宽×最高×件数"顺序或总计体积填写。

(17)运费。在 PP 下方打(×)表示预付;CC 下方打(×)表示到付。

(18)杂费。同运费表示方法一样。

(19)其他费用。托运时可以不填写其他费用,但货运单上需填写金额并冠以规定的操作代号。

(20)托运人签字、盖章。由托运人或其他代理人签字盖章。

(21)日期和地点。由托运人填写开货运单的时间和地点。

缮制好的航空托运单如下:

SHIPPER'S INSTRUCTIONS TO ARRANGE FOR SHIPMENT OF GOODS
国际航空货物托运书

Shipper ("Company name, Add, attn"): Attn: Tel: Fax:	Mawb No:.	Hawb No.:
	\multicolumn{2}{l}{苏州市海威国际货运代理有限公司 SUZHOU HI-TECH WAYLOGISTICS CO., LTD 苏州保税物流中心 N 栋 507 室 Tel:0512-33873198 Fax:33873199 E-mail:info@szjsjt.com}
Consignee Tel: Fax: Notify Party:	\multicolumn{2}{l}{Please Receive the undermentioned cargo for delivery by air in accordance with the terms and conditions overleaf and the conditions and provisions states or referred to on the airway bill form of the carrier(s). In the case of shipments requiring transportation by air through air carriers in the united states from the transshipment point(s) to final destination. I/we further agree to accept the limit of liability of that domestic air carrier as full settlement in the event of loss and/or damage of goods.}

Name of Carrier	Departure Airport	Air freight Charges: ☐ Prepaid Collect	Other Charges: ☐ Prepaid Collect
Destination	Airline Counter-Signature ☐ Yes ☐ No	\multicolumn{2}{l}{Country of Origin (Goods): CHINA}

Marks and Numbers of Packages; Description of Goods	Gross Weight	Measurement

Specify Currency	Declared Value for Customs	Declared Value for Carriage	Insurance Amount	Shipper's C. O. D

Special Instructions:	We hereby guarantee payment of all freight collect charges due to the fowarders or to the carrier. If the shipment is abandoned, refused by consignee. Retumed at our request, confiscated by the customs or for any other reason can't be delivered within a reasonable time. We also agree that the forwards shall have all right of lien upon doc and/or goods of our company for unpaid freight and charges and such lien shall apply until all unpaid accounts are fully settled. We also guarantee that payment should be made right after job execution, latest 7 days after invoice date. We shall guarantee interest on all overdue accounts at 12% annum and pay reasonable legal charges in the event of judicial proceedings to enforce collection. Other arrangements: In case of any other of special arrangements we agree to hold the forwarders examp from any liability what soever arising out of unforeseen circumstaces and/or acts of nature. ect
Documents accompanying Airway Bill: ☐ Packing List ☐ Certificate of Origin ☐ Commercial Invoice ☐ Consular Invoice	Signatory's Name in Block Letters:

2. 航空运单的含义、作用和缮制规范

(1)航空运单的概念。航空运单(airway bill)是指由托运人或者托运人委托承运人或其代理人填制的,托运人和承运人之间为在承运人的航线上承运托运人货物所订立运输合同的凭证,是办理货物运输的依据,是计收货物运费的财务票证,也是货主银行结汇文件之一。由于航空运输操作要求高,专业性强,因此通常情况下,航空运单由货运代理人代为填制。

(2)航空运单的性质、作用。航空运单是由承运人或其代理人签发的重要的货物运输单据,是承托双方的运输合同,其内容对双方均具有约束力。航空运单不可转让,持有航空运单也并不能说明可以对货物要求所有权。

①航空运单是发货人与航空承运人之间的运输合同。与海运提单不同,航空运单不仅证明航空运输合同的存在,而且航空运单本身就是发货人与航空运输承运人之间缔结的货物运输合同,在双方共同签署后产生效力,并在货物到达目的地交付给运单上所记载的收货人后失效。

②航空运单是承运人签发的已接收货物的证明。航空运单也是货物收据,在发货人将货物发运后,承运人或其代理人就会将其中一份交给发货人(即发货人联),作为已经接收货物的证明。除非另外注明,它是承运人收到货物并在良好条件下装运的证明。

③航空运单是承运人据以核收运费的账单。航空运单分别记载着属于收货人负担的费用、属于应支付给承运人的费用和应支付给代理人的费用,并详细列明费用的种类、金额,因此可作为运费账单和发票。承运人往往也将其中的承运人联作为记账凭证。

④航空运单是报关单证之一。出口时航空运单是报关单证之一。在货物到达目的地机场进行进口报关时,航空运单也通常是海关查验放行的基本单证。

⑤航空运单同时可作为保险证书。如果承运人承办保险或发货人要求承运人代办保险,则航空运单也可用来作为保险证书。

⑥航空运单是承运人内部业务的依据。航空运单随货同行,证明了货物的身份。运单上载有有关该票货物发送、转运、交付的事项,承运人会据此对货物的运输做出相应安排。

航空运单的正本一式三份,每份都印有背面条款,其中一份交发货人,是承运人或其代理人接收货物的依据;第二份由承运人留存,作为记账凭证;最后一份随货同行,在货物到达目的地,交付给收货人时作为核收货物的依据。

(3)航空运单的分类。

①航空主运单(master airway bill, MAWB)。凡由航空运输公司签发的航空运单就称为航空主运单。它是航空运输公司据以办理货物运输和交付的依据,是航空公司和托运人订立的运输合同,每一批航空运输的货物都有自己相对应的航空主运单。

②航空分运单(house airway bill, HAWB)。集中托运人在办理集中托运业务时签发的航空运单被称作航空分运单。在集中托运的情况下,除了航空运输公司签发航空主运单外,集中托运人还要签发航空分运单。

在这中间,航空分运单作为集中托运人与托运人之间的货物运输合同,合同双方分别为货主A、B和集中托运人;而航空主运单作为航空运输公司与集中托运人之间的货物运输合同,当事人则为集中托运人和航空运输公司。货主与航空运输公司没有直接的契约关系。不仅如此,由于在启运地货物由集中托运人将货物交付航空运输公司,在目的地由集中托运人或其代理从航空运输公司处提取货物,再转交给收货人,因而货主与航空运输公司也没有直接的货物交接关系。

(4)航空运单的构成。货运单一式八联。其中正本三联,副本五联。三联正本具有同等法律效力。

第一联:正本3,蓝色,为托运人联,作为托运人支付货物运费,并将货物交由承运人运输的凭证。

第二联:正本1,绿色,为财务联,作为收取货物运费的凭证交财务部门。

第三联:副本7,白色,为第一承运人联,由第一承运人留交其财务部门作为结算凭证。

第四联:正本2,粉红色,为收货人联,在目的站交收货人。

第五联:副本4,黄色,为货物交付联,收货人提取货物时在此联签字,由承运人留存,作为货物已经交付收货人的凭证。

第六联:副本5,白色,为目的站联,由目的站机场留存,也可作为第三承运人联,由第三承运人留交其财务部门作为结算凭证。

第七联:副本6,白色,为第二承运人联,由第二承运人留交其财务部门作为结算凭证。

第八联:副本8,白色,为代理人联(存根联),由货运单填置人留存备查。

货运单的三联正本具有同等法律效力,一联交承运人,一联交收货人,一联交托运人,分别由托运人签字或盖章,由承运人接受货物后签字或盖章。

(5)航空运单的内容。航空运单与海运提单类似也有正面、背面条款之分,不同的航空公司也会有自己独特的航空运单格式。所不同的是,海运提单可能千差万别,但各航空公司所使用的航空运单则大多借鉴IATA所推荐的标准格式,差别并不大。所以我们这里只介绍这种标准格式,也称中性运单。下面就有关需要填写的栏目说明如下:

①编号(airway bill No.)。航空运单最上方的编号由航空公司填制。编号的前三位一般是各国航空公司的代号,如中国民航的代号为999,日本航空公司的代号为131等。

②承运人(carrier)。承运人即航空公司。根据UCP600规定,若信用证要求空运单据,银行将接受表面标明承运人名称的单据。

③发货人名址(shipper's name and address)。托收方式下发货人名址按合同的卖方名址填列;信用证方式下发货人名址则必须与受益人名址一致。

④发货人账号(shipper's account number)。发货人账号一般可不填。

⑤收货人名址(consignee's name and address)。托收方式下,若以代收行为收货人,须事先征取代收行同意。在实务操作中多以合同的买方为收货人。信用证方式下,有的以买方为收货人,有的以开证行为收货人,应根据信用证的规定填写;但最好以开证行为收货人,以防进口方借口拒付或延付而货物却被提走。

⑥收货人账号(consignee's account number)。收货人账号一般可不填。

⑦签发运单的承运人的代理人名称和城市(issuing carrier's agent name and city)。若运单由承运人的代理人签发时,本栏填实际代理人名称及城市名;如果运单直接由承运人本人签发,此栏则可空白不填。

⑧代理人国际航空运输协会的代号(agent's IATA code)。一般可不填。

⑨代理人账号(account number)。如需要时可填代理人账号,供承运人结算时使用;一般可不填。

⑩启航机场和指定航线(airport of departure and requested routing)。一般仅填启航机场名

称即可。

⑪会计事项(accounting information)。会计事项是指与费用结算的有关事项,如运费预付、到付或发货人结算使用信用卡号、账号以及其他必要的情况。

⑫转运机场/一程承运人/路线和目的地(to/by first carrier/routing and destination)。此项目在货物运输途中需转运时按实际情况填写。

⑬目的地机场(airport of destination)。目的地机场即货物运载的最终目的机场。

⑭航班/日期(仅供承运人使用)[flight/date (for carrier use only)]。航班/日期即飞机航班号及其实际起飞日期。但本栏所填的内容只能供承运人使用,因而该起飞日期不能视为货物的装运日期(一般以航空运单的签发日期作为装运日期)。

⑮货币及费用代码(currency & CHGS code)。货币及费用代码即支付费用使用的货币国际标准电码表示,如 HKD、USD 等,费用代码一般不填。

⑯运费/声报价值费及其他费用(WT/VAL & other)。"声报价值费"(valuation charge)是指下列第17栏向承运人声报了价值时,必须与运费一起交付声明价值费。若该栏费用是预付,则在"PPD"(prepaid)栏下打"×";若是待付,则在"COLL"(collect)栏下打"×"。此栏应注意与第11栏保持一致。

⑰运输申报价值(declared value for carriage)。填写托运货物总价值,一般可按发票额填列,如不愿申报,则填"NVD"(no value declared,无申报价值)。

根据《统一国际航空运输某些规则的公约》(《华沙公约》)规定,托运人在交运货物时有特别声明货物价值者,如果货物因承运人的责任而造成毁灭、遗失或损坏等损失,承运人则按其声明价值赔偿。如无声明价值,承运人即按统一规定的每千克定额赔偿,但其定额不超过该货到达后的价值。

⑱海关申报价值(declared value for customs)。此栏所填价值是提供给海关的征税依据。当以出口货物报关单或商业发票作为征税时,本栏可空白不填或填"As Per INV.";如果货物系样品等数量少且无商业价值,可填"NCV"(no commercial value)。

⑲保险金额(amount of insurance)。如发货人根据本运单背面的条款要求保险,则在本栏内注明保险金额,若无则可填"NIL"。

⑳处理情况(handling information)。可利用本栏填写所需要注明的内容:被通知人;飞机随带的有关商业单据名称;包装情况;发货人对货物在途时的某些特别指示;对第二承运人的要求等。

㉑件数(No. of pieces)。正确地填入所装载的包装件数。(附样中本栏的 RCP 系"rate combination point"的缩写,意即税率组成点。)

㉒毛重/千克或磅(gross weight/kg/b)。填列以千克或磅为计量单位的货物毛重。("kg",也可填作"K"。)

㉓费率等级(rate class)。根据航空公司有关运价资料,按实际填列费率等级的代号,费率等级代号有 M、N、Q、C、R、S 六种。

M——Minimum Charge,即货物的起运费率。

N——Normal Under 45kgs Rate,即45千克以下普通货物的费率。

Q——Quantity Over 45kgs Rate,即45千克以上普通货物的费率。

上述以45千克为计算界限,因此称为重量分界点(weight break point)。

C——Special Commodity Rate,即特种货物费率。

R——Redueed Class Rate Less than Normal Rate,即折扣费率。对少数货物,可按"N"费率给予一定百分比的折扣。

S——Surcharged Class Rate,More than Normal Rate,即加价费率。对少数货物,按"N"费率加一定的百分比。

㉔商品编号(commodity item No.)。按费率等级填列商品编号,一般也可不填。

㉕计费重量(chargeable weight)。填列货物实际毛重,若属于M费率等级和以尺码计费者,则可空白此栏。

㉖费率(rate/charge)。填写实际计费的费率。

㉗运费总额(total)。填计收运费的总额,即计费重量与费率的乘积。

㉘货物品名和数量(包括体积或容积)[nature and quantity of goods(including dimension or volume)]。填合同或信用证中规定的货物名称、唛头、数量及尺码。

㉙计重运费(预付/待付)[weight charge (prepaid/collect)]。在对应的"预付"或"待付"栏内填入按重量计算的运费额。

㉚其他费用金额(other charges)。当发生诸如运单费、危险货物费、起运地仓储费和目的地仓储费等费用时填写;若无此类费用则空白不填。

㉛声报价值费(valuation charge)。一般空白不填。

㉜因代理人需要而产生的费用(total other charges due agent)。一般空白不填。

㉝因承运人需要而产生的其他费用(total other charges due carrier)。一般填写"As Arranged"。

㉞预付费用总额/待付费用总额(total prepaid/total collect)。即预付或待付的运费及其他费用总额,可在相应栏内填列"As Arranged"。

㉟发货人或其代理人签名(signature of shipper on his agent)。签名后以示保证所托运的货物并非危险品。

㊱承运人或其代理人签字及签发运单日期、地点[executed on (date) at (place),signature of issuing carrier or it's agent]。签单以后正本航空运单方能生效。本栏所表示的日期为签发本运单的日期,也就是本批货物的装运日期。如果信用证规定运单必须注明实际起飞日期,则以该所注的实际起飞日期作为装运日期。本栏的日期不得晚于信用证规定的装运日期。

以代理人身份签章时,如同提单一样,需在签章处加注"AS AGENTS";承运人签章时则加注"AS CARRIER"。

㊲正本(original)。航空运单正本按国际惯例为一式三份。第一份"ORIGNAL 1(FOR ISSUING CARRIER)",由航空公司留存;第二份"ORIGNAL 2(FOR CONSIGNEE)",随飞机转给收货人;第三份"ORIGINAL 3(FOR SHIPPER)"。交给发货人。虽然正本签发三份,但银行允许只提交一份正本。副本共9份,由航空公司按规定和需要分发。

已填制好的航空运单如下：

MAWB Shipper's Name and Address Shipper's Account Number	Not negotiable Air consignment note HELLMANN WORLDWIDE LOGISTICS issued by Copies1.2 and 3 of this Air Waybill are originals and have the same validity
Consignee's Name and Address Consignee's Account Number	It is agreed that the goods described herein are accepted in apparent good order and condition (except as noted) for carriage SUBJECT TO THE CONDITIONS OF CONTRACT ON THE REVERSE HEREOF. ALL GOODS MAY BE CARRIED BY ANY OTHER MEANS. INCLUDING ROAD OR ANY OTHER CARRIER UNLESS SPECIFIC CONTRARY INSTRUCTIONS ARE GIVEN HEREON BY THE SHIPPER. THE SHIPPER'S ATTENTION IS DRAWN TO THE NOTICE CONCERNING CARRIER'S LIMITATION OF LIABILITY. Shipper may increase such limitation of liability by declaring a higher value for carriage and paying a supplemental charge if required.
Issuing Carrier's Agent Name and City Agents IATA Code / Account No.	Accounting Information Reference number / Optional shipping information
To / By First Carrier / Routing and Destination / To / By / To / By	Currency / chgs code / WT/VAL (PPD, COLL) / Other (PPD, COLL) / Declared Value for Carriage / Declared Value for Carriage
Airport of Destination / Flight/Date / For Carrier Use only / Flight/Date	Amount of Insurance / INSURANCE IF carrier offers insurance and such insurance is requested in accordance with the conditions thereof indicate amount to be insured in figures in box marked amount of insurance.
Handling Information	

No.of Pieces RCP	Gross Weight	Kg ib		Rate Class Commodity item number		Chargeable Weight		Rate /charge		Total		Nature and Quantity of Goods (incl. Dimensions or Volume)

Prepaid	Weight charge	Collect	Other Charges
	Valuation Charge		
	Tax		
	Total other Charges Due Agent		Shipper certifies that the particulars on the face hereof are correct and that insofar as any part of the consignment contains dangerous goods, such part is properly described by name and is in proper condition for carriage by air according to the applicable Dangerous Goods Regulations.
	Total other Charges Due Carrier		
Total Prepaid		Total Collect	
Currency Conversion Rates		Charges in Dast Currency	Executed on(date) At(place) Signature of issuing Carrier or its Agent
For Carrier's Use only at Destination		Charges at Destination	Total Collect Charges / AWB No.

二、国际多式联运单据

1. 多式联运单据的含义

多式联运单据是指证明多式联运合同以及证明多式联运经营人接管货物并负责按照合同条款交付货物的单据。多式联运单据由承运人或其代理人签发，其作用与海运提单相似，既是货物收据也是运输契约的证明，在单据作成指示抬头或不记名抬头时，可作为物权凭证，经背书可以转让。多式联运单据表面上和联运提单相仿，但联运提单承运人只对自己执行的一段负责，而多式联运承运人对全程负责;联运提单由船公司签发,包括海洋运输在内的全程运输,多式联运单据由多式联运承运人签发,也包括全程运输,但多种运输方式中,可以不包含海洋运输。

2. 多式联运单据的分类

(1)可转让的多式联运单据。①多式联运单据以可转让的方式签发时,应列明按指示或向持票人交付;如列明按指示交付,须经背书后转让;如列明向持票人交付,无须背书即可转让;如签发一套一份以上的正本,应注明正本份数;如签发任何副本,每份副本均应注明"不可转让副本"字样。②只有交出可转让多式联运单据,并在必要时经正式背书,才能向多式联运经营人或其代表提取货物。③如签发一套一份以上的可转让多式联运单据正本,而多式联运经营人或其代表已正当地按照其中一份正本交货,该多式联运经营人便已履行其交货责任。

(2)不可转让的多式联运单据。多式联运单据以不可转让的方式签发时,应指明记名的收货人;多式联运经营人将货物交给此种不可转让的多式联运单据所指明的记名收货人或经收货人通常以书面正式指定的其他人后,该多式联运经营人即已履行其交货责任。

3. 多式联运单据的内容

(1)货物品类、识别货物所必需的主要标志。如属危险货物,其危险特性的明确声明、包数或件数、货物的毛重或其他方式表示的数量等,所有这些事项均由发货人提供。

(2)货物外表状况。

(3)多式联运经营人的名称和主要营业所。

(4)发货人名称。

(5)如经发货人指定收货人,则需收货人名称。

(6)多式联运经营人接管货物的地点和日期。

(7)交货地点。

(8)如经双方明确协议,则需在交付地点交货的日期或期间。

(9)表示该多式联运单据为可转让或不可转让的声明。

(10)多式联运单据的签发地点和日期。

(11)多式联运经营人或经其授权的人的签字。

(12)如经双方明确协议,则需每种运输方式的运费;或者应由收货人支付的运费,包括用以支付的货币;或者关于运费出自收货人支付的其他说明。

(13)如在签发多式联运单据时已经确知,则需预期经过的路线、运输方式和转运地点。

(14)如不违背签发多式联运单据所在国的法律,则需双方同意列入多式联运单据的任何其他事项。

但是以上一项或者多项内容的缺乏,不影响单据作为多式联运单据的性质。如果多式联运经营人知道或者有合理的根据怀疑多式联运单据所列的货物品类、标志、包数或者数量、重量等没有准确地表明实际接管货物的状况,或者无适当方法进行核对的,多式联运经营人应在多式联运单据上作出保留,注明不符合之处及怀疑根据或无适当核对方法。如果不加批注,则应视为已在多式联运单据上注明货物外表状况的良好。

4. 多式联运单据的签发

(1)多式联运经营人接管货物时,应签发一项多式联运单据,该单据应依发货人的选择,或为可转让单据或为不可转让单据。

(2)多式联运单据应由多式联运经营人或经他授权的人签字。

(3)多式联运单据上的签字,如不违背签发多式联运单据所在国的法律,可以是手签、手签笔迹的复印、打透花字、盖章、符号,或用任何其他机械或电子仪器打出。

(4)经发货人同意,可以用任何机械或其他保存《联合国国际货物多式联运公约》第8条所规定的多式联运单据应列明的事项的方式,签发不可转让的多式联运单据。在这种情况下,多式联运经营人在接管货物后,应交给发货人一份可以阅读的单据,载有用此种方式记录的所有事项,就《联合国国际货物多式联运公约》而言,这份单据应视为多式联运单据。

5. 多式联运单据的保留

(1)如果多式联运经营人或其代表知道,或有合理的根据怀疑多式联运单据所列货物的品类、主要标志、包数或件数、重量或数量等事项没有准确地表明实际接管货物的状况,或无适当方法进行核对,则该多式联运经营人或其代表应在多式联运单据上作出保留,注明不符之处、怀疑的根据,或无适当核对方法。

(2)如果多式联运经营人或其代表未在多式联运单据上对货物的外表状况加以批注,则应视为其已在多式联运单据上注明货物的外表状况良好。

技能训练

(一)名词解释

1. 海运提单　　2. 航空运单　　3. 承运货物收据

(二)简答题

1. 在实际业务中,装货单的作用有哪些?
2. 提单的核心功能是什么?
3. 为什么在海运提单中有被通知人(notified party)栏目?

(三)实务操作题

请根据下面"海运提单"提供的内容填空。

(1)托运人:＿＿＿＿＿　　　　(2)收货人:＿＿＿＿＿
(3)目的港:＿＿＿＿＿　　　　(4)总毛重:＿＿＿＿＿
(5)运费支付情况:＿＿＿＿＿　(6)正本提单份数:＿＿＿＿＿
(7)船名:＿＿＿＿＿　　　　　(8)装运港:＿＿＿＿＿
(8)唛头:＿＿＿＿＿　　　　　(10)提单日期及签发地点:＿＿＿＿＿

BILL OF LADING

Shipper 金诚贸易有限公司	B/L No.
	Combined Transport BILL OF LADING
Consignee TO ORDER	
Notify Address …	For delivery of goods please apply to:
Pre-carriage by	Place of Receipt	
Ocean Vessel Voy. No. "菊花"	Port of Loading 青岛	

Port of Discharge 纽约	Place of Delivery	Final Destination for the Merchant's Reference only	
Container, Seal No. & Marks & Numbers LST NEW YORK SY—2001—897 NOS 3000	No. of Package & Description of Goods 300 吨 2001 年产红小豆	Gross Weight (Kgs)	Measurement (m³)
FREIGHT & CHARGES 运费已付	Revenue Tons	Rate Per	Prepaid	Collect

(left side vertical: articulars Furnished dy Merchants)

Ex. Rate.	Prepaid at	Payable at	Place and date of issue 青岛 2001 年 9 月 28 日
	Total Prepaid	No. of Original B(s)/L 两份	Stamp & Signature

LADEN ON BOARD. THE VESSEL

Date

By··························

(TERMS CONTINUED ON BACK HERE OF)　　(KENWA. STANDARD)

任务五　制作报检单

学习目标

能力目标

能够根据合同或 L/C 条款和其他相关信息,正确填制出口报检单和检验证书

知识目标

1. 了解检验检疫机构的种类和我国质检总局的业务范围
2. 掌握检验证书的作用,熟悉法定检验的相关规定

任务设计

2010 年 6 月 15 日,常州市亚峰进出口有限公司和美国 LOOKING(罗京)公司的签订了出售钩针地毯的合同。合同如下:

1. 售货合同

SALES CONFIRMATION

卖方 Seller: CHANGZHOU YAFENG IMP. & EXP. CO., LTD. 　　3 GEHU MIDDLE ROAD, CHANG-ZHOU, JIANGSU CHINA Telex:0985　Fax:6332136　Tel:6332138	NO.:04F3—786 DATE: JUN.15,2010 SIGNED IN: CHANGZHOU,CHINA
买方 Buyer:THE LOOKING HANDCRAFT, INC 　　138 SAN MATEC AVENUE, SAN FRANCISCO 　　CA—94080—6501,U.S.A.	
经买卖双方同意成交下列商品,订立条款如下: This contract is made by and agreed between the BUYER and SELLER, in accordance with the terms and conditions stipulated below.	

唛头 Marks and Numbers	名称及规格 Description of Goods	数量 Quantity	单价 Unit Price CIFSAN FRANCISCO	金额 Amount (USD)
N/M	HOOK RUG ART. NO. CZ212　2×3' ART. NO. CZ287　3×5' ART. NO. CZ310　2×3'	2 000PCS 1 000PCS 1 000PCS	17.1 18.1 19.1	34 200.00 18 100.00 19 100.00

总值 TOTAL：	4 000PCS	USD 71 400.00
Transshipment（转运）：	☑ Allowed（允许）	☐ not allowed（不允许）
Partial shipments（分运）：	☐ Allowed（允许）	☑ not allowed（不允许）

Shipment date（装运期）：DURING JULY, 2010

Insurance（保险）：
由卖方按发票金额110%投保一切险，另加保　　　险至　　　为止。
to be covered by theSeller FOR 110% of the invoice value covering All Risks additional　　　from　　　to　　　.

Shipping advice（装运通知）：
一旦装运完毕，卖方应即电告买方合同号、商品名、已装载数量、发票总金额、毛重、运输工具名称及启运日期等。
The sellers shall immediately, upon the completion of the loading of the goods, advise the buyers of the Contract No., names of commodity, loaded quantity, invoice values, gross weight. names of vessel and shipment date by TELEX/FAX.

Disputes settlement（争议之解决方式）：
凡因执行本合约或有关本合约所发生的一切争执，双方应协商解决。如果协商不能得到解决，应提交仲裁。仲裁地点在被告方所在国内，或者在双方同意的第三国。仲裁裁决是终局的，对双方都有约束力，仲裁费用由败诉方承担。
All disputes in connection with this contract of the execution thereof shall be amicably settled through negotiation. In case no amicable settlement can be reached between the two parties, the case under dispute shall be submitted to arbitration, which shall be held in the country where the defendant resides, or in third country agreed by both parties. The decision of the arbitration shall be accepted as final and binding upon both parties. The Arbitration Fees shall be borne by the losing party.

Versions（文字）：
本合同中、英两种文字具有同等法律效力，在文字解释上，若有异议，以中文解释为准。
This contract is made out in both Chinese and English of which version is equally effective. Conflicts between these two languages arising therefrom, if any, shall be subject to Chinese version.

本合同共 __ 份，自双方代表签字(盖章)之日起生效。
This contract is in copies, effective since being singed/sealed by both parties.

The Buyer	The Seller
John Smith	*林擎*

2010年7月2日，进口方通过银行开来号码为0419049的信用证一份。

2. 信用证

	Issue of a Documentary Credit:	
	DOMINION BANK LTD. ,SAN FRANCISCO	
SEQUENCE OF TOTAL	27:	1/1
FORM OF DOC. CREDIT	40A:	IRREVOCABLE
DOC. CREDIT NUMBER	20:	0419049
DATE OF ISSUE	31C:	20100702
EXPIRY	31D:	DATE JUL. 30,2010 AT OUR COUNTER
APPLICANT	50:	THE LOOKING HANDCRAFT, INC.
		138 SAN MATEC AVENUE, SAN FRANCISCO
		CA－94080－6501,U. S.
BENEFICIARY	59:	CHANGZHOU YAFENG IMP. & EXP. CO. , LTD.
		3 GEHU MIDDLE ROAD, CHANGZHOU, JIANGSU CHINA
		Telex:0985 Fax:6332136 Tel:6332138
AMOUNT	32B:	CURRENCY USD AMOUNT 71 400. 00
AVAILABLE WITH/BY	41D:	BANK OF CHINA, CHANGZHOU BRANCH
		BY NEGOTIATION
DRAFTS AT	42C:	AT SIGHT FOR FULL INVOICE VALUE
DRAWEE	42A:	DOMINION BANK LTD. , SAN FRANCISCO
PARTIAL SHIPMENTS	43P:	PROHIBITED
TRANSSHIPMENT	43T:	ALLOWED
LOADING IN CHARGE	44A:	ANY CHINESE PORT
FOR TRANSPORT TO	44B:	SAN FRANCISCO
LATEST DATE OF SHIP	44C:	100730
DESCRIPT. OF GOODS	45A:	4 000 PCS HOOK RUG AS PER S/C NO. 04F3－780
		ART. NO. CZ212 2×3' 2 000 PCS @ USD17. 10 PER PC
		ART. NO. CZ287 3×5' 1 000 PCS @ USD18. 10 PER PC
		ART. NO. CZ310 2×3' 1 000 PCS @ USD19. 10 PER PC
		CIFSAN FRANCISCO
DOCUMENTS REQUIRED	46A:	(1)FULL SET 3/3 CLEAN ON BOARD BILL OF LADING MADE OUT TO ORDER OF SHIPPER, ENDORSED IN BLANK, MARKED "FREIGHT PREPAID" AND NOTIFY APPLICANT.
		(2)MANUALLY SIGNED COMMERCIAL INVOICE IN TRIPLICATE.
		(3)INSURANCE POLICY/CERTIFICATE FOR 110PCT OF INVOICE VALUE, BLANK ENDORSED, COVERING ALL RISKS AND WAR RISKS AS PER PICC DATED 1. 1. 81, UP

	TO SAN FRANCISCO, IF INCURRED, CLAIMS, IF ANY, PAYABLE IN U.S.A. (4) WEIGHT/PACKING LIST IN 3 FOLD INDICATING DETAILED PACKING OF EACH CARTON. (5) QUALITY CERTIFICATE. (6) QUANTITY CERTIFICATE. (7) SHIPMENT ADVICE WITH FULL DETAILS INCLUDING SHIPPING MARKS, CTN NUMBERS, VESSEL'S NAME, B/L NUMBER, VALUE AND QUANTITY OF GOODS MUST BE SENT ON THE DATE OF SHIPMENT TO U.S.A. (8) BENEFICIARY'S CERTIFICATE EVIDENCING THAT TWO COPIES OF NON-NEGOTIABLE B/L WILL BE DESPATCHED TO APPLICANT WITHIN TWO DAYS AFTER SHIPMENT.
ADDITIONAL COND	47A: (1) ONE SET OF N/N DOCUMENTS MUST BE AIRMAILED TO OPENER AFTER DATE OF SHIPMENT AND POST EVIDENCE TO THIS EFFECT IS REQUIRED. (2) ALL INVOICES MUST INDICATE LICENCE NO. CN617032. (3) EXCEPT SO FAR AS OTHERWISE EXPRESSLY STATE, THIS DOCUMENTARY CREDIT IS SUBJECT TO UNIFORM CUSTOMS AND PRACTICE FOR DOCUMENTARY CREDIT ICC PUBLICATION NO. 600.
DETAILS OF CHARGES	71B: ALL BANKING CHARGES OUTSIDE U.S.A. INCLUDING REIMBURSEMENT COMMISSION ARE FOR ACCOUNT OF BENEFICIARY.
PRESENTATION PERIOD	48: DOCUMENTS WILL BE DULY HONORED PRESENTATION WITHIN 5 DAYS AFTER THE DATE OF SHIPMENT BUT WHTHIN THE LIFE OF THIS CREDIT.
CONFIRMATION	49: WITHOUT
INSTRUCTIONS:	78: THE NEGOTIATION BANK MUST FORWARD THE DRAFTS AND ALL DOCUMENTS BY REGISTERED AIRMAIL DIRECT TO US IN TWO CONSECUTIVE LOTS, UPON RECEIPT OF THE DRAFTS AND DOCUMENTS IN ORDER, WE WILL REMIT THE PROCEEDS AS INSTRUCTED BY THE NEGOTIATION BANK.

出口方根据信用证制作的商业发票和装箱单如下：

3. 商业发票

ISSUER CHANGZHOU YAFENG IMP. & EXP. CO., LTD. 3 GEHU MIDDLE ROAD, CHANGZHOU, JIANGSU CHINA Telex:0985 Fax:6332136 Tel:6332138			常州亚峰进出口有限公司 商 业 发 票 COMMERCIAL INVOICE ORIGINAL	
TO THE LOOKING HANDCRAFT, INC 138 SAN MATEC AVENUE, SAN FRANCISCO CA—94080—6501, U.S.A			NO. F93002897	DATE JUL. 3, 2010
TRANSPORT DETAILS FROM SHANGHAI TO SAN FRANCISCO BY SEA			S/C NO. 04F3—786	L/C NO. 0419049
^			TERMS OF PAYMENT L/C AT SIGHT	
Marks and Numbers	Number and Kind of Package Description of Goods	Quantity	Unit Price	Amount
N/M	CIF SAN FRANCISCO			
	4 000PCS HOOK RUG AS PER S/C NO. 04F3—780 ART. NO. CZ212 2×3' ART. NO. CZ287 3×5' ART. NO. CZ310 2×3'	2 000PCS 1 000PCS 1 000PCS	USD 17.1 USD 18.1 USD 19.1	USD 34 200.00 USD 18 100.00 USD 19 100.00
	TOTAL:	4 000PCS		USD 71 400.00
SAY TOTAL: SAY U.S. DOLLARS SEVENTY ONE THOUSAND FOUR HUNDRED ONLY				
We certify that the goods named above have been supplied in conformity with Order No. 04F3—786, and the goods named herein are of Chinese Origin. LICENCE NO. CN617032				

4. 装箱单

ISSUER CHANGZHOU YAFENG IMP. & EXP. CO., LTD. 3 GEHU MIDDLE ROAD, CHANGZHOU, JIANGSU CHINA Telex:0985 Fax:6332136 Tel:6332138			常州亚峰进出口有限公司 装箱单 PACKING LIST ORIGINAL				
TO THE LOOKING HANDCRAFT, INC 138 SAN MATEC AVENUE, SAN FRANCISCO CA－94080－6501, U.S.A			INVOICE NO. F93002897			DATE JUL. 3, 2010	
Marks and Numbers	Number and Kind of package Description of Goods		Quantity	Package	G.W (KGS)	N.W (KGS)	Meas (M3)
N/M	HOOK RUG AS PER S/C NO. 04F3－780 ART. NO. CZ212　2×3' ART. NO. CZ287　3×5' ART. NO. CZ310　2×3' PACKING: 10PCS/CTN		2 000PCS 1 000PCS 1 000PCS	20CTNS 10CTNS 10CTNS	12.0 16.5 12.0	11.5 16.0 11.5	@0.08
SAY TOTAL: PACKED IN 40CARTONS ONLY							
THE L/C NUMBER: 0419049 CENTRAL BANK CONTROL NUMBER: 278701255020							

任务分解

1. 读懂合同和信用证条款，看懂发票和装箱单
2. 缮制出口报检单

任务描述

进出口商品检验检疫是进出口业务的一个重要环节。及时办理出口货物的报检手续，能保证出口货物按时、按质、按量出运，利于出口商及时收汇。根据合同或信用证的要求，以及出口货物的相关资料，如发票、装箱单等，准确地制作出口货物报检单，及时送到指定部门报检，是单证员必备的基本技能。

操作示范

第一步：读懂合同和信用证条款，看懂发票和装箱单的各个栏目
第二步：根据合同、信用证、发票和装箱单，缮制出口报检单

出口报检单的样式如下：

中华人民共和国出入境检验检疫
出境货物报检单

报检单位（加盖公章）　　　　　　　　　　　　　　＊编　　号：
报检单位登记号：　联系人：　电话：　报检日期：　年　月　日

发货人	（中文）
	（外文）
收货人	（中文）
	（外文）

货物名称（中/外文）	H.S编码	产地	数/重量	货物总值	包装种类及数量

运输工具名称号码		贸易方式		货物存放地点	

合同号		信用证号		用途	

发货日期		输往国家（地区）		许可证/审批号	
启运地		到达口岸		生产单位注册号	

集装箱规格、数量及号码	

合同、信用证订立的检验检疫条款或特殊要求	标记及号码	随附单据（划"√"或补填）
		□合同　　　　　　包装性能结果单 □信用证　　　　　□许可/审批文件 □发票　　　　　　□ □换证凭单　　　　□ □装箱单　　　　　□ □厂检单

需要证单名称（划"√"或补填）	检验检疫费

— 91 —

□品质证书 ＿正＿副 □重量证书 ＿正＿副 □数量证书 ＿正＿副 □兽医卫生证书＿正＿副 □健康证书 ＿正＿副 □卫生证书 ＿正＿副 □动物卫生证书＿正＿副	□植物检疫证书＿正＿副 □熏蒸/消毒证书＿正＿副 □出境货物换证凭单	总金额 (人民币元)	
		计费人	(签署)
		收费人	(签署)
报检人郑重声明： 1.本人被授权报检。 2.上列填写内容正确属实，货物无伪造或冒用他人的厂名、标志、认证标志，并承担货物质量责任。 签名：＿＿＿＿		领取证单	
		日 期	
		签 名	

注：有"＊"号栏由出入境检验检疫机关填写　　◆国家出入境检验检疫局制

报检人(报检员)要认真填写"出境货物报检单"，内容应按合同、出口发票、装箱单等单据上的内容填写，报检单应填写完整、无漏项、字迹清楚，不得涂改，且中英文内容一致，并加盖申请单位公章。

(1)编号：由检验检疫机构报检受理人员填写，前六位为检验检疫机关代码，第七位为报检类代码，第八、九位为年份代码，第十至十五位为流水号。

(2)报检单位：指经国家质量监督检验检疫总局审核，获得许可、登记，并取得国家质检总局颁发的《自理报检单位备案登记证明书》或《代理报检单位备案登记证明书》的企业。

本案填写：常州亚峰进出口有限公司

(3)报检单位登记号：报检单位在国家质检总局登记的10位数登记证号码。

本案填写：625419577

(4)联系人：报检人员的姓名；电话：报检人员的联系电话。

(5)报检日期：检验检疫机构接受报检当天的日期。本栏填制的报检日期统一用阿拉伯数字来表示。

本案填写：2010年7月3日

(6)发货人：外贸合同中的供货商或商业发票上的出票人。本栏分别用中、英文分行填报发货人名称。

本案填写：

发货人	(中文)常州亚峰进出口有限公司
	(外文)CHANGZHOU YAFENG IMP. & EXP. CO., LTD.

(7)收货人：外贸合同中的收购商或商业发票上的受票人。本栏分别用中、英文分行填报发货人名称。

本案填写：

收货人	(中文)罗京手工艺品股份有限公司
	(外文)THE LOOKING HANDCRAFT, INC.

(8)货物名称(中/外文):被申请报检的出境货物名称、规格、型号、成分以及英文对照,应与合同、信用证、发票所列一致,如为废旧货物应注明。

(9)H.S编码:出口货物的商品编码。以当年海关公布的商品税则编码分类为准。

(10)产地:在出境货物报检单中指货物生产地、加工制造地的省、市、县名。该栏在进境货物报检单中指进口货物的原产国家或地区。本栏填报出境货物生产地的省、市、县的中文名称。

(11)数/重量:指以商品编码分类中计量标准项下的实际检验检疫数量、重量。

本栏按实际申请检验检疫的数/重量填写,重量还需列明毛/净/皮重。

本栏可以填报一个以上计量单位,如第一计量单位:"个",第二计量单位:"公斤"。

(12)货物总值:指出境货物的商业总值及币种,应与合同、发票或报关单上所列的货物总值一致。注意:本栏不需要填报价格术语如CIF等。

(13)包装种类及数量:指货物实际运输外包装的种类及数量。若有托盘集中包装,除了填报托盘种类及数量外,还应填报托盘上小包装数量级及包装种类。

本案中(8)~(13)各栏的填写如下:

货物名称 (中/外文)	H.S编码	产地	数/重量	货物总值	包装种类 及数量
钩针地毯 HOOK RUG	5702.4100	无锡	4 000PCS 3 070M²	USD71 400.00	500CTNS

(14)运输工具名称号码:指载运出境货物运输工具的名称和运输工具的编号。

本栏填制实际出境运输工具的名称及编号,如船名航次等。若报检申请时未定运输工具的名称及编号时,可以填制笼统运输方式总称,如填报"船舶"或"飞机"等。

(15)贸易方式:本栏填报与实际情况一致的海关规范贸易方式。常见的贸易方式有"一般贸易"、"来料加工贸易"等。

(16)货物存放地点:指出口货物的生产企业存放出口货物的地点。

本栏按实际情况填报具体地点、仓库。

本案(14)~(16)栏的填写如下:

运输工具 名称号码	HANJIN V.014E	贸易方式	一般贸易	货物存放地点	无锡新区 500号

(17)合同号:指对外贸易合同、订单或形式发票的号码。

(18)信用证号:指信用证方式下,填写信用证号,其他结算方式不填。

(19)用途:指从以下9个选项中选择符合实际出境货物用途来填报:①种用或繁殖;②食用;③奶用;④观赏或演艺;⑤伴侣动物;⑥试验;⑦药用;⑧饲料;⑨其他。

本案(17)~(19)各栏的填报如下:

合同号	04F3-780	信用证号	0419049	用途	其他

(20)发货日期:指货物实际出境的日期。按实际开船日或起飞日等填报发货日期,以年、月、日的顺填报。

(21)输往国家(地区):指出口货物直接运抵的国家(地区),是货物的最终销售或消费国家。

本栏填报输往国家(地区)的中文名称。

提单/运单号:指货物海运提单号或空运单号,有二程提单的应同时填写。

(22)许可证/审批号:需办理出境许可证或审批的货物应填写有关许可证号或审批号。

本案(20)~(22)各栏的填写如下：

发货日期	2010年7月14日	输往国家（地区）	美国	许可证/审批号	CN617032

(23)启运地:本栏填报出境货物最后离境的口岸的中文名称。卸毕日期:货物在口岸的卸毕日期。

(24)到达口岸:指出境货物运往境外的最终目的港,填报中文名称。

(25)生产单位注册号:指出入境检验检疫机构签发给生产单位的卫生注册书编号或加工仓库的注册编号。

本案(25)~(26)各栏的填写如下：

启运地	上海	到达口岸	旧金山	生产单位注册号	625419577

(26)集装箱规格、数量及号码:指货物若以集装箱运输应填写集装箱的规格、数量及号码。填写规则:"数量"ד规格"/"箱号"。

(27)合同、信用证订立的检验检疫条款或特殊要求:指在合同中订立的有关检验检疫的特殊条款及其他要求应填入此栏。

(28)标记及号码:指货物的标记号码,应与合同、发票等有关外贸单据保持一致。若没有标记号码则填"N/M"。

(29)随附单据指在随附单据的种类前划"√"或补填。

本案(27)~(29)的填写如下：

合同、信用证订立的检验检疫条款或特殊要求	标记及号码	随附单据（划"√"或补填）	
	S.H.I 0419049 SAN FRANCISCO NO.1—500	☑ 合同 ☑ 信用证 ☑ 发票 ☐ 换证凭单 ☑ 装箱单 ☐ 厂检单	包装性能结果单 ☐ 许可/审批文件 ☐ ☐

(30)签名:由持有报检员证的报检人员手签。

(31)检验检疫费:由检验检疫机构计费人员核定费用后填写。

(32)领取证单:报检人在领取检验检疫机构出具的有关检验检疫证单时填写领证日期及领证人姓名。

填制好的出境货物报检单如下:

中华人民共和国出入境检验检疫
出境货物报检单

报检单位：常州亚峰进出口有限公司　　　　编　　号：

报检单位登记号：625419577　联系人：林峰　　报检日期：2010年7月3日

发货人	(中文)常州亚峰进出口有限公司						
	(外文)CHANGZHOU YAFENG IMP. & EXP. CO., LTD.						
收货人	(中文)罗京手工艺品股份有限公司						
	(外文)THE LOOKING HANDCRAFT, INC.						
货物名称(中/外文)	H.S编码		产地	数/重量	货物总值		包装种类及数量
钩针地毯 HOOK RUG	5702.4100		无锡	4 000PCS 3 070M2	USD71 400.00		500CTNS
运输工具名称号码	HANJIN V.014E		贸易方式	一般贸易	货物存放地点		无锡新区500号
合同号	04F3—780			信用证号	0419049	用途	其他
发货日期	2010年 7月14日	输往国家(地区)		美国	许可证/审批号		CN617032
启运地	上海	到达口岸		旧金山	生产单位注册号		625419577
集装箱规格、数量及号码							
合同、信用证订立的检验检疫条款或特殊要求		标记及号码				随附单据(划"√"或补填)	
		S.H.I 0419049 SAN FRANCISCO NO.1—500				√合同　　　包装性能结果单 √信用证　　□许可/审批文件 √发票　　　□ □换证凭单　□ √装箱单 □厂检单	
需要证单名称(划"√"或补填)						检验检疫费	

☑ 品质证书 __正__ 副 ☐ 重量证书 __正__ 副 ☑ 数量证书 2正2副 ☐ 兽医卫生证书 __正__ 副 ☐ 健康证书 __正__ 副 ☐ 卫生证书 __正__ 副 ☐ 动物卫生证书 __正__ 副	☐ 植物检疫证书 __正__ 副 ☐ 熏蒸/消毒证书 __正__ 副 ☐ 出境货物换证凭单	总金额 （人民币元）	1 200.00 元
		计费人	（签署）
		收费人	（签署）
报检人郑重声明： 1. 本人被授权报检。 2. 上列填写内容正确属实，货物无伪造或冒用他人的厂名、标志、认证标志，并承担货物质量责任。 签名：_____		领取证单	
		日 期	
		签 名	

注：有"＊"号栏由出入境检验检疫机关填写　　◆国家出入境检验检疫局制

必备知识

一、商检基础知识

1. 出入境检验检疫的含义

出入境检验检疫工作是国家出入境检验检疫部门依照国家检验检疫法律法规规定，对进出境的商品（包括动植物产品），以及运载这些商品、动植物和旅客的交通工具、运输设备，分别实施检验、检疫、鉴定、监督管理和对出入境人员实施卫生检疫及口岸卫生监督的统称。

2. 出入境检验检疫工作的主要内容和目的

(1)对进出口商品进行检验、鉴定和监督管理，保证进出口商品符合质量（标准）要求、维护对外贸易有关各方的合法权益，促进对外经济贸易的顺利发展。

(2)对出入境动植物及其产品，包括其运输工具、包装材料的检疫和监督管理，防止危害动植物的病菌、害虫、杂草种子及其他有害生物由国外传入或由国内传出，保护本国农、林、渔、牧业生产和国际生态环境和人类的健康。

(3)对出入境人员、交通工具、运输设备以及可能传播检疫传染病的行李、货物、邮包等物品实施国境卫生检疫和口岸卫生监督，防止传染病由国外传入或者由国内传出，保护人类健康。

3. 商检机构的种类

进行商品检验的机构主要有以下三类：其一，是由国家设立的商品检验机构，在我国就是国家进出口商品检验局；其二，是由私人或同业公会、协会开设的公证行；其三，是生产、制造厂商或产品的使用部门设立的检验机构。

我国从事进出口商品检验的机构有中华人民共和国国家出入境检验检疫局及其设在全国各地的商检机构。

4. 我国商检机构的业务范围

中国国家进出口商品检验局（The China I/E Commodity Inspection Bureau，CCIB）是我国

最主要的官方检验机构。国家进出口商品检验局在各省、自治区、直辖市及进出口商品口岸、集散地都设立进出口商品检验局及其分支机构。此外,我国还设立了专门从事动植物、食品卫生、药物、船舶、飞机、计量器具等检验或检疫的检验机构。

根据《商检法》(1989年8月1日颁布实施)及1992年底发布的《中华人民共和国进出口商品检验实施条例》的规定,我国商检机构有三项基本任务:

(1)实施法定检验。实施法定检验是指依法进行的强制性的检验或检疫,对大宗的关系国计民生的重要进出口商品、易发生质量问题的商品和涉及安全卫生的商品要进行法定检验。目前,实施法定检验的商品都列成表并进行分类。

(2)办理公证鉴定。公证鉴定是非强制性的,只证明货物的实在状态,并不是检验是否合格的依据。一般公证鉴定证明书不是海关放行的依据。

(3)实施监督管理。实施监督管理主要是通过行政手段,与海关配合打击走私,进行伪劣、假冒产品的查处。对进出口商品未经检验合格的不准销售或进出口。

5. 境外著名的商检机构及其业务范围

在国际贸易中,从事商检的机构很多。官方的有国家设立的检验机构;非官方的有私人或同业公会、协会等开设的检验机构,如公证人、公证行,还有工厂企业、用货单位设立的化验室、检验室等。目前国际上比较著名的商检机构有:美国粮谷检验署、美国食品药物管理局(FDA)、法国国家实验室检测中心、日本通商产业检查所、香港特别行政区的商品检验机构等官方所设立的检验机构,以及美国保险人实验室(UL)、瑞士日内瓦通用鉴定公司、英国劳合氏公证行、日本海事鉴定协会等民间或社团检验机构。

二、报检基础知识

1. 报检的含义和报检单位

报检是指进出口货物收发货人或其代理人,依照有关法律、行政法规的规定,在规定的地点和期限内,以书面或电子申报方式向出入检验检疫机构报告其法定检验检疫物的情况,随附有关单证,并接受出入境检验检疫机构对其法定检验检疫物实施检验检疫以获得出入境通关放行凭证及其他证单的行为。

我国自2000年1月1日起,实施"先报检,后报关"的检验检疫货物通关制度,海关凭检验检疫机构签发的"货物通关单"验放。

报检单位包括自理报检单位和代理报检单位。自理报检单位是指根据我国法律法规规定办理出入境检验检疫报检或委托代理报检单位办理出入境报检手续的货物收发货人、进出口货物的生产、加工和经营单位等。代理报检单位是指经国家工商行政部门注册的境内企业法人再经国家质检总局注册登记,取得代理报检资质,并依法接受进出口货物收货人、发货人、货主等相关对外贸易法人的委托,为其向出入境检验检疫机构代理办理出入境检验检疫报检手续的单位。

报检单位的范围主要包括:

(1)有进出口经营权的国内企业。

(2)进口货物的收货人或其代理人。

(3)出口货物的生产企业。

(4)出口货物运输包装及出口危险货物运输包装生产企业。

(5)中外合资、中外合作、外商独资企业。

(6)国外(境外)企业、商社驻中国代表机构。

(7)进出境动物隔离饲养和植物繁殖生产单位。

(8)进出境动植物产品的生产、加工、存储、运输单位。

(9)对进出境植物、动物产品进行药剂熏蒸和消毒服务的单位。

(10)从事集装箱的储存场地和中转场(库)、清洗、卫生除害处理、报检的单位。

(11)有进出境交换业务的科研单位。

(12)其他报检单位。

2. 入境货物报检应提供的单据

申请入境货物报检时,应填写入境货物报检单并提供合同、发票、提单等有关单据。有下列情况,报检时还应按要求提供有关文件。

(1)凡实施安全质量许可、卫生注册,或其他需审批审核的货物,应提供有关证明。

(2)进行品质检验的,还应提供国外品质证书或质量保证书、产品使用说明书及有关标准和技术资料;凭样成交的,应加附成交样品;以品级或公量计价结算的,应同时申请重量鉴定。

(3)报检入境废物时,还应提供国家环保部门签发的"进口废物批准证书"和经认可的检验机构签发的装运前检验合格证书等。

(4)申请残损鉴定的还应提供理货残损单、铁路商务记录、空运事故记录或海事报告等证明货损情况的有关单证。

(5)申请重(数)量鉴定的还应提供重量明细单、理货清单等。

(6)货物经收、用货部门验收或其他单位检测的,应随附验收报告或检测结果以及重量明细单等。

(7)入境的动植物及其产品,在提供贸易合同、发票、产地证书的同时,还必须提供输出国家或地区官方的检疫证书;需办理入境检疫审批手续的,还应提供入境动植物检疫许可证。

(8)过境动植物及其产品报检时,应持货运单和输出国家或地区官方出具的检疫证书;运输动物过境时,还应提交国家检验检疫局签发的动植物过境许可证。

(9)报检入境运输工具、集装箱时,应提供检疫证明,并申报有关人员健康状况。

(10)入境旅客、交通员工携带伴侣动物的,应提供入境动物检疫证书及预防接种证明。

(11)因科研等特殊需要,输入禁止入境物的物品,必须提供国家检验检疫局签发的特许审批证明。

(12)入境携带特殊物品时,应提供有关的批件或规定的文件。

3. 出境货物报检应提供的单据

申请出境货物报检时,应填写出境货物报检单并提供对外贸易合同(售货确认书或函电)、信用证、发票、装箱单等必要的单据。有下列情况,报检时还应按要求提供有关文件。

(1)凡实施质量许可、卫生注册或需经审批的货物,应提供有关证明。

(2)出境货物需经生产者或经营者检验合格并加附检验合格证或检测报告;申请重量鉴定的,应加附重量明细单或磅码单。

(3)凭样成交的货物,应提供经买卖双方确认的样品。

(4)出境人员应向检验检疫机构申请办理国际旅行健康证明书及国际预防接种证书。

(5)报检出境运输工具、集装箱时,还应提供检疫证明,并申报有关人员健康状况。

(6)生产出境危险货物包装容器的企业,必须向检验检疫机构申请包装容器的性能鉴定。

(7)生产出境危险货物的企业,必须向检验检疫机构申请危险货物包装容器的使用鉴定。

(8)报检出境危险货物时,必须提供危险货物包装容器性能鉴定结果单和使用鉴定结果单。
(9)申请原产地证明书和普惠制原产地证明书的,应提供商业发票等资料。
(10)出境特殊物品的,根据法律法规规定应提供有关的审批文件。

4. **出入境货物报检的时限和地点**

(1)入境报检的时限和地点。入境货物应在入境前或入境时向入境口岸、指定的或到达站的检验检疫机构办理报检手续;入境货物需对外索赔出证的,应在索赔有效期前不少于20天内向到货口岸或货物到达地的检验检疫机构报检。

(2)出境报检的时限和地点。出境货物最迟应于报关或装运前7天报检。对于个别检验检疫周期较长的货物,应留有相应的检验检疫时间。

拓展知识

一、商品检验检疫证书的含义、种类和作用

1. **含义**

商品检验检疫证书是指进出口商品经商品检验检疫机构检验、鉴定后出具的证明检验检疫结果的书面文件。商品检验检疫证书的种类很多,在实际进出口商品交易中,应在检验检疫条款中规定检验检疫证书的类别及其商品检验检疫的要求。

2. **种类和作用**

商品检验检疫证书的种类和用途主要有:

(1)品质检验证书。品质检验证书是出口商品交货结汇和进口商品结算索赔的有效凭证,是法定检验商品的证书,也是进出口商品报关、输出输入的合法凭证。商检机构签发的放行单和在报关单上加盖的放行章有与商检证书同等通关效力,签发的检验情况通知单同为商检证书性质。

(2)重量/数量检验证书。重量/数量检验证书是出口商品交货结汇、签发提单和进口商品结算索赔的有效凭证,是出口商品的重量证书,也是国外报关征税和计算运费、装卸费用的证件。

(3)兽医检验证书。兽医检验证书是证明出口动物产品或食品经过检疫合格的证件,适用于冻畜肉、冻禽、禽畜罐头、冻兔、皮张、毛类、绒类、猪鬃、肠衣等出口商品,是对外交货、银行结汇和进口国通关输入的重要证件。

(4)卫生/健康证书。卫生/健康证书是证明可供人类食用的出口动物产品、食品等经过卫生检验检疫合格的证件,适用于肠衣、罐头、冻鱼、冻虾、食品、蛋品、乳制品、蜂蜜等,是对外交货、银行结汇和通关验放的有效证件。

(5)消毒检验证书。消毒检验证书是证明出口动物产品经过消毒处理,保证安全卫生的证件,适用于猪鬃、马尾、皮张、山羊毛、羽毛、人发等商品,是对外交货、银行结汇和国外通关验放的有效凭证。

(6)熏蒸证书。熏蒸证书是用于证明出口粮谷、油籽、豆类、皮张等商品,以及包装用木材与植物性填充物等,已经过熏蒸灭虫的证书。

(7)残损检验证书。残损检验证书是证明进口商品残损情况的证件,适用于进口商品发生残、短、渍、毁等情况,可作为受货人向发货人或承运人或保险人等有关责任方索赔的有效证件。

(8)积载鉴定证书。积载鉴定证书是证明船方和集装箱装货部门正确配载积载货物,作为证明履行运输契约义务的证件,可供货物交接或发生货损时处理争议之用。

(9)财产价值鉴定证书。财产价值鉴定证书是作为对外贸易关系人和司法、仲裁、验资等有关部门索赔、理赔、评估或裁判的重要依据。

(10)船舱检验证书。船舱检验证书用来证明承运出口商品的船舱清洁、密固、冷藏效能及其他技术条件是否符合保护承载商品的质量和数量完整与安全的要求,可作为承运人履行租船契约适载义务,对外贸易关系方进行货物交接和处理货损事故的依据。

(11)生丝品级及公量检验证书。生丝品级及公量检验证书是出口生丝的专用证书,其作用相当于品质检验证书和重量/数量检验证书。

(12)产地证明书。产地证明书是出口商品在进口国通关输入、享受减免关税优惠待遇和证明商品产地的凭证。

(13)舱口装/卸载证书、舱口检视证书、监视装/卸载证书、舱口封识证书、油温空距证书、集装箱监装/拆证书。以上证书作为证明承运人履行契约义务,明确责任界限,是便于处理货损货差责任事故的证明。

(14)价值证明书。价值证明书作为进口国管理外汇和征收关税的凭证,在发票上签盖商检机构的价值证明章与价值证明书具有同等效力。

(15)货载衡量检验证书。货载衡量检验证书是证明进出口商品的重量、体积吨位的证件,可作为计算运费和制订配载计划的依据。

(16)集装箱租箱证书、集装箱租箱交货检验证书、租船交船剩水/油重量鉴定证书。以上证书可作为契约双方明确履约责任和处理费用清算的凭证。

二、检验检疫证书的格式

正如上文所述,检验检疫证书的种类很多,常用的是数量检验证书和质量检验证书,它们的格式如下:

1. 数量检验证书

中华人民共和国出入检验检疫
ENTRY—EXIT INSPECTION AND QUARANTINE
OF THE PEOPLE'S REPUBLIC OF CHINA
数量检验证书
QUANTITY CERTIFICATE

正 本
ORGINAL

编号
No.:

发货人:
Consignor:

收货人:
Consignee:

品名: 标记及号码
Description: Marks & Numbers:

报检数量/重量:
Quantity/Weight Declared:

包装种类及数量:
Number and Type of Packages:

运输工具:
Means of Conveyance:

检验结果:
Results of Inspection: (签署)

2. 质量检验证书

中华人民共和国出入检验检疫
ENTRY—EXIT INSPECTION AND QUARANTINE
OF THE PEOPLE'S REPUBLIC OF CHINA

正 本
ORGINAL

编 号 No.:

质量检验证书
QUALITY CERTIFICATE

发货人：
Consignor：

收货人：
Consignee：

品名：
Description of Goods：

报检数量/重量：
Quantity/Weight Declared：

包装种类及数量：
Number and type of Packages：

运输工具：　　　　　　　　　　　　　标记及号码：
Means of Conveyance：　　　　　　　Marks & Numbers：

装运日期：
Date of Loading：

发票号：
Invoice No.：

合同号：
Contract No.：

检验结果：
Results of Inspection：

印章：　　　　　　签证地点：　　　　　　签证日期：
Official Stamp：　　Place of Issue：　　　Date of Issue：

　　授权签字人 Authorized Officer　　　　　签名 Signature

技能训练

(一)训练资料

2010年4月16日,常州亚峰进出口有限公司委托南通盛通食品厂报检,申请签发出境货物换证凭单与健康证书。

1. 商品资料

中文名称: 碎片蘑菇罐头
英文名称: CANNED MUSRHOOMS PIECES & STEMS
商品描述: 24 TINS * 425 GRAMS NET WEIGHT
包装纸箱: 长45mm 宽20mm 高14.9mm
海关编码: 2003.1011
商品毛重: 按净重的1.1倍计算
装运日期: 2010年4月25日
发票编号: 2010SDT001

2. 外销合同

<table>
<tr><td colspan="4" align="center">**销售合同**
SALES CONTRACT</td></tr>
<tr><td rowspan="3">卖方
SELLER:</td><td rowspan="3">CHANGZHOU YAFENG IMP. & EXP. CO., LTD.
3 GEHU MIDDLE ROAD, CHANGZHOU, JIANGSU CHINA
Telex:0985 Fax:6332136 Tel:6332138</td><td>编号 NO.:</td><td>04F3—787</td></tr>
<tr><td>日期 DATE:</td><td>MAR. 28, 2010</td></tr>
<tr><td>地点
SIGNED IN:</td><td>CHANGZHOU, CHINA</td></tr>
<tr><td>买方
BUYER:</td><td colspan="3">THE LOOKING HANDCRAFT, INC 138 SAN MATEC AVENUE, SAN FRANCISCO CA—94080—6501, U.S.A.</td></tr>
<tr><td colspan="4">买卖双方同意以下条款达成交易:
This contract is made by and agreed between the BUYER and SELLER, in accordance with the terms and conditions stipulated below.</td></tr>
<tr><td align="center">1.品名及规格
Commodity & Specification</td><td align="center">2.数量
Quantity</td><td align="center">3.单价及价格条款
Unit Price &
Trade Terms</td><td align="center">4.金额
Amount</td></tr>
<tr><td colspan="4" align="right">CFR NEWYORK PORT, U.S.A.</td></tr>
</table>

CANNED MUSRHOOMS PIECES & STEMS 24 TINS×425 GRAMS NET WEIGHT		1 700CARTONS	USD7.80	USD13 260.00
Total：		1 700CARTONS		USD13 260.00
允许 With	5%	溢短装，由卖方决定 More or less of shipment allowed at the sellers' option		
5.总值 Total Value		U.S. DOLLARS THIRTEEN THOUSAND TWO HUNDRED AND SIXTY ONLY		
6.包装 Packing		EXPORTED BROWN CARTON		
7.唛头 Shipping Marks		ROSE BRAND 178/2010 RIYADH		
8.装运期及运输方式 Time of Shipment & means of Transportation		Not Later Than Apr.30, 2010 BY VESSEL		
9.装运港及目的地 Port of Loading & Destination		From：SHANGHAI PORT, CHINA To：NEWYORK PORT, U.S.A		
10.保险 Insurance		TO BE COVERED BY THE BUYER.		
11.付款方式 Terms of Payment		The Buyers shall open through a bank acceptable to the Seller an Irrevocable Letter of Credit payable at sight of reach the seller 30 days before the month of shipment, valid for negotiation inChina until the 15th day after the date of shipment.		
12.备注 Remarks				

The Buyer　　　　　　　　　　　　　　　　　　　　　　　　　　　　The Seller

(二)根据上述资料,制作出境货物报检单,要求格式清楚、内容完整

中华人民共和国出入境检验检疫
出境货物报检单

报检单位(加盖公章)　　　　　　　　　　　　　＊编　号:

报检单位登记号:　　联系人:　　电话:　　报检日期:　年　月　日

发货人	(中文)					
	(外文)					
收货人	(中文)					
	(外文)					
货物名称(中/外文)	H.S编码	产地	数/重量	货物总值	包装种类及数量	
运输工具名称号码		贸易方式		货物存放地点		
合同号		信用证号		用途		
发货日期		输往国家(地区)		许可证/审批号		
启运地		到达口岸		生产单位注册号		
集装箱规格、数量及号码						

合同、信用证订立的检验检疫条款或特殊要求	标记及号码	随附单据(划"√"或补填)	
		□合同 □信用证 □发票 □换证凭单 □装箱单 □厂检单	包装性能结果单 □许可/审批文件 □ □ □

需要证单名称(划"√"或补填)		检验检疫费	
□品质证书　__正__副 □重量证书　__正__副 □数量证书　__正__副 □兽医卫生证书　__正__副 □健康证书　__正__副 □卫生证书　__正__副 □动物卫生证书　__正__副	□植物检疫证书　__正__副 □熏蒸/消毒证书　__正__副 □出境货物换证凭单	总金额(人民币元)	
		计费人	(签署)
		收费人	(签署)

报检人郑重声明: 1.本人被授权报检。 2.上列填写内容正确属实,货物无伪造或冒用他人的厂名、标志、认证标志,并承担货物质量责任。 　　　　　　　　　签名:_____	领取证单	
	日　期	
	签　名	

任务六 制作原产地证

学习目标

能力目标

学会用英文准确、规范地缮制一般原产地证书和普惠制产地证

知识目标

1. 掌握产地证书的含义、作用、缮制方法
2. 熟悉原产地证书的基本内容、申领手续

任务设计

上海宏达进出口公司向挪威 OSJORD 公司出口货物灭火器商品共 9 250 只,按合同从上海海运至挪威 STAVANGER 港。该公司于 2010 年 9 月 27 日持原产地申请书和商业发票,向上海出入境检验检疫局申请原产地证,当日被发证。根据提供的资料缮制一般原产地证。

商业发票资料

Receiving unit: Hongda Import & Export Co. ,Ltd.
　　　　　　　　No. 596,Changjiang Road,Shanghai
Buying Unit:　OSJORD AS LURAMYRVEIEN
　　　　　　　　64,Postorks 152N－4065
　　　　　　　　Stavanger,Norway
　　　　　　　　Tel No. :147 5163 7200
Shipping Marks: N/M
Descriptions: Extinguisher
Quantity: 9 250PCS
Packing: 5 862 Cartons
Invoice No. : SJ100927
Invoice date: Sept. 27, 2010
　　其他资料
签证机构: 中华人民共和国出入境检验检疫局(Entry-Exit Inspection & Quarantine Bureau of the People's Republic of China)
　　签证号码: 04C3100A0936/00014
　　商品编号: 84241000

任务分解

1. 读懂所给资料
2. 根据所给资料,制作一般原产地证

任务描述

一般原产地证通常用于不使用海关发票或领事发票的国家(地区),以确定对货物征税的税率。根据合同、信用证相关条款以及相关单据准确、规范地制作一般原产地证书是单证员必备的一项技能,在实际业务中,要确保一般原产地证的内容与合同、信用证的一致性,确保一般原产地证与其他单据的一致性。

操作示范

第一步:读懂所给资料
第二步:根据所给资料,制作一般原产地证
一般原产地证的格式如下:

1. Goods Consigned from (Exporter's full name, address and country)			CERTIICATE No.: **CERTIFICATE OF ORIGIN OF THE PEOPLE'S REPUBLIC OF CHINA**		
2. Goods Consigned to (Consignee's full name, address and country)					
3. Means of Transport and Route (as far as known)			5. For Certifying Authority Use Only		
4. Country/ Region of Destination					
6. Marks and Numbers of Packages	7. Number and Kind of Pkgs; Description of Goods		8. H. S. Code	9. Quantity or Weight	10. Number and Date of Invoice
11. Declaration by the exporter 　　The undersigned hereby declares that the above details and statements are correct; that all the goods were produced in China and that they comply with the Rules of Origin of the People's Republic of China. —————————— Place and date, signature and stamp of certifying authority			12. Certification 　　It is hereby certified that the declaration by the exporter is correct. —————————— Place and date, signature and stamp of certifying authority		

1. **出口方的名称、地址、国家**［exporter(full name,address and country)］

此栏应填报出口方的企业全称、详细地址、国家全称。

(1)此栏不能填报境外中间商名称,即使信用证有规定也不可以。

(2)出口方名称要完整。若信用证项下,一般为受益人;若托收项下,一般为托收人。

(3)地址要详细完整,包括街道名称、门牌号码和邮政编码。

本案中,该栏应填写:HONGDA IMPORT&EXPORT CO.,LTD.
　　　　　　　　　　NO.596 CHANGJIANG ROAD,SHANGHAI CHINA

2. **收货人名称、地址、国家**［consignee(full name,address and country)］

本栏填报该批货物最终目的地收货人的名称、地址、国家全称。

收货人通常是合同的买方或信用证规定的提单通知人。但由于外贸需要,有时信用证所有单证收货人一栏留空。在这种情况下,有以下两种方法:

(1)此栏加注:"to whom it may concern"。

(2)此栏加注:"to order"。

如果需要填写转口商,可在收货人后面加注"VIA"＋转口商名称、地址、国家。

在本案中,该栏应填写:OSJORD AS LURAMYRVEIEN
　　　　　　　　　　64,Postorks 152N－4065
　　　　　　　　　　Stavanger,Norway

3. **运输方式和路线**(means of transport and route)

本栏填报装运地、目的地、中转地的名称,并说明运输方式。

例一:From Shanghai to Humburg by sea

例二:By S.S. fromShanghai to Humburg via Hong Kong

有时还需要加注预计离开中国的日期,此日期必须真实,不得捏造。

例三:On/After Nov.6,2003 From Shantou to Hong Kong By Truck.

在本案中,该栏应填写:FROM SHANGHAI PORT TO STAVANGER PORT BY SEA

4. **运抵国/地区**(country/region of destination)

一般按合同或信用证规定的目的港和国家填报。例如:NewYork,U.S.A.在转口贸易时,一般不能填报转口商的国家,而填报最终进口国的国名(地区)。

在本案中,该栏应填写:NORWAY。

5. **供签证机构使用**(for certifying authority use only)

本栏供签证机构对后发证书、补发证书、签发副本或其他事项加注声明时使用,证书申领单位应将此栏留空。

6. **唛头和包装号**(marks and numbers)

(1)填报的唛头应按信用证或合同中的规定填写,且与商业发票和提单的该项内容填写一致。如唛头过多此栏不够,可填报在第7栏、第8栏、第9栏、第10栏的空白处。

(2)唛头不能出现中国以外的国家(地区)制造的字样,如:"made in Hong Kong"等。

(3)若没有唛头,应填写"N/M"或"No Marks"。

在本案中,该栏应填写:"N/M"或"No Marks"。

7. **商品名称、包装件数和种类**(number and kind of packages;description of goods)

填报的商品名称应系发票中所描述的货物。包装件数和种类与货运单据一致的外包装数量及相应包装种类。若散装货,用"in bulk"表示。

(1)商品名称必须具体,其详细程度应可以在商品编码 H.S. CODE 的 8 位数中找到,不能填报笼统名称,因为笼统名称无法确定商品编码。

(2)与商品名称有关的商标、品牌无需显示,因为这些与商品编码和海关税则无关。

(3)商品名称填完后,在下一行加上结束的符号"＊＊＊＊＊＊",以防伪造。有时国外信用证要求在产地证上显示信用证号,可加注在此栏结束符号下方。

(4)包装件数和包装种类必须用英文大写和阿拉伯数字同时表示。如:"ONE HUNDRED AND TWENTY(120) CARTONS OF WORKING GLOVES"。

在本案中,该栏应填写:

FIVE THOUSAND EIGHT HUNDRED AND SIXTY TWO(5862) CARTONS OF EXTINGUISHER

＊＊＊＊＊＊＊＊＊＊＊＊＊＊＊＊＊＊＊＊＊＊＊＊＊＊＊＊＊＊

8. **商品编码**(H.S. code)

根据《中华人民共和国进出口商品的目录对照表》中规定的商品名称和编码,本栏应按正确的商品编码填入 8 位数或 10 位数。

(1)同一张产地证中包含几种不同商品时,应分别标明不同的商品编码,全部填报。

(2)此栏有时候填报 10 位商品编码,其中最后两位为补充编码。

(3)填报的商品编码,必须准确无误。

在本案中,此栏应填写:84241000。

9. **毛重或其他数量**(quantity or weight)

依据发票和货运单据中显示的毛重或其他数量来填报。

(1)若计量单位为重量,应标明毛重或净重。例如:"G.W. 400kg"或"N.W. 400kg"。

(2)用规范英文或缩写表示计量单位。如件(Pieces/PCS)、打(Dozen/DOZ)等。

本案中,没有显示重量,所以应填写:9 250PCS。

10. **发票号码及日期**(number and date of invoice)

按发票实际号码及日期填写,发票日期不得迟于出货日期。

(1)月份一律用英文缩写表示,顺序为:月、日、年。例:OCT.17,2003

(2)发票号与日期分行填报。一般第一行为发票号,第二行为日期。此栏不得为空。

在本案中,该栏应填写:INVOICE NO:SJ100927

INVOICE DATE:SEPT.27,2010

11. **出口方声明**(declaration by the exporter)

出口方声明已事先印制,内容为:"兹出口方声明以上所列内容正确无误,本批出口商品的生产地在中国,完全符合中华人民共和国原产地规则。"

出口方在此声明栏空白处,由法人或手签人员签字并盖公章(有中英文)。并且还需填制申报地点、申报日期。(此栏日期不得早于本证第 10 栏内的发票日期)

本案中,2010 年 9 月 27 日向上海出入境检验检疫局申请原产地证,该栏应填写:SHANG-

HAI,SEPT. 27,2010,×××。

12. 签证机构证明(certification)

签证机构证明已事先印制,内容为:"兹证明出口方的声明是正确无误的"。签证机构在此加盖签证机构印章并由授权人签名,两者不得重叠。签证机构在此注明签发地点和签发日期,签发日期不得早于发票日期和申请日期。

由贸促会签发的产地证书一般在机构印章中还加注下列声明:China Council for the Promotion of International Trade(CCPIT)is China Chamber of International Commerce.

在本案中,该栏应填写:SHANGHAI, SEPT. 27,2010 或 9 月 27 日后至出口前的一个日期。

根据任务设计中的信息,填制好的一般原产地证如下:

1. Goods Consigned from (Exporter's full name, address and country) HONGDA IMPORT & EXPORT CO. ,LTD. NO. 596 CHANGJIANG ROAD, SHANGHAI CHINA			Certificate No. 04C3100A0936/00014 **CERTIFICATE OF ORIGIN OF THE PEOPLE'S REPUBLIC OF CHINA**		
2. Goods Consigned to (Consignee's full name, address and country) OSJORD AS LURAMYRVEIEN 64,POSTORKS 152N－4065 STAVANGER,NORWAY					
3. Means of Transport and Route (as far as known) FROM SHANSHAI PORT TO STAVANGER PORT BY SEA 4. Country/ Region of Destination NORWAY			5. For Certifying Authority Use Only		
6. Marks and Numbers of Packages N/M	7. Number and Kind of Pkgs; Description of Goods FIVE THOUSAND EIGHT HUNDRED AND SIXTY TWO (5862) CARTONS OF EXTINGUISHER *	8. H. S Code 84241000	9. Quantity or Weight 9 250PCS	10. Number and Date of Invoices INVOICE NO. ;SJ100927 INVOICE DATE: SEPT. 27, 2010	

11. Declaration by the Exporter 　　The undersigned hereby declares that the above details and statements are correct; that all the goods were produced in China and that they comply with the Rules of Origin of the People's Republic of China. **申请单位盖印** SHANGHAI, SEPT. 27, 2010, ××× ———————————————— Place and date, signature and stamp of authorized signatory	12. Certification 　　It is hereby certified that the declaration by the exporter is correct. **CIQ** SHANGHAI, SEPT. 27, 2010 ———————————————— Place and date, signature and stamp of certifying authority

必备知识

一、产地证明书概述

1. 含义

原产地证明书(certificate of origin, C/O),简称产地证书,是由出口国政府有关机构签发的一种证明货物的原产地或制造地的法律文件。它主要用于进口国海关实行差别关税,实施进口限制、不同进口税率和不同进口配额等不同国别政策的书面依据。

我国出口商可以向以下三大机构申领原产地证明书:

(1)中华人民共和国国家质量监督检验检疫总局,以下简称质检总局(Genernal Administration of Quality Supervision Inspection and Quarantine of the People's Republic of China, AQSIQ)。

(2)中国国际贸易促进委员会,以下简称贸促会(China Council for the Promotion of International Trade, CCPIT)。

(3)中华人民共和国商务部,以下简称商务部,(Ministry of Commerce of the People's Republic of China, MOFCOM)。

2. 作用

(1)证明出口货物符合《中华人民共和国出口货物原产地规则》,确系中国制造。

(2)进口国海关以此作为差别关税、进口限制和不同进口配额与不同税率的依据文件。

(3)出口通关、结汇和进行贸易统计的重要依据。

3. 基本内容

原产地证书的基本内容有12项,主要包括:货物的商品名称、数量、包装、原产地、制造地;包括出口商的名称、地址、国别和声明;包括与装运相关的运输方式、路线和运输时间;还包括发证机构的签署、盖章和证明文件。

4. 种类

根据原产地证书的签发机构不同、使用范围不同、证书格式不同,分为以下几种类型:

	简称	签发机构	证书格式
一般原产地证书	C/O 产地证	贸促会、质检总局	商务部统一格式
普惠制原产地证书	GSP 产地证	质检总局	格式 A、格式 59A、格式 APR
欧共体纺织品专用产地证	EEC 产地证	商务部	统一格式
对美国出口纺织品声明书	DCO 声明书	出口商	格式 A、格式 B、格式 C

二、一般原产地证书的申领手续

1. 一般原产地证书的形式

一般原产地证书(certificate of origin of the People's Republic of China),简称"产地证",又称"普通产地证书"。

通常用于不使用海关发票或领事发票的国家(地区),以确定对货物征税的税率。若信用证或合同未作具体规定,一般由质检总局出具。

另外,根据进口商的不同要求,进口国海关除了认可由质检总局或贸促会签发的"中华人民共和国原产地证"外,有时也认可由出口商、生产厂家等单位出具证明货物原产地的文件。因此,一般原产地证书有四种形式:①质检总局出具的《中华人民共和国原产地证书》;②贸促会出具的《中华人民共和国原产地证书》;③出口商出具的《原产地证书》;④生产厂家出具的《原产地证书》。其中,以第一种、第二种形式最具权威性。

2. 申领时间

根据我国有关规定,出口企业最迟于货物出运 3 天前,持签证机构规定的正本文件,向签证机构申请办理原产地证书。

3. 申领所需要的文件

(1)提供规定格式并已缮制的《一般原产地证明书申请单》一份。

(2)提供缮制完毕的《中华人民共和国原产地证明书》一套(一正三副)。

(3)提供出口商业发票正本一份。

(4)提供发证机构所需的其他证明文件,如《加工工序清单》等。

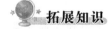 拓展知识

一、普惠制产地证书

1. 含义

普惠制原产地证(generalized system of preferences certificate of origin),简称 GSP 产地证,又称为 FORM A(格式 A)。

普遍优惠制度是发达国家给予发展中国家出口制成品和半制成品(包括某些初级产品)普遍

的、非歧视性的、非互惠的一种关税优惠制度。普惠制产地证是一种受惠国有关机构就本国出口商品向给惠国出口受惠商品而签发的用以证明原产地的证明文件。

在我国，普惠制产地证由各口岸的检验检疫机构或贸促会办理签证、发证和管理工作。出口商在对给惠国出口"可受惠商品"时，不管信用证是否要求提供 GSP 产地证，都应申领此证交收货人，使其能享受普惠制的待遇。全球有 30 个给惠国，近年来除了美国、匈牙利、保加利亚对我国不给此种待遇，其他 27 国家均给予中国产品以普惠制待遇。其主要有德国、比利时、荷兰、卢森堡、法国、意大利、丹麦、爱尔兰、英国、希腊、西班牙、葡萄牙、奥地利、芬兰、挪威、瑞典、澳大利亚、新西兰、日本、加拿大等国。

普惠制产地证主要有三种格式：普惠制产地证格式 A（FORM A）、普惠制产地证格式 59A（FORM 59A）和普惠制产地证格式 APR（FORM 59A）；其中，"格式 A"（FORM A）使用范围较广。

需要说明的是在给惠国中，有两个国家的证书格式特殊，要引起注意。新西兰只用 FORM 59A；澳大利亚则不用任何规定的格式，只需在商业发票上加注指定声明文句即可。例句："Declare: A, that the final process of manufacture of the goods for which special parts are claimed has been performed in China and B, that not less than one half of the factory cost of the goods is represented by the value of labour and material of China."

2. 申领手续

(1) 申领时间。根据我国质检总局有关规定，出口企业最迟于货物出运 5 天前，持签证机构规定的正本文件，向签证机构申请办理普惠制产地证书。

(2) 申领所需要的文件。

① 提供规定格式并已缮制的《普惠制产地证明书申请单》一份；

② 提供缮制完毕的《普惠制产地证明书 FORM A》一套（一正两副）；

③ 提供出口商《商业发票》正本一份；

④ 发证机构所需的其他证明文件，如《加工工序清单》等；

⑤ 如果出口商品含有进口成分，还应交纳《含进口成分受惠国商品成本明细单》一式两份。

3. 缮制规范

《普惠制产地证 FORM A》共有 12 项内容，其中，证书右上角标题栏已显示潜在机构所编制的证书号（reference No.），在标题横线上方必须填上"中华人民共和国签发"的英文字样，即"issued in The People's Republic of China"。

(1) 出口商的名称、地址、国家〔goods consigned from（exporter's full name, address and country）〕。此栏带有强制性，应填报在中国境内的出口商的名称、详细地址，包括门牌号、街道名、邮政编码、城市、国家。若信用证项下，一般按信用证规定的受益人全称、地址、国别填制。

(2) 收货人名称、地址、国家〔goods consigned to（consignee's name, address and country）〕。本栏显示本批货物最终目的地给惠国收货人的名称、地址、国别。

若信用证项下，一般为开证申请人。如果不确定最终收货人，则可显示提单上通知人或发票抬头人。银行接受开证申请人、提单通知人、发票抬头人等作为收货人，一般银行也接受下列表述"to whom it may concern"。

需要提醒的是：不可将中间商的名称填入此栏；收货人应是在给惠国。

(3) 运输方式和路线，就所知而言〔means of transport and route（as far as known）〕。填本批货物装运地、目的地的名称，并说明运输方式。

①如因运输的需要而发生转运,应注明转运地。不明确转运地时用"W/T"表示。

②若目的地为内陆地,则允许产地证上目的地名称与提运单上的卸货港名称不一致。

③对于输往没有海岸的给惠国,如瑞士、奥地利等,如确系海运,填证时需注明:"从××港口经转××港口抵达××给惠国"。

④有时本栏还需要加注预计离开中国的日期,此日期必须真实,不得捏造。例如:2009年10月6日,从上海港经汉堡港转运至瑞士,产地证运输方式和路线填报如下:

Country/Region of Destination:

On/After Oct. 6, 2006 by Sea from Shanghai to Hamburg Transit to Switzerland.

(4) 供签证方使用(for offcial use。)本栏留空,供签证机构加注说明时用。若为"后发"证书,签证机关在此栏加盖"ISSUED RETROSPECTIVELY"红色印章。若为副本证书,签证机构在此栏加盖"DUPLICATE"印章同时还注明"本证为某月某日签发第××号证书的副本,原证书作废"字样。(This Certificate is in Replacement of Certificate of Original No... Dated... which Cancelled.)

(5) 商品顺序号(items number)。如果同一批出口货物由不同种类商品品种,则按每一项商品归类品种后,用阿拉伯数字"1"、"2"、"3"……编一个顺序编号填入此栏。单项商品用"1"表示,或省略不填。

(6) 唛头和包装号(marks and number of packages)。与一般原产地证相应栏目填法相同。

(7) 商品名称、包装件数及种类(number and kind of packages;description of goods)。与一般原产地证相应栏目填法相同。

(8) 原产地标准[origin criterion(see notes overleaf)]。此栏文字最少,但却是国外海关审核的核心项目。对含有进口成分的商品,国外要求严格而极容易退证。一般应根据原产地标准选择正确代码填报此栏。

原产地标准及填报代码

填报代码	出口国家	原产地标准
P	所有给惠国	完全原产品
WHS	欧盟、挪威、瑞士、日本	产品列入给惠国"加工清单",并符合其加工条件
		产品未列入"加工清单"但产品使用的进口原料或零部件经过充分加工,产品HS号不同于原材料或零部件的HS号。
F	加拿大	有进口成分,但进口成分价值未超过产品出厂价的40%
WHS	波兰	有进口成分,但进口成分价值未超过离岸价的50%
Y	俄罗斯、乌克兰、哈萨克斯坦、捷克、斯洛伐克	有进口成分,但进口成分价值未超过离岸价的50%
	澳大利亚、新西兰	

(9) 毛重或其他数量(gross weight or quantity)。此栏依据合同、发票和货运单据中显示的毛重或其他数量来填报。

①若计量单位为重量,应标明毛重或净重。例如:"G.W.400kg"或"N.W.400kg"。
②用规范英文或缩写表示计量单位。例如:件(Pieces/PCS)、打(Dozen/DOZ)等。
(10)发票号码及日期(number and date of invoice)。与一般原产地证相应栏目填法相同。
(11)签证机构证明(certification)。签证机构证明已事先印制,内容为:"兹证明出口商的声明是正确无误的,本批货物已由承运人运出。"

签证机构批注四项内容:
①中华人民共和国出入境检验检疫局公章;只签一份正本,副本不予盖章;
②由机构授权人手签;
③签发日期,即与原产地证合理概念一致的日期;
④签发地点,具体的城市名和国家。

(12)出口商声明(declaration by the exporter)。出口商声明已事先印制,内容大意为:"兹出口商声明以上所列内容正确无误"。本栏须填写四项内容:
①用英文填报生产国国名;
②用英文填报进口国国名;
③申报单位签署,且加盖申报单位公章(正副本均须手签并盖章);
④申报日期、地点,应填写申报的具体日期及城市名、国别,申报日期应合理。

二、其他原产地证书

(1)欧洲经济共同体纺织品专用产地证(Europe Economic Community Certificate of Origin)(以下简称 EEC 纺织品产地证书)。EEC 纺织品产地证书专门用于需要配额的纺织类商品,是欧共体进口国海关控制配额的主要依据。EEC 纺织品产地证书与 EEC 纺织品出口许可证内容一致,我国专门由商务部签发。

(2)对美国出口的原产地声明书(Declaration of Country Origin)(以下简称 DCO 产地证,又称为美国产地证)。凡出口至美国的纺织品,出口方必须向进口方提供该类原产地声明书,作为进口方清关的单据之一。声明书主要有 A、B、C 三种格式:

格式 A:为单一国家产地声明书,一般适用于本国原料并由本国生产的产品。
格式 B:为多国产地声明书,一般用于来料加工、来件装配的产品,由多国生产。
格式 C:非多种纤维纺织品声明书,一般适用于纺织品原料是丝、麻类或者其中羊毛含量不超过 17% 的纺织品。

技能训练

训练项目一

(一)训练资料

1. 信用证

LETTER OF CREDIT

FORM OF DOCUMENTARY CREDIT 40A: IRREVOCABLE TRANSFERABLE
DOCUMENTARY CREDIT NUMBER 20: 70/1/5822
DATE OF ISSUE   31C: 051007
DATE AND PLACE OF EXPIRY   31D: DATE 060115 PLACE CHINA
APPLICANT BANK   51D: SUN BANK

		P. O. BOX 201 GDANSK, POLAND
APPLICANT	50:	BBB TRADING CO.
		P. O. BOX 203 GDANSK, POLAND
BENEFICIARY	59:	AAA IMPORT AND EXPORT CO.
		222 JIANGUO ROAD
		DALIAN, CHINA
AMOUNT	32B:	USD 45 600.00
AVAILABLE WITH/BY	41A:	BANK OF CHINA DALIAN BRANCH BY DEFERRED PAYMENT
DEFERRED PAYMENT	42P:	60 DAYS AFTER B/L DATE
DRAWEE	42D:	ISSUING BANK
PARTIAL SHIPMENTS	43P:	ALLOWED
TRANS SHIPMENT	43T:	NOT ALLOWED
LOADING IN CHARGE	44E:	DALIAN, CHINA
FOR TRANSPORT TO	44F:	GDANSK
LATEST DATE OF SHIPMENT	44C:	051231
DESCRIPTION OF GOODS	45A:	65% POLYESTER 35% COTTON LADIES SKIRTS
		STYLE NO. A101 200DOZ@USD60/DOZ
		STYLE NO. A102 400DOZ@USD84/DOZ
		ALL OTHER DETAILS OF GOODS ARE AS PER CONTRACT NO. LT07060 DATED AUG. 10, 2005
		DELIVERY TERMS: CIFGDANSK
DOCUMENTS REQUIRED	46A:	
		+MANUALLY SIGNED COMMERCIAL INVOICE IN 2 ORIGINALS PLUS 1 COPY MADE OUT TO DDD TRADING CO. P. O. BOX 211, GDANSK, POLAND.
		+FULL SET OF ORIGINAL CLEAN ON BOARD BILL OF LADING PLUS 3/3 NON NEGOTIABLE COPIES. MADE OUT TO ORDER, AND BLANK ENDORSED. MARKED FREIGHT PREPAID AND NOYIFY APPLICANT.
		+PACKING LIST IN 2 ORIGINALS PLUS 1 COPY.
		+CERTIFICATE OF ORIGIN IN 1 ORIGINAL PLUS 2 COPIES SIGNED BY CCPIT.

	+INSURANCE POLICIES OR CERTIFICATES IN DUPLICATE, ENDORSED IN BLANK
	FOR 110 PERCENT OF INVOICE VALUE COVERING F. P. A RISKS OF PICC CLAUSES INDICATING CLAIMS PAYABLE IN POLAND.
ADDITIONAL CONDITIONS 47A:	
	+ALL DOCS MUST BE ISSUED IN ENGLISH.
	+SHIPMENTS MUST BE EFFECTED BY FCL.
	+B/L MUST SHOWING SHIPPINGMARKS: BBB, S/C LT07060, GDANSK, C/NO.
	+ALL DOCS MUST NOT SHOW THIS L/C NO. 70/1/5822.
PRESENTATION PERIOD 48:	15 DAYS AFTER B/L DATE BUT WITHIN L/C VALIDITY.
CONFIRMATION 49:	WITHOUT
INSTRUCTIONS 78:	WE SHALL REIMBURSE AS PER YOUR INSTRUCTIONS.

2. 其他补充资料

(1)货物数量7 200PCS(600DOZ)。
(2)740CTNS。
(3)GROSS WEIGHT:3 700KGS。
(4)NET WEIGHT:2 960KGS。
(5)MEASUREMENT:22.2CBM。
(6)货物于12月10日备妥,12月15日装船。
(7)12月10号制作发票,发票号码为CBA001。

(二)根据以上资料,用英文制作一般原产地证书

1. Goods Consigned from (Exporter's full name, address and country)	Cetificate No. CCPIT 064814623			
	CERTIFICATE OF ORIGIN			
2. Goods Consigned from (Consignee's full name, address and country)	**OF**			
	THE PEOPLE'S REPUBLIC OF CHINA			
3. Means of Transport and Route (as far as known)	5. For Certifying Authority Use Only			
4. Country / Region of Destination				
6. Marks and Numbers of Packages	7. Number and Kind of Packages; Description of Goods	8. H. S. Code	9. Quantity or Weight	10. Number and Date of Invoices

11. Declaration by the exporter	12. Certification
The undersigned hereby declares that the above details and statements are correct; that all the goods were produced in China and that they comply with the Rules of Origin of the People's Republic of China. ———————————— Place and date, signature and stamp of certifying authority	It is hereby certified that the declaration by the exporter is correct. CCPIT ———————————— Place and date, signature and stamp of certifying authority

训练项目二

(一)训练资料

1. 货物明细 商品名称：Trolley Cases

货号

TS503214　　　　　　TS503215　　　　　　TS503216

(1)产地：Dalian China

(2)商标：TAISHAN

(3)包装：1 pc in 1 PE bag; 3pcs/CTN

(4)每个箱子尺寸：0.157 3cbm　　　0.151cbm　　　0.122 5cbm

(5)箱子尺寸(总)：57.886 4cbm　　　57.833cbm　　　58.8cbm

(6)净重/毛重(个)：4KG/4.6KG　　　3.5KG/4KG　　　3KG/3.5KG

(7)净重/毛重(总)：4 416KG/5 078.4KG　　4 021.5KG/4 596KG　　4 320KG/5 040KG

(8)数量：1 104PCS　　　　　1 149PCS　　　　　1 440PCS

(9)单价：USD6.50　　　　　USD6.00　　　　　USD5.80

(10)金额：USD7 176　　　　USD6 894　　　　USD8 352

(11)集装箱容量：Qty/40'FCL:368ctns　　Qty/40'FCL:383ctns　　Qty/40' FCL:480ctns

(12)发票号码：TSI0801005　　发票日期：2008-8-5　授权签字人：张平

(13)装运船名:DONGFENG 航次:V.369 装船日期:2008-8-23

(14)运输标志:ORTAI
     TSI0601005
     NEW YORK
     C/NO.1-1231

(15)原产地标准:"P"

2. 信用证

SEQUENCE OF TOTAL	27:	1/1
FORM OF DOCUMENTARY CREDIT	40A:	IRREVOCABLE
DOCUMENTARY CREDIT NUMBER	20:	N5632405TH11808
DATE OF ISSUE	31C:	080715
DATE AND PLACE OF EXPIRY	31D:	080909 CHINA
APPLICANT BANK	51D:	CITY NATIONAL BANK
		133 MORNINGSIDE AVE NEW YORK, NY 10027 TEL:001-212-865-4763
APPLICANT	50:	ORTAI CO., LTD.
		30 EAST 40TH STREET, NEW YORK, NY 10016
		Tel:001-212-992-9788
		FAX:001-212-992-9789
BENEFICIARY	59:	DALIAN TAISHAN SUITCASE & BAG CO., LTD.
		66 ZHONGSHAN ROAD DALIAN 116001, CHINA TEL:0086-0411-84524789
CURRENCY CODE AMOUNT	32B:	USD22 422.00
AVAILABLE WITH/BY	41D:	ANY BANK IN CHINA BY NEGOTIATION
DRAFTS AT	42C:	SIGHT
DRAWEE	42D:	ISSUING BANK
PARTIAL SHIPMENTS	43P:	NOT ALLOWED
TRANSHIPMENT	43T:	NOT ALLOWED
PORT OF LOADING	44E:	DALIAN,CHINA
PORT OF DISCHARGE	44F:	NEW YORK,U.S.A
LATEST DATE OF SHIPMENT	44C:	080825

DESCRIPTION OF GOODS AND/OR SERVICES 45A: CIF NEWYORK TROLLEY CASES
            AS PER SC NO. TSSC0801005

DOCUMENTS REQUIRED 46A: +MANUALLY SIGNED COMMERCIAL INVOICE
         IN 2 COPYES INDICATING L/C NO. AND CON-

TRACT NO. CERTIFYING THE CONTENTS IN THIS INVOICE ARE TRUE AND CORRECT.

+FULL SET OF ORIGINAL CLEAN ON BOARD MARINE BILLS OF LADING MADE OUT TO ORDER, ENDORSED IN BANK MARKED FREIGHT PREPAID AND NOYIFY APPLICANT.

+PACKING LIST IN 2 COPYES ISSUED BY THE BENEFICIARY.

+ORIGINAL GSP FORM A CERTIFICATE OF ORIGIN ON OFFICIAL FORM ISSUED BY A TRADE AUTHORITY OR GOVERNMENT BODY.

+INSURANCE POLICIES OR CERTIFICATES IN DUPLICATE, ENDORSED IN BANK FOR 110 PERCENT OF INVOICE VALUE COVERING ICC CLAUSES(A).

+MANUFACTURER'S QUALITY CERTIFICATE CERTIFYING THE COMMODITY IS IN GOOD ORDER.

+BENEFICIARY'S CERTIFICATE CERTIFYING THAT ONE SET OF COPIES OF SHIPPING DOCUMENTS HAS BEEN SENT TO APPLICANT WHTHIN 5 DAYS AFTER SHIPMENT.

ADDITIONAL CONDITIONS 47A: +UNLESS OTHERWISE EXPRESSLY STATED, ALL DOCUMENTS MUST BE IN ENGLISH.

+ANY PROCEEDS OF PRESENTATIONS UNDER THIS DC WILL BE SETTLED BY TELETRANSMISSION AND A CHARGE OF USD50.00（OR CURRENCY EQUIVALENT）WILL BE DEDUCTED.

CONFIRMATION INSTRUCTIONS 49: WITHOUT
ADVISE THROUGH BANK 57D: BANK OF CHINA DALIAN BRANCH
SENDER TO RECEIVER INFORMATION 72: DOCUMENTS TO BE DESPATCHED BY COURIER
SERVICE IN ONELOT TO CITY NATIONAL BANK

(二)请根据以上资料,缮制普惠制原产地证书

1. Goods Consigned from (Exporter's full name address and, country)	Reference No. : **GENERALIZED SYSTEM OF PREFERENCES CERTIFICATE OF ORIGIN** (**Combined declaration and certificate**) **FORM A**
2. Goods Consigned to (Consignee's full name, address and country)	Issued in _____ (Country)
3. Means of Transport and Route (as far as known)	4. For Certifying Authority Use only See Notes. Overleaf

5. Item Number	6. Marks and Numbers of Packages	7. Number and Kind of Packages; Description of Goods	8. Origin Criterion (see notes overleaf)	9. Gross Weight or other Quantity	10. Number and Date of Invoice

11. Certification It is hereby certified that the declaration by the exporter is correct. _____ Place and date, signature and stamp of certifying authority	12. Declaration by the exporter The undersigned hereby declares that the above details and statements are correct, that all the goods were produced in _____ (country) and that they comply with the origin requirements specified for those goods in the generalized system of preferences for goods exported to _____ (importing country) _____ Place and date, signature and stamp of certifying authority

任务七　制作出口收汇核销单和出口货物报关单

学习目标

能力目标
能根据相关单据和信息,熟练地制作出口收汇核销单和出口货物报关单,并办理相关手续

知识目标
熟悉出口收汇核销单和出口货物报关单的格式,掌握制作要求

任务设计

2010年6月10日天津四海纺织品进出口公司同新加坡的T公司签订了一份出口漂布的出口合同,现履行出口合同并缮制了出口所需单据,其中商业发票内容如下:

INVOICE

SOLD TO	
SHIPPING MARKS: O.T.C. SC300762 SINGAPORE NO.1—70	INVOICE NO.：SH10063—01 L/C NO.：DPCLBM030854 CONTACT NO.：SH2010063

VESSEL XIANG QIANG V.0010		PORT OF LOADING TIANJIN CHINA		
PORT OF DISCHARGE： SINGAPORE				
DESCRIPTION OF GOODS	QUANTITY	N.W(KG)	UNIT PRICE	AMOUNT
FOB XINGANG 1　BRAND	7 000 YARDS	20	1.5	USD 10 500.00
TOTAL	7 000			10 500.00
G.W 1 400KG				
QTY	1×20	集装箱号:BHLU1234567		
B/L NO.	TJ2010WN01			

天津四海纺织品进出口公司(海关注册号:432393××××)向新加坡出口的漂布,共计70包,核销单号:1250012345,单位代码:0312010,生产企业:天津纺织十厂。该企业报关员于2010年10月11日向海关申报,海关当日接受申报,装运货物的运输工具于2010年10月12日从天津新港海关离境,漂布的商品编码为1376.0001。该企业业务人员及时办理出口手续,填制出口收汇核销单和出口货物报关单。

任务分解

1. 读懂商业发票条款，掌握操作程序
2. 根据商业发票和背景材料，正确制作出口收汇核销单和出口货物报关单

任务描述

出口合同签订之后，及时履行合同，缮制合同履行各个环节所需的单证，是单证员必备的一项基本技能。出口收汇核销单和出口货物报关单缮制得准确与否，直接决定了能否顺利通关和结汇。因此，单证员务必在读懂发票条款和掌握实践操作程序的基础上，缮制出口收汇核销单和出口货物报关单，确保出口收汇核销单和出口货物报关单的内容与实际业务和相关单据的一致。

操作示范

第一步：读懂发票条款和掌握实践操作环节

认真仔细地阅读发票，弄清实践操作的程序及时间，为准确缮制出口收汇核销单和出口货物报关单做好准备。

第二步：根据材料和商业发票，正确制作出口收汇核销单

出口收汇核销单是指由国家外汇管理局制发，出口企业和受托行及解付行填写，海关凭以受理报关，各级外汇管理部门凭以核销外汇的有顺序号的凭证。如实、准确地填制核销单，对提高核销业务的办事效率，加速出口收汇有十分重要的作用。

出口收汇核销单分为存根、正联、退税联三部分，出口收汇核销单如下：

出口收汇核销单 存根 （秦）编号	出口收汇核销单 （秦）编号	出口收汇核销单 出口退税专用 （秦）编号
出口单位：	出口单位：	出口单位：
单位代码：	单位代码：	单位代码：
出口币种总价：	银行签审：类别／币种金额／日期／盖章	货物名称／数量／币种总价
收汇方式：		
预计收款日期：		
报关日期：		
备注：	海关签注栏：	报关单编号：
此单报关有效期截止到	外汇局签注栏 年 月 日（签章）	外汇局签注栏 年 月 日（签章）

各部分填写方法如下:
1. 核销单存根的缮制
(1)编号。出口收汇核销单上已印刷好,无需填写。本案中,编号是 1250012345。

(2)出口单位。填写领取核销单的单位的名称。本案中,填写天津四海纺织品进出口公司。

(3)单位代码。填写领取核销单的单位在外汇管理局备案的号码。本案中,填写 0312010。

(4)出口币种总价。此栏填写出口成交货物总价及使用币种。一般情况下,总价需与报关单一致。溢短装出口时,总价可以不一致,但需提供该笔出口的货运提单副本(提单上有实际出口的数量和重量,根据发票或报关单上的单价与提单上的重量或数量相乘,即可得出实际出口的总金额)。本案中,填写 USD10 500.00。

(5)收汇方式。填写信用证、托收、汇付。本案中,填写信用证。

(6)预计收款日期。依付款期限、地点不同填写:

①即期信用证和即期托收项下的货款,从寄单之日起,近洋地区(香港和澳门)20 天内,远洋地区(香港和澳门以外的地区)30 天内结汇或收账。如港澳地区,2010 年 11 月 1 日寄单,预计收款日期即应填写 2010 年 11 月 21 日。

②远期信用证和远期托收项下货款,从汇票规定的付款日起,港澳地区 30 天内,远洋地区 40 天内结汇或收账。如港澳地区,预计收款日期为寄单日期加上邮程日期加上汇票规定的远期天数加上 30 天。如:寄单日期为 2010 年 6 月 1 日,汇票为远期 180 天,则预计收款日期应为 2010 年 6 月 1 日+10 天+180 天+30 天,则为 2011 年 1 月 8 日。本案中,填写 2010 年 11 月 10 日。

(7)报关日期。同出口报关单右上角的出单日期。本案中,报关日期为 2010 年 10 月 11 日。

(8)备注。填写出口单位就应核销单项下需说明的事项。如:上海华康进出口公司代北京旭东进出口公司出口,收汇后,原币划转北京旭东进出口公司,则该事项连同该受托公司的联系地址和电话应批注在备注栏内,并加盖批注单位的公章。本案中,没有需要特殊说明的事项,所以不填。

(9)有效期。自领单之日起 4 个月。此栏由外汇管理局填写。本案中,企业人员不填写,留给外汇管理局填写。

2. 核销单正联的缮制
(1)出口单位。同存根。

(2)单位代码。同存根。

(3)银行签审。填写收汇方式、币种总价、收结汇日期、银行盖章。本案中,企业人员不填写,留给银行工作人员填写。

(4)海关签注栏。海关验放该核销单项下的出口货物后,在该栏目内加盖"放行"或"验讫"章,并填写放行日期。如遇退关,海关需在该栏目加盖有关更正章。本案中,企业人员不填写,留给海关工作人员填写。

(5)外汇管理局签注栏。由外汇管理部门将核销单、报关单、发票等配对审核无误后,在该栏内签注意见,并由核销人员签字,加盖"已核销"章。本案中,企业人员不填写,留给外汇管理局填写。

3. 核销单退税联的缮制
(1)编号。同存根。

(2)出口单位。同存根。

(3)单位代码。同存根。

(4)货物名称。同报关单。本案中,填写漂布。

(5)出口数量。同报关单。本案中,填写 7 000 码。

(6)币种总价。同存根。

(7)报关单编号。同存根。

(8)外汇局签注栏。同正联。

4. 制作好的出口收汇核销单

| 出口收汇核销单 存根 (津)编号 1250012345 | 出口收汇核销单 正联 (津)编号 1250012345 | 出口收汇核销单 出口退税专用 (津)编号 1250012345 |

出口单位 天津四海纺织品进出口公司		
单位代码 0312010		
出口币种总价 USD 10 500.00		
收汇方式 信用证		
预计收款日 2010 年 11 月 10 日		
报关日期 2010 年 10 月 11 日		
备注		
此单报关有效期截止到		

出口单位 天津四海纺织品进出口公司
单位代码 0312010

类别	币种金额	日期	盖章
银行签审			

海关签注栏:

外汇局签注栏

　　　　　年　　月　　日(盖章)

出口单位 天津四海纺织品进出口公司
单位代码 0312010

货物名称	数 量	币种总价
漂布	7 000 码	USD 10 500.00

报关单编号:

外汇局签注栏

　　　　　年　　月　　日(盖章)

第三步:根据材料和商业发票,正确制作出口货物报关单

出口报关单的格式如下:

中华人民共和国海关出口货物报关单

预录入编号：　　　　　　　　　　　　　　　海关编号：

出口口岸		备案号		出口日期		申报日期	
经营单位		运输方式		运输工具名称		提运单号	
发货单位		贸易方式		征免性质		结汇方式	
许可证号		运抵国（地区）		指运港		境内货源地	
批准文号		成交方式		运费		保费	杂费
合同协议号		件数		包装种类		毛重（公斤）	净重（公斤）
集装箱号		随附单据				生产厂家	
标记唛码及备注							

项号	商品编号	商品名称、规格号	数量及单位	最终目的国（地区）	单价	总价	币制	征免

税费征收情况			
录入员 录入单位	兹声明以上申报无讹并承担法律责任	海关审单批注及放行日期（签章） 审单　　　　审价	
报关员 单位地址　　申报单位（签章） 邮编　　电话　　填制日期		征税　　　　统计	
		查验　　　　放行	

出口报关单各栏目的填写如下：

1. **预录入编号**

本栏目填报预录入报关单的编号，预录入编号规则由接受申报的海关决定。本案中，报关员不用填写，由接受申报的海关电脑自动生成。

2. **海关编号**

本栏目填报海关接受申报时给予报关单的编号，一份报关单对应一个海关编号。

报关单海关编号为18位，其中第1—4位为接受申报海关的编号（海关规定的《关区代码表》

中相应海关代码),第5—8位为海关接受申报的公历年份,第9位为进出口标志("1"为进口,"0"为出口;集中申报清单"I"为进口,"E"为出口),后9位为顺序编号。

本案中,报关员不用填写,由接受申报的海关电脑自动生成。

3. 进口口岸/出口口岸

本栏目应根据货物实际进出境的口岸海关,填报海关规定的《关区代码表》中相应口岸海关的名称及代码。特殊情况填报要求如下:

进口转关运输货物应填报货物进境地海关名称及代码,出口转关运输货物应填报货物出境地海关名称及代码。按转关运输方式监管的跨关区深加工结转货物,出口报关单填报转出地海关名称及代码,进口报关单填报转入地海关名称及代码。

在不同海关特殊监管区域或保税监管场所之间调拨、转让的货物,填报对方特殊监管区域或保税监管场所所在的海关名称及代码。

其他无实际进出境的货物,填报接受申报的海关名称及代码。本案中,填写新港海关0202。

4. 备案号

本栏目填报进出口货物收发货人在海关办理加工贸易合同备案或征、减、免税备案审批等手续时,海关核发的《中华人民共和国海关加工贸易手册》、电子账册及其分册(以下统称《加工贸易手册》)、《进出口货物征免税证明》(以下简称《征免税证明》)或其他备案审批文件的编号。

一份报关单只允许填报一个备案号。具体填报要求如下:

(1)加工贸易项下货物,除少量低值辅料按规定不使用《加工贸易手册》及以后续补税监管方式办理内销征税的外,填报《加工贸易手册》编号。

(2)涉及征、减、免税备案审批的报关单,填报《征免税证明》编号。

(3)涉及优惠贸易协定项下实行原产地证书联网管理(香港CEPA、澳门CEPA,下同)的报关单,填报原产地证书代码"Y"和原产地证书编号。

(4)减免税货物退运出口,填报《减免税进口货物同意退运证明》的编号;减免税货物补税进口,填报《减免税货物补税通知书》的编号;减免税货物结转进口(转入),填报《征免税证明》的编号;相应的结转出口(转出),填报《减免税进口货物结转联系函》的编号。

(5)涉及构成整车特征的汽车零部件的报关单,填报备案的Q账册编号。本案中,无需填写。

5. 合同协议号

本栏目填报进出口货物合同(包括协议或订单)编号。本案中,填写SH2010063。

6. 进口日期/出口日期

进口日期是指填报运载进口货物的运输工具申报进境的日期。

出口日期是指指运载出口货物的运输工具办结出境手续的日期,本栏目供海关签发打印报关单证明联用,在申报时免予填报。

无实际进出境的报关单填报海关接受申报的日期。

本栏目为8位数字,顺序为年(4位)、月(2位)、日(2位)。本案中,出口日期填写2010.10.11。

7. 申报日期

申报日期是指海关接受进出口货物收发货人、受委托的报关企业申报数据的日期。以电子数据报关单方式申报的,申报日期为海关计算机系统接受申报数据时记录的日期。以纸质报关单方式申报的,申报日期为海关接受纸质报关单并对报关单进行登记处理的日期。

申报日期为8位数字,顺序为年(4位)、月(2位)、日(2位)。本栏目在申报时免予填报。本案中,填写2010.10.11。

8. 经营单位

本栏目填报在海关注册登记的对外签订并执行进出口贸易合同的中国境内法人、其他组织或个人的名称及海关注册编码。

特殊情况下填制要求如下:

(1)进出口货物合同的签订者和执行者非同一企业的,填报执行合同的企业。

(2)外商投资企业委托进出口企业进口投资设备、物品的,填报外商投资企业,并在标记唛码及备注栏注明"委托某进出口企业进口"。

(3)有代理报关资格的报关企业代理其他进出口企业办理进出口报关手续时,填报委托的进出口企业的名称及海关注册编码。本案中,填写天津四海纺织品进出口公司432393××××。

9. 收货单位/发货单位

(1)收货单位填报已知的进口货物在境内的最终消费、使用单位的名称,包括自行从境外进口货物的单位、委托进出口企业进口货物的单位。

(2)发货单位填报出口货物在境内的生产或销售单位的名称,包括自行出口货物的单位、委托进出口企业出口货物的单位。

(3)有海关注册编码或加工企业编码的收、发货单位,本栏目应填报其中文名称及编码;没有编码的应填报其中文名称。使用《加工贸易手册》管理的货物,报关单的收、发货单位应与《加工贸易手册》的"经营企业"或"加工企业"一致;减免税货物报关单的收、发货单位应与《征免税证明》的"申请单位"一致。本案中,填写天津四海纺织品进出口公司432393××××。

10. 申报单位

自理报关的,本栏目填报进出口企业的名称及海关注册编码;委托代理报关的,本栏目填报经海关批准的报关企业名称及海关注册编码。

本栏目还包括报关单左下方用于填报申报单位有关情况的相关栏目,包括报关员、报关单位地址、邮政编码和电话号码等栏目。本案中,填写天津四海纺织品进出口公司432393××××。

11. 运输方式

运输方式包括实际运输方式和海关规定的特殊运输方式。前者指货物实际进出境的运输方式,按进出境所使用的运输工具分类;后者指货物无实际进出境的运输方式,按货物在境内的流向分类。

本栏目应根据货物实际进出境的运输方式或货物在境内流向的类别,按照海关规定的《运输方式代码表》选择填报相应的运输方式。

(1)特殊情况填报要求如下:

①非邮件方式进出境的快递货物,按实际运输方式填报。

②进出境旅客随身携带的货物,按旅客所乘运输工具填报。

③进口转关运输货物,按载运货物抵达进境地的运输工具填报;出口转关运输货物,按载运货物驶离出境地的运输工具填报。

④不复运出(入)境而留在境内(外)销售的进出境展览品、留赠转卖物品等,填报"其他运输"(代码9)。

(2)无实际进出境货物在境内流转时,根据实际情况选择填报《运输方式代码表》中的运输方式。本案中,填写水路运输。

12. 运输工具名称

本栏目填报载运货物进出境的运输工具名称或编号。填报内容应与运输部门向海关申报的舱单(载货清单)所列相应内容一致。具体填报要求如下：

(1)直接在进出境地或采用"属地申报,口岸验放"通关模式办理报关手续的报关单填报要求如下：

①水路运输:填报船舶编号(来往港澳小型船舶为监管簿编号)或者船舶英文名称。

②公路运输:填报该跨境运输车辆的国内行驶车牌号,深圳提前报关模式的报关单填报国内行驶车牌号+"/"+"提前报关"。

③铁路运输:填报车厢编号或交接单号。

④航空运输:填报航班号。

⑤邮件运输:填报邮政包裹单号。

⑥其他运输:填报具体运输方式名称,如管道、驮畜等。

(2)转关运输货物的报关单填报要求如下：

①进口。

a. 水路运输:直转、提前报关填报"@"+16位转关申报单预录入号(或13位载货清单号);中转填报进境英文船名。

b. 铁路运输:直转、提前报关填报"@"+16位转关申报单预录入号;中转填报车厢编号。

c. 航空运输:直转、提前报关填报"@"+16位转关申报单预录入号(或13位载货清单号);中转填报"@"。

d. 公路及其他运输:填报"@"+16位转关申报单预录入号(或13位载货清单号)。

e. 以上各种运输方式使用广东地区载货清单转关的提前报关货物填报"@"+13位载货清单号。

②出口。

a. 水路运输:非中转填报"@"+16位转关申报单预录入号(或13位载货清单号),如多张报关单需要通过一张转关单转关的,运输工具名称字段填报"@"。

中转货物,境内水路运输填报驳船船名;境内铁路运输填报车名(主管海关4位关别代码+"TRAIN");境内公路运输填报车名(主管海关4位关别代码+"TRUCK")。

b. 铁路运输:填报"@"+16位转关申报单预录入号(或13位载货清单号),如多张报关单需要通过一张转关单转关的,填报"@"。

c. 航空运输:填报"@"+16位转关申报单预录入号(或13位载货清单号),如多张报关单需要通过一张转关单转关的,填报"@"。

d. 其他运输方式:填报"@"+16位转关申报单预录入号(或13位载货清单号)。

(3)采用"集中申报"通关方式办理报关手续的,报关单本栏目填报"集中申报"。

(4)无实际进出境的报关单,本栏目免予填报。本案中,填写 XIANG QIANG。

13. 航次号

本栏目填报载运货物进出境的运输工具的航次编号。具体填报要求如下：

(1)直接在进出境地或采用"属地申报,口岸验放"通关模式办理报关手续的报关单

①水路运输:填报船舶的航次号。

②公路运输:填报运输车辆的8位进出境日期〔顺序为年(4位)、月(2位)、日(2位),下同〕。

③铁路运输:填报列车的进出境日期。

④航空运输:免予填报。
⑤邮件运输:填报运输工具的进出境日期。
⑥其他运输方式:免予填报。

(2)转关运输货物的报关单。

①进口。

a.水路运输:中转转关方式填报"@"+进境干线船舶航次;直转、提前报关免予填报。

b.公路运输:免予填报。

c.铁路运输:填报"@"+8位进境日期。

d.航空运输:免予填报。

e.其他运输方式:免予填报。

②出口。

a.水路运输:非中转货物免予填报。中转货物:境内水路运输填报驳船航次号;境内铁路、公路运输填报6位启运日期〔顺序为年(2位)、月(2位)、日(2位)〕。

b.铁路拼车拼箱捆绑出口:免予填报。

c.航空运输:免予填报。

d.其他运输方式:免予填报。

(3)无实际进出境的报关单,本栏目免予填报。本案中,填写/0010。

14. 提运单号

本栏目填报进出口货物提单或运单的编号。一份报关单只允许填报一个提单或运单号,一票货物对应多个提单或运单时,应分单填报。

具体填报要求如下:

(1)直接在进出境地或采用"属地申报,口岸验放"通关模式办理报关手续。

①水路运输:填报进出口提单号。如有分提单的,填报进出口提单号+"*"+分提单号。

②公路运输:免予填报。

③铁路运输:填报运单号。

④航空运输:填报总运单号+"_"+分运单号,无分运单的填报总运单号。

⑤邮件运输:填报邮运包裹单号。

(2)转关运输货物的报关单。

①进口。

a.水路运输:直转、中转填报提单号。提前报关免予填报。

b.铁路运输:直转、中转填报铁路运单号。提前报关免予填报。

c.航空运输:直转、中转货物填报总运单号+"_"+分运单号。提前报关免予填报。

d.其他运输方式:免予填报。

e.以上运输方式进境货物,在广东省内用公路运输转关的,填报车牌号。

②出口。

a.水路运输:中转货物填报提单号;非中转货物免予填报;广东省内汽车运输提前报关的转关货物,填报承运车辆的车牌号。

b.其他运输方式:免予填报。广东省内汽车运输提前报关的转关货物,填报承运车辆的车牌号。

(3)采用"集中申报"通关方式办理报关手续的,报关单填报归并的集中申报清单的进出口起止日期〔按年(4位)月(2位)日(2位)年(4位)月(2位)日(2位)〕。

(4)无实际进出境的,本栏目免予填报。本案中,填写 TJ2010WN01。

15. 贸易方式（监管方式）

本栏目应根据实际对外贸易情况按海关规定的《监管方式代码表》选择填报相应的监管方式简称及代码。一份报关单只允许填报一种监管方式。

特殊情况下加工贸易货物监管方式填报要求如下：

(1)进口少量低值辅料(即 5000 美元以下,78 种以内的低值辅料)按规定不使用《加工贸易手册》的,填报"低值辅料"。使用《加工贸易手册》的,按《加工贸易手册》上的监管方式填报。

(2)外商投资企业为加工内销产品而进口的料件,属非保税加工的,填报"一般贸易"。外商投资企业全部使用国内料件加工的出口成品,填报"一般贸易"。

(3)加工贸易料件结转或深加工结转货物,按批准的监管方式填报。

(4)加工贸易料件转内销货物以及按料件办理进口手续的转内销制成品、残次品、半成品,应填制进口报关单,填报"来料料件内销"或"进料料件内销";加工贸易成品凭《征免税证明》转为减免税进口货物的,应分别填制进、出口报关单,出口报关单本栏目填报"来料成品减免"或"进料成品减免",进口报关单本栏目按照实际监管方式填报。

(5)加工贸易出口成品因故退运进口及复运出口的,填报"来料成品退换"或"进料成品退换";加工贸易进口料件因换料退运出口及复运进口的,填报"来料料件退换"或"进料料件退换";加工贸易过程中产生的剩余料件、边角料退运出口,以及进口料件因品质、规格等原因退运出口且不再更换同类货物进口的,分别填报"来料料件复出"、"来料边角料复出"、"进料料件复出"、"进料边角料复出"。

(6)备料《加工贸易手册》中的料件结转转入加工出口《加工贸易手册》的,填报"来料加工"或"进料加工"。

(7)保税工厂加工贸易进出口货物,根据《加工贸易手册》填报"来料加工"或"进料加工"。

(8)加工贸易边角料内销和副产品内销,应填制进口报关单,填报"来料边角料内销"或"进料边角料内销"。

(9)加工贸易进口料件不再用于加工成品出口,或生产的半成品(折料)、成品因故不再出口,主动放弃交由海关处理时,应填制进口报关单,填报"料件放弃"或"成品放弃"。本案中,填写一般贸易。

16. 征免性质

本栏目应根据实际情况按海关规定的《征免性质代码表》选择填报相应的征免性质简称及代码,持有海关核发的《征免税证明》的,应按照《征免税证明》中批注的征免性质填报。一份报关单只允许填报一种征免性质。

加工贸易货物报关单应按照海关核发的《加工贸易手册》中批注的征免性质简称及代码填报。特殊情况填报要求如下：

(1)保税工厂经营的加工贸易,根据《加工贸易手册》填报"进料加工"或"来料加工"。

(2)外商投资企业为加工内销产品而进口的料件,属非保税加工的,填报"一般征税"或其他相应征免性质。

(3)加工贸易转内销货物,按实际情况填报(如一般征税、科教用品、其他法定等)。

(4)料件退运出口、成品退运进口货物填报"其他法定"(代码 0299)。

(5)加工贸易结转货物,本栏目免予填报。本案中,填写一般征税。

17. 征税比例/结汇方式

进口报关单本栏目免予填报。

出口报关单填报结汇方式,按海关规定的《结汇方式代码表》选择填报相应的结汇方式名称或代码。本案中,结汇方式填写信用证。

18. 许可证号

本栏目填报以下许可证的编号：进(出)口许可证、两用物项和技术进(出)口许可证、两用物项和技术出口许可证(定向)、纺织品临时出口许可证、出口许可证(加工贸易)、出口许可证(边境小额贸易)。

一份报关单只允许填报一个许可证号。本案中,不涉及许可证,所以不填。

19. 启运国(地区)/运抵国(地区)

启运国(地区)填报进口货物启始发出直接运抵我国或者在运输中转国(地)未发生任何商业性交易的情况下运抵我国的国家(地区)。

运抵国(地区)填报出口货物离开我国关境直接运抵或者在运输中转国(地区)未发生任何商业性交易的情况下最后运抵的国家(地区)。

本栏目应按海关规定的《国别(地区)代码表》选择填报相应的启运国(地区)或运抵国(地区)中文名称及代码。

无实际进出境的,填报"中国"(代码142)。本案中,运抵国填写新加坡。

20. 装货港/指运港

装货港填报进口货物在运抵我国关境前的最后一个境外装运港。

指运港填报出口货物运往境外的最终目的港；最终目的港不可预知的,按尽可能预知的目的港填报。

本栏目应根据实际情况按海关规定的《港口航线代码表》选择填报相应的港口中文名称及代码。装货港/指运港在《港口航线代码表》中无港口中文名称及代码的,可选择填报相应的国家中文名称或代码。

无实际进出境的,本栏目填报"中国境内"(代码142)。本案中,指运港填写新加坡。

21. 境内目的地/境内货源地

境内目的地填报已知的进口货物在国内的消费、使用地或最终运抵地,其中最终运抵地为最终使用单位所在的地区。最终使用单位难以确定的,填报货物进口时预知的最终收货单位所在地。

境内货源地填报出口货物在国内的产地或原始发货地。出口货物产地难以确定的,填报最早发运该出口货物的单位所在地。

本栏目按海关规定的《国内地区代码表》选择填报相应的国内地区名称及代码。本案中,根据实际情况,境内货源地填写河北区。

22. 批准文号

进口报关单中本栏目免予填报。

出口报关单中本栏目填报出口收汇核销单编号。本案中,填写1250012345。

23. 成交方式

本栏目应根据进出口货物实际成交价格条款,按海关规定的《成交方式代码表》选择填报相应的成交方式代码。

无实际进出境的报关单,进口填报CIF,出口填报FOB。本案中,填写FOB。

24. 运费

本栏目填报进口货物运抵我国境内输入地点起卸前的运输费用和出口货物运至我国境内输出地点装载后的运输费用。进口货物成交价格包含前述运输费用或者出口货物成交价格不包含前述运输费用的,本栏目免予填报。

运费可按运费单价、总价或运费率三种方式之一填报,注明运费标记(运费标记"1"表示运费率,"2"表示每吨货物的运费单价,"3"表示运费总价),并按海关规定的《货币代码表》选择填报相应的币种代码。

运保费合并计算的,填报在本栏目。本案中,不填。

25. 保费

本栏目填报进口货物运抵我国境内输入地点起卸前的保险费用和出口货物运至我国境内输出地点装载后的保险费用。进口货物成交价格包含前述保险费用或者出口货物成交价格不包含前述保险费用的,本栏目免予填报。

保费可按保险费总价或保险费率两种方式之一填报,注明保险费标记(保险费标记"1"表示保险费率,"3"表示保险费总价),并按海关规定的《货币代码表》选择填报相应的币种代码。

运保费合并计算的,本栏目免予填报。本案中,不填。

26. 杂费

本栏目填报成交价格以外的、按照《中华人民共和国进出口关税条例》相关规定应计入完税价格或应从完税价格中扣除的费用。可按杂费总价或杂费率两种方式之一填报,注明杂费标记(杂费标记"1"表示杂费率,"3"表示杂费总价),并按海关规定的《货币代码表》选择填报相应的币种代码。

应计入完税价格的杂费填报为正值或正率,应从完税价格中扣除的杂费填报为负值或负率。本案中,不填。

27. 件数

本栏目填报有外包装的进出口货物的实际件数。特殊情况填报要求如下:

(1)舱单件数为集装箱的,填报集装箱个数。

(2)舱单件数为托盘的,填报托盘数。

本栏目不得填报为零,裸装货物填报为"1"。本案中,填写70。

28. 包装种类

本栏目应根据进出口货物的实际外包装种类,按海关规定的《包装种类代码表》选择填报相应的包装种类代码。本案中,填写包(捆)。

29. 毛重(千克)

本栏目填报进出口货物及其包装材料的重量之和,计量单位为千克,不足一千克的填报为"1"。本案中,填写1 400。

30. 净重(千克)

本栏目填报进出口货物的毛重减去外包装材料后的重量,即货物本身的实际重量,计量单位为千克,不足一千克的填报为"1"。本案中,填写1 400。

31. 集装箱号

本栏目填报装载进出口货物(包括拼箱货物)集装箱的箱体信息。一个集装箱填一条记录,分别填报集装箱号(在集装箱箱体上标示的全球唯一编号)、集装箱的规格和集装箱的自重。非集装箱货物填报为"0"。本案中,填写 BHLU1234567/20/2270。

第二篇　国际贸易单证制作基础篇——信用证下国际贸易单证制作

32. 随附单证

本栏目根据海关规定的《监管证件代码表》选择填报除本规范第18条规定的许可证件以外的其他进出口许可证件或监管证件代码及编号。

本栏目分为随附单证代码和随附单证编号两栏,其中代码栏应按海关规定的《监管证件代码表》选择填报相应证件代码,编号栏应填报证件编号。

(1)加工贸易内销征税报关单,随附单证代码栏填写"c",随附单证编号栏填写海关审核通过的内销征税联系单号。

(2)含预归类商品报关单,随附单证代码栏填写"r",随附单证编号栏填写"××关预归类书××号"。本案中,不填。

33. 用途/生产厂家

进口货物本栏目填报用途,应根据进口货物的实际用途按海关规定的《用途代码表》选择填报相应的用途代码。

出口货物本栏目填报其境内生产企业。本案中,填写天津纺织十厂。

34. 标记唛码及备注

本栏目填报要求如下:

(1)填报标记唛码中除图形以外的文字、数字。

(2)填报受外商投资企业委托代理其进口投资设备、物品的进出口企业名称。

(3)与本报关单有关联关系的,同时在业务管理规范方面又要求填报的备案号,填报在电子数据报关单中"关联备案"栏。

加工贸易结转货物及凭《征免税证明》转内销货物,其对应的备案号应填报在"关联备案"栏。

减免税货物结转进口(转入),报关单"关联备案"栏应填写本次减免税货物结转所申请的《减免税进口货物结转联系函》的编号。

减免税货物结转出口(转出),报关单"关联备案"栏应填写与其相对应的进口(转入)报关单"备案号"栏中《征免税证明》的编号。

(4)与本报关单有关联关系的,同时在业务管理规范方面又要求填报的报关单号,填报在电子数据报关单中"关联报关单"栏。

加工贸易结转类的报关单,应先办理进口报关,并将进口报关单号填入出口报关单的"关联报关单"栏。

办理进口货物直接退运手续的,除另有规定外,应当先填写出口报关单,再填写进口报关单,并将出口报关单号填入进口报关单的"关联报关单"栏。

减免税货物结转出口(转出),应先办理进口报关,并将进口(转入)报关单号填入出口(转出)报关单的"关联报关单"栏。

(5)办理进口货物直接退运手续的,本栏目填报《准予直接退运决定书》或者《责令直接退运通知书》编号。

(6)申报时其他必须说明的事项填报在本栏目。本案中,填写实际的唛头。

35. 项号

本栏目分两行填报及打印。第一行填报报关单中的商品顺序编号;第二行专用于加工贸易、减免税等已备案、审批的货物,填报和打印该项货物在《加工贸易手册》或《征免税证明》等备案、审批单证中的顺序编号。

优惠贸易协定项下实行原产地证书联网管理的报关单:第一行填报报关单中的商品顺序编

号,第二行填报该项商品对应的原产地证书上的商品项号。

加工贸易项下进出口货物的报关单:第一行填报报关单中的商品顺序编号,第二行填报该项商品在《加工贸易手册》中的商品项号,用于核销对应项号下的料件或成品数量。其中第二行特殊情况填报要求如下:

(1)深加工结转货物,分别按照《加工贸易手册》中的进口料件项号和出口成品项号填报。

(2)料件结转货物(包括料件、制成品和半成品折料),出口报关单按照转出《加工贸易手册》中进口料件的项号填报;进口报关单按照转进《加工贸易手册》中进口料件的项号填报。

(3)料件复出货物(包括料件、边角料、来料加工半成品折料),出口报关单按照《加工贸易手册》中进口料件的项号填报;如边角料对应一个以上料件项号时,填报主要料件项号。料件退换货物(包括料件、不包括半成品),进出口报关单按照《加工贸易手册》中进口料件的项号填报。

(4)成品退换货物,退运进境报关单和复运出境报关单按照《加工贸易手册》原出口成品的项号填报。

(5)加工贸易料件转内销货物(以及按料件办理进口手续的转内销制成品、半成品、残次品)应填制进口报关单,填报《加工贸易手册》进口料件的项号;加工贸易边角料、副产品内销,填报《加工贸易手册》中对应的进口料件项号。如边角料或副产品对应一个以上料件项号时,填报主要料件项号。

(6)加工贸易成品凭《征免税证明》转为减免税货物进口的,应先办理进口报关手续。进口报关单填报《征免税证明》中的项号,出口报关单填报《加工贸易手册》原出口成品项号,进、出口报关单货物数量应一致。

(7)加工贸易料件放弃或成品放弃,本栏目应填报《加工贸易手册》中的进口料件或出口成品项号。半成品放弃的应按单耗折回料件,以料件放弃申报,本栏目填报《加工贸易手册》中对应的进口料件项号。

(8)加工贸易副产品退运出口、结转出口或放弃,本栏目应填报《加工贸易手册》中新增的变更副产品的出口项号。

(9)经海关批准实行加工贸易联网监管的企业,按海关联网监管要求,企业需申报报关清单的,应在向海关申报进出口(包括形式进出口)报关单前,向海关申报"清单"。一份报关清单对应一份报关单,报关单上的商品由报关清单归并而得。加工贸易电子账册报关单中项号、品名、规格等栏目的填制规范比照《加工贸易手册》。本案中,填写01。

36. **商品编号**

本栏目应填报由《中华人民共和国进出口税则》确定的进出口货物的税则号列和《中华人民共和国海关统计商品目录》确定的商品编码,以及符合海关监管要求的附加编号组成的10位商品编号。本案中,填写13760001。

37. **商品名称、规格型号**

本栏目分两行填报及打印。第一行填报进出口货物规范的中文商品名称,第二行填报规格型号。

具体填报要求如下:

(1)商品名称及规格型号应据实填报,并与进出口货物收发货人或受委托的报关企业所提交的合同、发票等相关单证相符。

(2)商品名称应当规范,规格型号应当足够详细,以能满足海关归类、审价及许可证件管理要求为准,可参照《中华人民共和国海关进出口商品规范申报目录》中对商品名称、规格型号的要求进行填报。

(3)加工贸易等已备案的货物,填报的内容必须与备案登记中同项号下货物的商品名称一致。

(4)由同一运输工具同时运抵同一口岸并且属于同一收货人、使用同一提单的多种进口货物,按照商品归类规则应当归入同一商品编号的,应当将有关商品一并归入该商品编号。商品名称填报一并归类后的商品名称;规格型号填报一并归类后商品的规格型号。

(5)加工贸易边角料和副产品内销、边角料复出口,本栏目填报其报验状态的名称和规格型号。本案中,填写漂布。

38. 数量及单位

本栏目分三行填报及打印。

(1)第一行应按进出口货物的法定第一计量单位填报数量及单位,法定计量单位以《中华人民共和国海关统计商品目录》中的计量单位为准。

(2)凡列明有法定第二计量单位的,应在第二行按照法定第二计量单位填报数量及单位。无法定第二计量单位的,本栏目第二行为空。

(3)成交计量单位及数量应填报并打印在第三行。本案中,填写7 000码。

39. 原产国(地区)/最终目的国(地区)

原产国(地区)是指进口货物的生产、开采或加工制造的国家(地区)。最终目的国(地区)是指出口货物的最终实际消费、使用或进一步加工制造国家(地区)。

本栏目应按海关规定的《国别(地区)代码表》选择填报相应的国家(地区)名称及代码。本案中,最终目的国家填写新加坡。

40. 单价

本栏目填报同一项号下进出口货物实际成交的商品单位价格。无实际成交价格的,本栏目填报单位货值。本案中,填写1.5。

41. 总价

本栏目填报同一项号下进出口货物实际成交的商品总价格。无实际成交价格的,本栏目填报货值。本案中,填写10 500.00。

42. 币制

本栏目应按海关规定的《货币代码表》选择相应的货币名称及代码填报,如《货币代码表》中无实际成交币种,需将实际成交货币按申报日外汇折算率折算成《货币代码表》列明的货币填报。本案中,填写美元。

43. 征免

本栏目应按照海关核发的《征免税证明》或有关政策规定,对报关单所列每项商品选择海关规定的《征减免税方式代码表》中相应的征减免税方式填报。

加工贸易货物报关单应根据《加工贸易手册》中备案的征免规定填报;《加工贸易手册》中备案的征免规定为"保金"或"保函"的,应填报"全免"。本案中,填写照章。

44. 税费征收情况

本栏目供海关批注进(出)口货物税费征收及减免情况。本案中,不填。

45. 录入员

本栏目用于记录预录入操作人员的姓名。本案中,报关员不填写,由录入人员自己签名。

46. 录入单位

本栏目用于记录预录入单位名称。本案中,报关员不填写,由录入人员自己填写。

47. 填制日期

本栏目填报申报单位填制报关单的日期。本栏目为8位数字,顺序为年(4位)、月(2位)、日(2位)。本案中,填写2010.10.11。

48. 海关审单批注及放行日期(签章)

本栏目供海关作业时签注。本案中,报关员不填,由海关工作人员填写。

填制好的出口报关单:

中华人民共和国海关出口货物报关单

预录入编号: _____   海关编号: _____

出口口岸 新港海关0202	备案号		出口日期 2010.10.11		申报日期 2010.10.11
经营单位 天津商实进出口公司 432393××××	运输方式 水路运输		运输工具名称 XIANG QIANG/0010		提运单号 TJ2010WN01
发货单位 天津商实进出口公司 432393××××	贸易方式 一般贸易		征免性质 一般征税		结汇方式 信用证
许可证号	运抵国(地区) 新加坡		指运港 新加坡		境内货源地 河北区
批准文号 1250012345	成交方式 FOB	运费	保费		杂费
合同协议号 SH2010063	件数 70	包装种类 包(捆)	毛重(公斤) 1 400		净重(公斤) 1 400
集装箱号 BHLU1234567/ 20/2270	随附单据				生产厂家 天津纺织十厂
标记唛码及备注 O.T.C. SC300762 SINGAPORE NO1—70					

项号	商品编号	商品名称、规格型号	数量及单位	最终目的国(地区)	单价	总价	币制	征免
01	13760001	漂布	7 000码	新加坡	1.5	10 500.00	美元	照章

税费征收情况		
录入员 录入单位	兹声明以上申报无讹并承担法律责任	海关审单批注及放行日期(签章) 审单　　　　　审价
责任报关员:张三 单位地址 邮编　　电话	申报单位(签章)　　(略) 填制日期　2010.10.11	 征税　　　　　统计 查验　　　　　放行

必备知识

一、出口收汇核销的基础知识

出口收汇核销是国家为了加强出口收汇管理,确保国家外汇收入,防止外汇流失,指定国家职能部门对出口企业的出口货物实施"跟单"核销管理和出口企业外汇收入情况进行监督检查的一种制度。

1. 出口收汇核销单的作用

我国自外汇管理部门对境内出口企业的一切出口收汇实施跟踪管理和监督收汇以来,出口企业无论是在货物报关、向银行交单收汇,还是向外汇管理部门办理核销,都必须使用出口收汇核销单。出口收汇核销单是实现一国货物进出管理和外汇管制的有效单据,也是外贸企业出口退税,获得国家出口补贴的必要单据。

2. 出口收汇核销的对象

出口收汇核销是指企业在货物出口后的一定期限内向当地外汇管理部门办理收汇核销,证实该笔出口价款已经收回或按规定使用的一项外汇业务。其核销的对象是经商务部及其授权单位批准的经营出口业务的公司、有对外贸易经营权的企业和外商投资企业,具体包括:

(1)出口企业委托有代理报关权的外贸企业代理报关,但由委托单位自己签订出口合同并收汇的,报关时应使用委托单位的出口收汇核销单;报关后,代理报关单位应将核销单、报关单等文件及时送委托单位,由其向外汇管理部门办理核销。

(2)对自身无对外贸易经营权或无该项商品出口权的企业,其委托外贸单位出口并代理报关、收汇的,由受托单位到当地外汇管理部门办理收汇核销手续。如委托单位与受托单位不在同一地区,需由受托单位将出口收汇划转到委托单位,则由受托单位在当地外汇管理部门办妥领取核销单和异地委托原笔划转的出口收汇通知手续,委托单位凭解付行收妥划转款所出具的结汇水单或收账通知,在其所在地外汇管理部门办理收汇核销手续。

3. 出口收汇核销单的缮制及核销程序

根据《出口收汇核销管理办法及其实施细则》的规定,出口收汇核销程序为:

（1）出口企业提前到外汇管理部门领取出口收汇核销单。

（2）出口企业报关时,向海关提交事先从外汇管理部门领取的有顺序编号的收汇核销单,经海关审核无误,在核销单和与核销单有相同编号的报关单上盖"验讫章"。

（3）报关后,出口企业在规定期限内将收汇核销单存根送回外汇管理局接受外汇管理部门对企业出口收汇情况的监督。

（4）货物出口后,出口企业将海关退还的收汇核销单、报关单和有关单据送交银行收汇。

（5）货款汇交至出口地银行以后,银行向出口单位出具结汇水单或收账通知并在结汇单或收账通知上填写有关收汇核销单编号。

（6）出口单位凭出口收汇核销单和出口收汇核销专用联的结汇水单或收账通知及其他规定的单据,到国家外汇管理部门办理核销手续。

（7）国家外汇管理部门按规定办理核销后,在收汇核销单上加盖"已核销章",并将其中的出口退税专用联退还给出口单位作为日后退税依据。

二、进出口货物报关的基础知识

1. 报关的含义

报关是指进出口货物收发货人、进出境运输工具负责人、进出境物品的所有人或者他们的代理人向海关办理货物、物品或运输工具进出境手续及相关海关事务的过程。

《中华人民共和国海关法》(以下简称《海关法》)规定:"进出境运输工具、货物、物品,必须通过设立海关的地点进境或者出境。"因此,由设立海关的地点进出境并办理规定的海关手续是运输工具、货物、物品进出境的基本规则,也是进出境运输工具负责人、进出口货物收发货人、进出境物品的所有人应履行的一项基本义务。

2. 报关单位

报关单位是指依法在海关注册登记的进出货物收发货人和报关企业。

《海关法》规定:"进出口货物收发货人、报关企业办理报关手续,必须依法经海关注册登记,报关人员必须依法取得报关资格。未依法经海关注册登记的企业和未依法取得报关从业资格的人员,不得从事报关业务。"法律明确规定了对向海关办理进出口货物报关手续的进出口货物收发货人、报关企业实行注册登记管理制度。因此,依法向海关注册登记是法人、其他组织或者个人成为报关单位的法定要求。

《海关法》将报关单位划分为两种类型,即进出口货物收发货人和报关企业。

（1）进出口货物收发货人。进出口货物收发货人是指依法直接进口或者出口货物的中华人民共和国关境内的法人、其他组织或者个人。

进出口货物收发货人经向海关注册登记后,只能为本单位进出口货物报关。

（2）报关企业。报关企业是指按照规定经海关准予注册登记,接受进出口货物收发货人的委托,以进出口货物收发货人的名义或者以自己的名义,向海关办理代理报关业务,从事报关服务的境内企业法人。

报关企业必须在经营规模、管理人员素质、报关员数量、守法状况、管理制度等几个方面符合海关规定的设立条件,并经海关注册登记行政许可,依法向海关办理注册登记。

目前,我国从事报关服务的报关企业主要有两类:一类是经营国际货物运输代理、国际运输工具代理等业务,兼营进出口货物代理报关业务的国际货物运输代理公司等;另一类是主营代理报关业务的报关行或报关公司。

3. **报关员**

报关员是指依法取得报关员从业资格,并在海关注册,向海关办理进出口货物报关业务的人员。

根据海关规定,只有向海关注册登记的进出口货物收发货人和报关企业才可以向海关报关,报关员必须受雇于一个依法向海关注册登记的进出口货物收发货人或者报关企业,并代表该企业向海关办理报关业务。因此,报关员不是自由职业者。我国有关法律规定禁止报关员非法接受他人委托从事报关业务。

4. **进出口货物报关的一般程序**

报关程序是指进出口货物收发货人、运输工具负责人、物品所有人或其代理人按照海关的规定,办理货物、物品、运输工具的进、出境及相关海关事务的手续和步骤。

进出口货物收发货人或其代理人应当采用纸质报关单形式和电子数据报关单形式向海关申报,即进出口货物收发货人或其代理人先向海关计算机系统发送电子数据报关单,接收到海关计算机系统发送的"接受申报"电子报文后,凭以打印纸质报关单,附必需的其他单证,提交给海关。在特殊情况下,进出口货物收发货人或其代理人也可以单独使用纸质报关单或单独使用电子数据报关单向海关申报。

在我国,货物的进出境须经过海关审单、查验、征税、放行四个作业环节。与之相适应,进出口货物收发货人或其代理人应当按照程序办理相应的进出口申报、配合查验、缴纳税费、提取或装运货物等手续,货物才能进出境。但是,这些程序还不能满足海关对所有进出境货物的实际监管要求。比如不是进入出口加工区和保税区的加工贸易货物进口,海关要求事先备案,因此不能在"申报"和"审单"这一阶段中完成上述工作,而必须有一个前期办理手续的阶段;如果上述原材料进口加工成品后出口,也不能在"放行"和"装运货物"离境时完成所有的工作,必须有一个后期办理核销等手续的工作阶段。因此,从海关对进出境货物进行监管的全过程来看,报关程序按时间先后可以分为三个阶段:前期阶段、进出境阶段、后续阶段。

(1)前期阶段。前期阶段是指根据海关对保税货物、特定减免税货物、暂准进出境货物、其他进出境货物的监管要求,进出口货物收发货人或其代理人在货物进出境以前,向海关办理备案手续的过程。

(2)进出境阶段。进出境阶段是指根据海关对进出境货物的监管制度,进出口货物收发货人或其代理人在货物进出境时向海关办理进出口申报、配合查验、缴纳税费、提取或装运货物手续的过程。

(3)后续阶段。后续阶段是指根据海关对保税货物、特定减免税货物、暂准进出境货物、部分其他进出境货物的监管要求,进出口货物收发货人或其代理人在货物进出境储存、加工、装配、使用、维修后,在规定的期限内,按照规定的要求,向海关办理上述进出口货物核销、销案、申请解除监管等手续的过程。

5. 进出口货物报关单填制的一般要求

进出境货物的收发货人或其代理人向海关申报时,必须填写并向海关提交进出口货物报关单。申报人在填制报关单时,应当依法如实向海关申报,对申报内容的真实性、准确性、完整性和规范性承担相应的法律责任。

(1)报关人必须按照《海关法》、《货物申报管理规定》和填制规范的有关要求,向海关如实申报。

(2)报关单的填报必须真实,做到"两个相符":一是单证相符,即所填报关单各栏目的内容必须与合同、发票、装箱单、提单以及批文等随附单据相符;二是单货相符,即所填报关单各栏目的内容必须与实际出口货物的情况相符,不得伪报、瞒报、虚报。

(3)报关单的填报要准确、齐全、清楚,报关单各栏目内容要逐项详细准确填报,字迹清楚、整洁、端正,不得用铅笔、红色和复写纸填写;若有更正,必须在更正项目上加盖校对章。

(4)不同批文或许可证以及不同合同的货物、同一批货物中不同贸易方式的货物、不同备案号的货物、不同提运单的货物、不同征免性质的货物、不同运输方式或相同运输方式但不同航次以及不同运输工具名称的货物等,均应分单填报。一份原产地证书只能对应一份报关单。同一份报关单上的商品不能同时享受协定税率和减免税。在一批货物中,对于实行原产地证书联网管理的,如涉及多分原产地证书或含非原产地证书商品,也应分单填报。

6. 报关单的类别

按货物的进出口状态、表现形式、贸易性质和海关监管方式的不同,进出口货物报关单可以分为以下几种类型:

(1)按进出口流向分类:进口货物报关单、出口货物报关单。

(2)按介质分类:纸质报关单、电子数据报关单。

(3)按海关监管方式分类:进料加工进(出)口货物报关单、来料加工及补偿贸易进(出)口货物报关单、一般贸易及其他贸易进(出)口货物报关单。

 拓展知识

电子报关

我国海关目前运用的电子通关系统是 H883 通关系统,它是我国海关利用计算机对进出口货物进行全面信息化管理,实现监管、征税、统计三大海关业务一体化管理的综合性信息利用项目。

H2000 通关系统是对 H883 通关系统的全面更新换代项目。H2000 通关系统在集中式数据库的基础上建立了全国统一的海关信息作业平台,不但提高了海关管理的整体效能,而且使进出口企业真正享受到简化报关手续的便利。进出口企业可以在其办公场所办理加工贸易登记备案、特定减免税证明申领、进出境报关等各种海关手续。

中国电子口岸系统又称口岸电子执法系统,简称电子口岸,是与进出口贸易管理有关的国家12个部委,利用现代计算机信息技术将各部委分别管理的进出口业务信息电子底账数据集中存放在公共数据中心,为政府管理机关提供跨部门、跨行业联网数据核查,为企业提供网上办理各种进出口业务的国家信息系统。

技能训练

(一)训练资料

现有某铝业有限公司(海关注册号:130393××××)向黎巴嫩的贝鲁特出口铝箔,共计28木箱,核销单号:135690406,该企业的报关员于2010年10月11日向海关申报,海关当日接受申报,装运货物的运输工具于2010年10月12日从连大窑湾海关离境,铝箔的商品编码为:76071100。

INVOICE

SOLD TO	INVOICE NO.:BH03-409
SHIPPING MARKS: SANITA-HALAT-LEBANON ORDER NO.:SANITA200911	L/C NO.:DPCLBM030854 CONTACT NO.:SANITA200911

VESSEL NAN FENG SHAN V.0010	PORT OF LOADING QINHUANGDAO CHINA

PORT OF DISCHARGE:
BEIRUT PORT, LEBANON

DESCRIPTION OF GOODS	QUANTITY:BOXES	N.W(MT)	UNIT PRICE	AMOUNT CIF BEIRUT
130CM × 12MICRONS	8	6.22	2 389.00	USD 14 859.58
245CM × 12MICRONS	6	5.024	2 389.00	USD 12 002.34
345CM × 10MICRONS	8	6.002	2 389.00	USD 14 338.78
50CM × 12MICRONS	4	3.122	2 389.00	USD 7 458.46
50CM × 10MICRONS	2	1.403	2 389.00	USD 3 351.77
TOTAL	28	21.771		

G.W 22 771KG
FREIGHT   2 000
INSURANCE VALUE   362.57
QTY   2×20   集装箱号:BHLU1234567、BHLU7654321
B/L NO.   QD116WN01

(二)根据训练资料完成出口货物报关单的缮制工作

1. 出口收汇核销单

存根　　　　　　　　　　　　　　　　　　　　　　　　　**出口退税专用**

(秦)编号　　　　　　　　　(秦)编号　　　　　　　　　(秦)编号

出口单位：
单位代码：
出口币种总价：
收汇方式：
预计收款日期：
报关日期：
备注：
此报关单有效期截止到

银行签审	类别	币种金额	日期	盖章

海关签注栏

外汇局签注栏

　　　　　年　月　日(签章)

出口单位：		
单位代码：		
货物名称	数量	币种总价

报关单编号

外汇局签注栏

　　　　　年　月　日(签章)

2. 出口报关单

中华人民共和国海关出口货物报关单

预录入编号：　　　　　　　　　海关编号：

出口口岸	备案号	出口日期	申报日期
经营单位	运输方式	运输工具名称	提运单号
发货单位	贸易方式	征免性质	结汇方式
许可证号	运抵国(地区)	指运港	境内货源地
批准文号	成交方式	运费	保费	杂费
合同协议号	件数	包装种类	毛重(公斤)	净重(公斤)
集装箱号	随附单据			生产厂家
标记唛码及备注				

项号	商品编号	商品名称、规格号	数量及单位	最终目的国(地区)	单价	总价	币制	征免

税费征收情况	
录入员 录入单位　兹声明以上申报无讹并承担法律责任	海关审单批注及放行日期（签章） 审单　　　　审价
报关员 单位地址　　　　申报单位（签章）	征税　　　　统计
	查验　　　　放行
邮编　　电话　　填制日期	

任务八　制作投保单和保险单据

学习目标

能力目标

1. 能够根据信用证的相关条款和其他相关信息,准确填制投保单和保险单
2. 能够根据相关条件计算保险金额和保险费

知识目标

1. 熟悉 UCP600 关于保险单的条款
2. 了解 ISBP681 中有关保险单据和保险范围的规定

任务设计

苏州泰山箱包有限公司外贸单证员李芳根据任务三中的信用证要求,需要填制作的有关条款如下:

1. 商业发票

<table>
<tr><td colspan="5" align="center">SUZHOUTAISHAN SUITCASE & BAG CO., LTD.
66,ZHONGSHAN ROAD SUZHOU, JIANGSU CHINA
TEL: 0086－0512－84524788　FAX: 0086－0512－84524788
COMMERCIAL INVOICE</td></tr>
<tr><td>TO:</td><td colspan="2">ORTAI CO., LTD.
30 EAST 40TH STREET, NEW YORK,NY 10016</td><td>Invoice No.:</td><td>TSI0801005</td></tr>
<tr><td></td><td colspan="2"></td><td>Invoice Date:</td><td>AUG.5,2009</td></tr>
<tr><td></td><td colspan="2"></td><td>S/C No.:</td><td>TSSC0801005</td></tr>
<tr><td></td><td colspan="2"></td><td>L/C No.:</td><td>N5632405TH11808</td></tr>
<tr><td>Transport Details:</td><td colspan="4">FROM SHANGHAI CHINA TO NEW YORK U.S.A. BY SEA</td></tr>
<tr><td>Marks and Numbers</td><td>Description of Goods</td><td>Quantity</td><td>Unit Price</td><td>Amount</td></tr>
<tr><td>ORTAI
TSI0601005
NEW YORK
C/NO.1-1231</td><td>Trolley Cases
TS503
TS504
TS505</td><td>1 104PCS
1 149PCS
1 440PCS</td><td>CIF NEWYORK
USD6.50/PC
USD6.00/PC
USD5.80/PC</td><td>USD7 176.00
USD6 894.00
USD8 352.00</td></tr>
</table>

	TOTAL:	3 693PCS		USD 22 422.00
TOTAL VALUE IN WORDS:		SAY U. S. DOLLARS TWENTY TWO THOUSAND FOUR HUNDRED AND TWENTY TWO ONLY.		
WE HEREBY CERTIFY THAT THE CONTENTS IN THIS INVOICE ARE TRUE AND CORRECT. SUZHOU TAISHAN SUITCASE & BAG CO., LTD. 张奇				

2. 装箱单

SUZHOUTAISHAN SUITCASE & BAG CO., LTD.
66,ZHONGSHAN ROAD SUZHOU, JIANGSU CHINA
TEL: 0086-0512-84524788 FAX: 0086-0512-84524788
PACKING LIST

TO:	ORTAI CO., LTD. 30 EAST 40TH STREET, NEW YORK, NY 10016		Invoice No.:	TSI0801005
			Invoice Date:	AUG. 5, 2009
			S/C No.:	TSSC0801005
			L/C No.:	N5632405TH11808

Transport Details: FROM SHANGHAI CHINA TO NEW YORK U.S.A BY SEA

Marks and Numbers	Number and Kind of Package; Description of Goods	PACKAGES	Quantity	G. W (KGS)	N. W (KGS)	MEAS. (CBM)
ORTAI TSI0601005 NEW YORK C/NO. 1-1231	Trolley Cases TS503 TS504 TS505 Packed in 3PCS/CTN, SHIPPED IN 3×40' FCL	368CTNS 383CTNS 480CTNS	1 104PCS 1 149PCS 1 440PCS	5 078.4 4 596 5 040	4 416 4 021.5 4 320	57.886 4 57.833 58.8
	Total:	1 231CTNS	3 693PCS	1 4714.4	1 2757.5	174.519
TOTALPACKAGES IN WORDS: SAY ONE THOUSAND TWO HUNDRED AND THIRTY ONE CARTONS ONLY. SUZHOU TAISHAN SUITCASE & BAG CO., LTD. 张奇						

3. 信用中的保险单条款

(1) INSURANCE POLICIES OR CERTIFICATES IN DUPLICATE, ENDORSED IN BLANK FOR 110 PERCENT OF INVOICE VALUE COVERING ICC CLAUSES(A).

(2) UNLESS OTHERWISE EXPRESSLY STATED, ALL DOCUMENTS MUST BE IN

ENGLISH.

4. 其他信息

(1) 启运日:AUG.8,2009

(2) 船名和航次:XING YUN HAO VOY:001

(3) 保单号:SZ123456

任务分解

1. 制作出口投保单
2. 制作出口保险单

任务描述

在国际货物贸易中,为了能够在货物发生风险导致损失后得到补偿,通常买卖双方中的一方要对国际贸易货物办理保险。根据信用证或合同中的保险条款以及其他信息,准确制作投保单,是单证员必备的基本技能。尽管保险单由保险公司出具,但是实务中不少保险公司让投保人自己制作保险单,然后由保险公司签署保险单的情况也较为常见,因此,单证员还必须掌握保险单的制作技能。

操作示范

第一步:读懂所给的条件

掌握信用证中同制作保险单有关的条款,从发票和装箱单中提取制作保险单所需要的金额、数量等信息。

第二步:制作投保单和保险单

不同保险公司投保单和保险单的格式可能有差异,但是内容都差不多。本案以中国大地财产保险股份有限公司的投保单和保险单为例,来讲解制作要点。由于投保单和保险单的诸多栏目类似,因此下面主要讲解保险单的制作。投保单和保险单的格式如下:

(1) 投保单。

货物运输保险投保单

APPLICATION FORM FOR CARGO TRANSPORTATION INSURANCE

投保单号:

被保险人:
INSURED:

发票号(INVOICE NO.):

合同号(CONTRACT NO.):

信用证号(L/C NO.):

发票金额(INSURANCE AMOUNT):   投保加成

兹有下列物品箱中国大地财产保险股份有限公司投保:(INSURANCE IS REQUIRED ON THE FOLLOWING COMMODITIES:)

标记 MARKS & NOS.	包装及数量 QUANTITY	保险货物项目 DESCEPTION OF GOODS	保险金额 AMOUNT INSURED

起运日期：　　　　　　　　　　　装载工具：
DATE OF COMMENCEMENT _____ PER CONVEYANCE _____
自　　　　　　　　经　　　　　　　　至
FROM _____　　VIA _____　　TO _____
提单号：　　　　　　　　　赔款偿付地点：
B/C NO. _____　　　CLAIM PAYBLE _____
投保险别:（PLEASE INDICATE THE CONDITIONS&OR SPECIAL COVERAGES）

请如实告知下列情况：(如"是"，在括号内打"×")IF ANY, PLEASE MARK "×"
1. 货物种类　袋装（　）　　散装（　）　冷藏（　）　液体（　）活动物（　）
　　GOODS　　BAG/CTN　　BULK　　REEFER　　LIQUID　　LIVE ANIMAL
　　　　　　机器/汽车（　）　危险品等级（　）
　　　　　　MACHINE/AUTO　DANGEROUS CLASS
2. 集装箱种类　普通（　）　开顶（　）框架（　）平板（　）冷藏（　）
　　CONTAINER　ORDINARY　OPEN　FRAME　FLAT　REFRIGERATOR
3. 转运工具　海轮（　）　飞机（　）驳船（　）火车（　）汽车（　）
　　BY TRANSIT SHIP　PLANE　BARGE　TRAIN　TRUCK
4. 船舶资料　　　　　　　船籍（　　）　　　　　船龄（　　）
　　PARTICULAR OF SHIP　　RIGISTRY _____　　AGE _____

备注：被保险人确认本保险合同条款和内容已经完全了解
THE ASSURED CONFIRMS HEREWITH THE TERMS AND CONDITONS OF THE INSURANCE CONTRACT FULLY UNDERSTOOD.

投保人（签名盖章）
APPLICANTS SIGNATURE

投保日期(DATE)　　　　　　电话(TEL)
　　　　　　　　　　　　　　地址(ADD)

本公司自用(FOR OFFICE USE ONLY)
费率　　　　　　　　　保费　　　　　　　　　　备注
RATEAS ARRANGED　　PREMIUM AS ARRANGED
经办人 BY _____　核保人 _____　负责人 _____
总公司地址：上海市浦东南路855号　电话:021-58369558
邮政编码:200120　网址:www.ccic-net.com.cn

(2) 保险单。

中国大地财产保险股份有限公司
China Contient Property & Casualty Insurance Company Ltd.
货物运输保险单
CARGO TRANSPORTATION INSURANCE POLICY

发票号(INVOICE NO.) 　　　　　　　　　保单号次(POLICY NO.)
合同号(CONTRACT NO.)
信用证号(L/C NO.)
被保险人(INSURED)_____

中国大地财产保险股份有限公司(以下简称本公司)根据被保险人的要求,由被保险人向本公司缴付约定的保险费,按照本保险单承保险别和背面所载条款与下列特款承保下述货物运输保险,特立本保险单。
THIS POLICY OF INSURANCE WITNESSES THAT CHINA CONTINENT PROPERTY & CASUALTY INSURANCE COMPANY LTD. OF CHINA (HEREIN AFTER CALLED "THE COMPANY") AT THE REQUEST OF THE INSURED AND IN CONSIDERATION OF THE AGREED PREMIUM PAID TO THE COMPANY BY THE INSUSRED, UNDERTAKES TO INSURE THE UNDERMENTIONED GOODS IN TRANSPORTATION SUBJECT TO THE CONDITIONS OF THIS POLICY AS PER THE CLAUSES PRINTED OVERLEAF AND OTHER SPECIAL CLAUSES ATTACHED HEREON.

标记 MARKS AND NUMBERS	包装及数量 QUANTITY	保险货物项目 DESCRIPTION OF GOODS	保险金额 AMOUNT INSURED

总保险金额 TOTAL AMOUNT INSURED:			
保费: PERMIUM	AS AR-RANGED	起运日期 DATE OF COMMENCEMENT	装载运输工具 PER CONVEYANCE
自 FROM		经 VIA	* * * 　　　至 TO

承保险别 CONDITIONS

所保货物,如发生保险单项下可能引起索赔的损失或损坏,应立即通知本公司下述代理人勘查。如有索赔,应向本公司提交保单正本(本保险单共有2份正本)及有关文件。如一份正本已用于索赔,其余正本自动失效。

赔款偿付地点 CLAIM PAYABLE AT		中国大地财产保险股份有限公司 ChinaContient Property & Casualty Insurance Company Ltd. 杨菲
日期和地点 DATE AND PLACE		（Authorized Signature）

IN THE EVENT OF LOSS OR DAMAGE WHICH MAY RESULT IN A CLAIM UNDER THIS POLICY, IMMEDIATE NOTICE MUST BE GIVEN TO THE COMPANY'S AGENT AS MENTIONED HEREUNDER. CLAIMS, IF ANY, ONE OF THE ORIGINAL POLICY WHICH HAS BEEN ISSUED IN TWO ORIGINAL(s) TOGETHER WITH THE RELEVANT DOCUMENTS SHALL BE SURRENDERED TO THE COMPANY. IF ONE OF THE ORIGINAL POLICY HAS BEEN ACCOMPLISHED, THE OTHERS TO BE VOID.

1. 保险单据名称

信用证要求提交"INSURANCE POLICIES OR CERTIFICATES"（保险单或保险证明），因此可以提交保险单或保险证明。UCP600 第 28 条 e 款规定："An insurance policy is acceptable in lieu of an insurance certificate or a declaration under an open cover."（可以接受保险单代替预约保险项下的保险证明或声明书）。因此，当信用证要求提交保险证明书时，可以提交保险单取代，反之则不行。

本案使用的是保险单。

CARGO TRANSPORTATION INSURANCE POLICY

2. 保单号

这是保险公司的业务流水号，由保险公司填制。

本案填写：

保单号次（POLICY NO.）SZ123456

3. 相关的业务参考号

发票号、合同号和信用证号，以及所给信息正确填写。

本案填写：

发票号（INVOICE NO.）TSI0801005

合同号（CONTRACT NO.）TSSC0801005

信用证号（L/C NO.）N5632405TH11808

4. 被保险人（insured）

被保险人，又称保险单的抬头人，该项填在保险单上的"at the request of 后面"，通常有以下几种填写方法：

(1)L/C 无特殊要求,或要求"ENDORSED IN BLANK",一般应填受益人名称,可不填详细地址,且受益人应在保险单背面背书。

(2)若 L/C 指定以×××公司为被保险人,则在此栏填写"IN FAVOUR OF ×××",或在此栏填写受益人名称接"HELD IN FAOVUR OF×××",受益人不需要背书。

(3)如果 L/C 规定保险单背书给特定方,如:"ENDORSED TO ORDER OF OPENING BANK",则在此栏填受益人,并在背面背书,注明:"CLAIMS, IF ANY, PAYABLE TO OR-DER OF OPENING BANK."

本案填写:

被保险人(INSURED). SUZHOU TAISHAN SUITCASE & BAG CO., LTD.

5. 唛头(marks and numbers)

保险单上唛头应与发票、装箱单、提单等单据上的一致,也可简单地填成"AS PER IN-VOICE NO.×××"。

6. 包装及数量(quantity)

此栏填写货物的最大包装件数;对煤炭、石油等散装货要注明净重;裸装货物要注明货物本身件数。

7. 保险货物项目(description of goods)

保险货物名称可以用统称,但不同类别的多种货物应该注明不同类别的各自统称。

本案第 5、6、7 栏的填写如下:

标记 (MARKS & NOS)	包装及数量 (QUANTITY)	保险货物项目 (DESCRIPTION OF GOODS)
ORTAI TSI0601005 NEW YORK C/NO.1—1231	1 231CTNS	Trolley Cases

8. 保险金额(amount insured)

保险金额按信用证的要求填制。UCP600 规定:①信用证对于投保金额为货物价值、发票金额或类似金额的某一比例的要求,将被视为对最低保额的要求;②如果信用证对投保金额未做规定,投保金至少为货物 CIF 或 CIP 价格的 110%;③如果从单据中不能确定 CIF 或 CIP 价格的,投保金额必须基于要求承付或议付的金额,或者基于发票上显示的货物总值来计算,两者之中取金额较高者。

保险金额填写时英注意:

(1)保险金额货币应与信用证一致。

(2)保险金额不要小数,出现小数时无论多少一律向上进位。

(3)若为含佣价,则以该价格作为计算保险金额的基础。

本案填写:USD24 665.00

9. 总保险金额(total amount insured)

该栏为保险金额的大写,大写必须准确反映小写金额。

本案填写：
SAY U.S. DOLLRS TWENTY THOUSAND SIX HUNDERED AND SIXTY FIVE ONLY.

10. 保费（premium）

该栏一般由保险公司填制或保险单本身已印制好"AS ARRANGED"字样。如信用证要求在保险单上显示"MARKED PREMIUM PREPAID"，则在此栏填入"PREPAID"，或把已印好的"AS ARRANGED"删去加盖校对章后打上"PAID"字样。

本案此栏已印有"AS ARRANGED"，因此无需填写。

11. 起运日期（date of commencement）

填写提单中的装船日，也可填写"AS PER B/L"。

12. 装载运输工具（per conveyance）

此栏按实际情况填写。当运输由两段或以上运程完成时，应把各程运输的船只明填在上面。

11、12栏本案的填写：

起运日期 DATE OF COMMENCEMENT	AUG. 8, 2009	装载运输工具 PER CONVEYANCE	XING YUN HAO, VOY. NO. 001

13. 起讫地点（from...via...to...）

此案填制货物实际的装运港口和目的港口名称。货物如转船，也应把转船的地点填上。如"FROM SHANGHAI, CHINA TO NEWYORK, USA VIA HONGKONG"。如海运至目的港，保险至内陆城市，应在目的港后注明该内陆城市名称。例如："FROM NINGBO TO LIVERPOOL AND THENCE TO BIRMINGHAM"。

本案填写：FROM SHANGHAI TO NEWYORK, USA

14. 承保险别（conditions）

此栏按信用证中的要求填写。

本案填写：COVERING ICC CLAUSES(A)

15. 赔款偿付地点（claim payable at...）

此栏应严格按信用证规定缮制。若信用证未规定，则应填目的港。如信用证规定不止一个目的港或赔付地，则应全部照填。

本案填写：NEWYORK USA

16. 日期和地点（date and palce）

日期填写保险单的签发日期，该日期一般应早于提单签发日。保险单签发地点即办理投保所在地，地点一般保险公司在印制保险单时已印制好。

本案填写：AUG. 8, 2009, SHANGHAI

17. 签字（authorized signature）

此栏由签发保险单的保险公司签字盖章。

根据所给条件，制作好的投保单和保险单如下：

(1) 投保单。

货物运输保险投保单
APPLICATION FORM FOR CARGO TRANSPORTATION INSURANCE

投保单号：

被保险人：
INSURED: SUZHOU TAISHAN SUITCASE & BAG CO., LTD.
发票号(INVOICE NO.): TSI0801005
合同号(CONTRACT NO.): TSSC0801005
信用证号(L/C NO.): N5632405TH11808
发票金额(INSURANCE AMOUNT): USD 22 422.00 投保加成 10%

兹有下列物品向中国大地财产保险股份有限公司投保：(INSURANCE IS REQUIRED ON THE FOLLOWING COMMODITIES:)

标记 MARKS of NOS.	包装及数量 QUANTITY	保险货物项目 DESCEPTION OF GOODS	保险金额 AMOUNT INSURED
ORTAI TSI0601005 NEW YORK C/NO. 1—1231	1 231CTNS	Trolley Cases	USD24 665.00

起运日期：   装载工具：
DATE OF COMMENCEMENT AUG. 10,2009   PER CONVEYANCE XING YUN HAO, VOY. NO. 001
自   经   至
FROM SHANGHAI   VIA   * * * *   TO NEW YORK U.S.A.
提单号：   赔款偿付地点：
B/C NO. AS PER B/L   CLAIM PAYBLE   AT NEWYORK
投保险别：(PLEASE INDICATE THE CONDITIONS & OR SPECIAL COVERAGES)
COVERING ICC CLAUSES(A).
◎INSURANCE POLICY MUST SHOW：
(1) IN ENGLISH
(2) THE CLIAIMING CURRENCY: USD

请如实告知下列情况：(如"是"，在括号内打"×")IF ANY, PLEASE MARK "×"
1. 货物种类   袋装(×)   散装( )   冷藏( )   液体( )   活动物( )
   GOODS   BAG/CTN   BULK   REEFER   LIQUID   LIVE ANIMAL
              机器/汽车( )   危险品等级( )
              MACHINE/AUTO   DANGEROUS CLASS
2. 集装箱种类 普通( )   开顶( )   框架( )   平板( )   冷藏( )
   CONTAINER ORDINARY   OPEN   FRAME   FLAT   REFRIGERATOR
3. 转运工具   海轮(×)   飞机( )   驳船( )   火车( )   汽车( )
   BY TRANSIT SHIP   PLANE   BARGE   TRAIN   TRUCK
4. 船舶资料   船籍( )   船龄( )
   PARTICULAR OF SHIP   RIGISTRY _____   AGE _____

备注：被保险人确认本保险合同条款和内容已经完全了解
THE ASSURED CONFIRMS HEREWITH THE TERMS AND CONDITONS OF THE INSURANCE CONTRACT FULLY UNDERSTOOD.

投保人（签名盖章）
APPLICANTS SIGNATURE

SUZHOU TAISHAN SUITCASE & BAG CO., LTD.

张奇

投保日期（DATE） AUG. 8, 2009

电话（TEL）0512—84524788
地址（ADD）66, ZHONGSHAN ROAD SUZHOU, JIANGSU CHINA

本公司自用（FOR OFFICE USE ONLY）
费率　　　　　　　保费　　　　　　备注
RATEAS ARRANGED　　PREMIUM AS ARRANGED
经办人 BY _____　核保人 _____　负责人 _____
总公司地址：上海市浦东南路 855 号　电话：021—58369558
邮政编码：200120　网址：www.ccic—net.com.cn

(2) 保险单。

中国大地财产保险股份有限公司

China Contient Property & Casualty Insurance Company Ltd.

货物运输保险单
CARGO TRANSPORTATION INSURANCE POLICY

发票号（INVOICE NO.）TSI0801005　　　保单号次（POLICY NO.）SZ123456
合同号（CONTRACT NO.）TSSC0801005
信用证号（L/C NO.）N5632405TH11808
被保险人（INSURED）. SUZHOU TAISHAN SUITCASE & BAG CO., LTD.
中国大地财产保险股份有限公司（以下简称本公司）根据被保险人的要求，由被保险人向本公司缴付约定的保险费，按照本保险单承保险别和背面所载条款与下列特款承保下述货物运输保险，特立本保险单。
THIS POLICY OF INSURANCE WITNESSES THAT CHINA CONTINENT PROPERTY & CASUALTY INSURANCE COMPANY LTD. OF CHINA (HEREIN AFTER CALLED "THE COMPANY") AT THE REQUEST OF THE INSURED AND IN CONSIDERATION OF THE AGREED PREMIUM PAID TO THE COMPANY BY THE INUSRED, UNDERTAKES TO INSURE THE UNDERMENTIONED GOODS IN TRANSPORTATION SUBJECT TO THE CONDITIONS OF THIS POLICY AS PER THE CLAUSES PRINTED OVERLEAF AND OTHER SPECIAL CLAUSES ATTACHED HEREON.

标记 MARKS & NOS	包装及数量 QUANTITY	保险货物项目 DESCRIPTION OF GOODS	保险金额 AMOUNT INSURED
ORTAI TSI0601005 NEW YORK C/NO.1－1231	1 231CTNS	Trolley Cases	USD24 665.00
总保险金额 TOTAL AMOUNT INSURED:		SAY U.S. DOLLARS TWENTY FOUR THOUSAND SIX HUNDRED AND SIXTY FIVE ONLY.	
保费： PERMIUM	AS AR-RANGED	起运日期 DATE OF COMMENCEMENT	AUG.8,2009	装载运输工具 PER CON-VEYANCE	XING YUN HAO,VOY. NO.001
自 FROM	SHANG-HAI	经 VIA	***	至 TO	NEW YORK, USA

承保险别 CONDITIONS
  COVERING ICC CLAUSES(A).

所保货物，如发生保险单项下可能引起索赔的损失或损坏，应立即通知本公司下述代理人勘查。如有索赔，应向本公司提交保单正本(本保险单共有2份正本)及有关文件。如一份正本已用于索赔，其余正本自动失效。

IN THE EVENT OF LOSS OR DAMAGE WHICH MAY RESULT IN A CLAIM UNDER THIS POLICY, IMMEDIATE NOTICE MUST BE GIVEN TO THE COMPANY'S AGENT AS MEN-TIONED HEREUNDER. CLAIMS, IF ANY, ONE OF THE ORIGINAL POLICY WHICH HAS BEEN ISSUED IN TWO ORIGINAL(s) TOGETHER WITH THE RELEVANT DOCU-MENTS SHALL BE SURRENDERED TO THE COMPANY. IF ONE OF THE ORIGINAL POLICY HAS BEEN ACCOMPLISHED, THE OTHERS TO BE VOID.

赔款偿付地点 CLAIM PAYABLE AT	NEWYORK IN USD	中国大地财产保险股份有限公司 ChinaContient Property & Casualty Insurance Company Ltd. 杨菲
日期和地点 DATE AND PLACE	AUG.8,2009, SHANGHAI	(Authorized Signature)

必备知识

一、货物运输风险和损失类型

1. 货物运输风险

(1)自然灾害,是指非常的自然界力量造成的灾害,如恶劣气候、雷电、洪水、地震、海啸等;

(2)意外事故,是指由于意料不到的原因所造成的事故。海运保险中,意外事故仅指搁浅、触礁、沉没、碰撞、火灾、爆炸和失踪等。

(3)一般外来风险,是指货物在运输途中由于偷窃、雨淋、短量、渗漏、破碎、受潮受热、霉变、串味、沾污、钩损、生锈、碰损等原因所导致的风险。

(4)特殊外来风险,是指由于战争、罢工、拒绝交付货物等政治、军事、国家禁令及管制措施所造成的风险与损失。如因政治或战争因素,运送货物的船只被敌对国家扣留而造成交货不到,某些国家颁布的新政策或新的管制措施以及国际组织的某些禁令,都可能造成货物无法出口或进口而造成损失。

2. 损失类型

被保险货物因遭受海洋运输中的风险所导致的损失称之为海损或海上损失。海损按损失程度的不同,可分为全部损失和部分损失。其中全损又分为实际全损和推定全损,部分损失按性质分为单独海损和共同海损。

(1)全部损失(total loss)。

①实际全损(actual total loss),又称绝对全损,是指保险标的物在运输途中全部灭失或等同与全部灭失。

②推定全损(constructive total loss),是指保险货物的实际全损已经不可避免,而进行施救、复原的费用已超过将货物运抵目的港的费用或已超出保险补偿价值的损失。

(2)部分损失(partial loss)。部分损失是指被保险货物的损失没有达到全部损失的程度。

①共同海损(general average),是指载货船舶在海运上遇难时,船方为了共同安全,以使同一航程中的船货脱离危险,有意而合理地作出的牺牲或引起的特殊费用,这些损失和费用被称为共同海损。

②单独海损(particular average),是指保险标的物在海上遭受承保范围内的风险所造成的部分灭失或损害,即指除共同海损以外的部分损失。这种损失只能由标的物所有人单独负担。

(二)保险条款和险别

1. 保险条款

常用的货物运输保险条款包括英国伦敦协会货物保险条款(Institute Cargo Clauses,ICC)和中国保险条款(China Insurance Clauses,CIC)。

2. 保险险别

保险险别一般分为主险(可单独投保,即基本险)、一般附加险和特别附加险(不可单独投保)。

(1)ICC 保险条款的险别。

①主险:协会货物(A)险条款[ICC(A)],协会货物(B)险条款[ICC(B)]和协会货物(C)险条

款[ICC(C)],还有协会货物险条款(航空)[instituite cargo clauses (air)]。

②附加险:协会货物战争险条款(institute war clauses－cargo),协会罢工险条款(intitute strikes clauses－cargo)和恶意损害险条款(malicious damage clauses),还有协会战争险条款(航空货物)[institute war clauses (air cargo)],协会罢工险条款(航空货物)[institute strikes clauses(air cargo)],协会战争险条款(邮包)[institute war clauses (spendings by post)]。

(2)CIC保险条款的险别。

①主险:海运运输货物保险条款(分为平安险、水渍险和一切险)、海洋运输冷藏货物保险条款、海洋运输散装桐油保险条款、陆上运输货物保险条款、陆上运输冷藏货物保险条款、航空运输货物保险条款、邮包险条款以及活牲畜、家禽的海上、陆上和航空运输保险条款等。

②一般附加险:包括偷窃提货不着险条款、淡水雨淋险条款、短量险条款、混杂玷污险条款、渗漏险条款、碰损破碎险条款、串味险条款、受潮受热险条款、钩损险条款、包装破裂险条款、锈损险条款等。

③特殊附加险:进口关税条款、舱面货物条款、拒收险条款、黄曲霉素险条款、易腐货物条款、交货不到条款、出口货物到港澳存仓火险责任扩展条款、海关检验条款、码头检验条款、战争险条款、战争险的附加费用、罢工险条款。

三、保险单据的作用和类别

保险单据是一份保险合同的证明,也是一份赔偿合同。保险单据经过背书后,还可以随货物所有权的转移而进行转让。根据UCP600,保险单据包括以下几种:

1. 保险单(insurance policy)

保险单又称大保单,是保险人和被保险人之间订立合同的一种正式证明。保险单的正面印制了海上保险所需的基本事项,如上述保险单所示。保险单的背面则列明了一般保险条款,规定保险人与被保险人的各项权利与义务、保险责任范围、除外责任、责任起讫、损失处理、索赔理赔、保险争议处理、时效条款等各项内容。

2. 保险证明书(insurance certificate)

保险证明书实质上是一种简化的保险单,与海上保险单具有同等的法律效力,又称小保单,用以证明海上货物运输保险合同的有效存在。其正面所列内容同海上保险单是一样的,但其背面是空白的,没有载明保险条款,在正面声明以同类海上保险单所载条款为准。

3. 保险申明书(insurance declaration)

保险申明书是预约保险项下的保险单据。预约保险(open cover)是一种长期性的货物运输保险合同,合同中规定了承保范围、险别、费率、责任、赔款等项目。凡属于预约保险项下的货物,在合同有效期内自动承保。

拓展知识

一、UCP600中涉及保险的相关条款

UCP600对保险单据的种类、保险单据的签字、保险单据的日期、投保货币与投保金额、承保的风险区间、投保的险别等均有具体的规定,这些规定体现在UCP600的第28条a~j款。

二、ISBP681中涉及保险的相关条款

ISBP681涉及保险的内容在第170段至第180段,对保险单据的出具人、投保风险、出具日期、投保的加成比例和投保金额、被保险人和背书作出了具体的规定。

技能训练

(一)训练资料

1. 信用证中同保险有关的条款

INSURANCE POLICY/CERTIFICATE FOR 110PCT OF INVOICE VALUE, BLANK ENDORSED, COVERING ALL RISKS AND WAR RISKS AS PER PICC DATED 1.1.81, UP TO SAN FRANCISCO, IF INCURRED, CLAIMS, IF ANY, PAYABLE IN U.S.

2. 商业发票

ISSUER CHANGZHOU YAFENG IMP. & EXP. CO., LTD. 3 GEHU MIDDLE ROAD, CHANGZHOU, JIANGSU CHINA Telex:0985 Fax:6332136 Tel:6332138				常州亚峰进出口有限公司 商 业 发 票 COMMERCIAL INVOICE	
TO THE LOOKING HANDCRAFT, INC 138 SAN MATEC AVENUE, SAN FRANCISCO CA—94080—6501, U.S.A.				NO. F93002897	DATE JUL. 3, 2010
TRANSPORT DETAILS FROMSHANGHAI TO SAN FRANCISCO BY SEA				S/C NO. 04F3—786	L/C NO. 0419049
^				TERMS OF PAYMENT L/C AT SIGHT	
Marks and Numbers	Number and Kind of Package Description of Goods		Quantity	Unit Price	Amount
N/M	CIF SAN FRANCISCO				
	4 000PCS HOOK RUG AS PER S/C NO. 04F3—780				
	ART. NO. CZ212 2×3'		2 000PCS	USD 17.1	USD 34 200.00
	ART. NO. CZ287 3×5'		1 000PCS	USD 18.1	USD 18 100.00
	ART. NO. CZ310 2×3'		1 000PCS	USD 19.1	USD 19 100.00
	TOTAL:		4 000PCS		USD 71 400.00
SAY TOTAL:	SAY U.S. DOLLARS SEVENTY ONE THOUSAND FOUR HUNDRED ONLY.				

We certify that the goods named above have been supplied in conformity with Order No. 04F3-786, and the goods named herein are of Chinese Origin.

LICENCE NO. CN617032

3. 装箱单

ISSUER CHANGZHOU YAFENG IMP. & EXP. CO., LTD. 3 GEHU MIDDLE ROAD, CHANG ZHOU, JIANGSU CHINA Telex:0985 Fax:6332136 Tel:6332138			常州亚峰进出口有限公司 装箱单 PACKING LIST	
TO THE LOOKING HANDCRAFT, INC 138 SAN MATEC AVENUE, SAN FRANCISCO CA-94080-6501, U.S.A.			INVOICE NO. F93002897	DATE JUL. 3, 2010
Marks and Numbers	Number and Kind of package Description of Goods	Quantity	Package	G.W (KGS)	N.W (KGS)	Meas (M3)

Marks and Numbers	Number and Kind of package Description of Goods	Quantity	Package	G.W (KGS)	N.W (KGS)	Meas (M3)
N/M	HOOK RUG AS PER S/C NO. 04F3-780 ART. NO. CZ212 2×3' ART. NO. CZ287 3×5' ART. NO. CZ310 2×3' PACKING:10PCS/CTN	2 000PCS 1 000PCS 1 000PCS	20CTNS 10CTNS 10CTNS	12.0 16.5 12.0	11.5 16.0 11.5	@0.08

SAY TOTAL: PACKED IN 40 CARTONS ONLY.

THE L/C NUMBER:0419049
CENTRAL BANK CONTROL NUMBER:278701255020

4. 其他信息

(1)运输工具名称:HANJIN V.014E

(2)起运日期:2010年7月14日

(3)保单号码:CZ001

(二)请根据以上信息制作投保单和出口保险单

(1)投保单。

货物运输保险投保单
APPLICATION FORM FOR CARGO TRANSPORTATION INSURANCE

投保单号：

被保险人：
INSURED：_____
发票号(INVOICE NO.)：
合同号(CONTRACT NO.)：
信用证号(L/C NO.)：
发票金额(INSURANCE AMOUNT)：_____ 投保加成 _____

兹有下列物品箱中国大地财产保险股份有限公司投保(INSURANCE IS REQUIRED ON THE FOLLOWING COMMODITIES：)

标记 MARKS & NOS.	包装及数量 QUANTITY	保险货物项目 DESCEPTION OF GOODS	保险金额 AMOUNT INSURED

起运日期：   装载工具：
DATE OF COMMENCEMENT _____ PER CONVEYANCE _____
自   经   至
FROM _____   VIA _____   TO _____
提单号：   赔款偿付地点：
B/C NO. _____   CLAIM PAYBLE _____
投保险别：(PLEASE INDICATE THE CONDITIONS & OR SPECIAL COVERAGES)

请如实告知下列情况：(如"是",在括号内打"X")IF ANY, PLEASE MARK "X"
1.货物种类   袋装( )   散装( )   冷藏( )   液体( )   活动物( )
   GOODS   BAG/CTN   BULK   REEFER   LIQUID   LIVE ANIMAL
             机器/汽车( )   危险品等级( )
             MACHINE/AUTO   DANGEROUS CLASS
2.集装箱种类 普通( )   开顶( )   框架( )   平板( )   冷藏( )
   CONTAINER ORDINARY   OPEN   FRAME   FLAT   REFRIGERATOR
3.转运工具   海轮( )   飞机( )   驳船( )   火车( )   汽车( )
   BY TRANSIT SHIP   PLANE   BARGE   TRAIN   TRUCK

4.船舶资料 PARTICULAR OF SHIP	船籍( ) RIGISTRY _____	船龄( ) AGE _____

备注:被保险人确认本保险合同条款和内容已经完全了解
THE ASSURED CONFIRMS HEREWITH THE TERMS AND CONDITONS OF THE INSURANCE CONTRACT FULLY UNDERSTOOD.

投保人(签名盖章)
APPLICANTS SIGNATURE

投保日期(DATE)　　　　　　　　　电话(TEL)
　　　　　　　　　　　　　　　　　地址(ADD)

本公司自用(FOR OFFICE USE ONLY)
费率　　　　　　　　保费　　　　　　　　备注
RATEAS ARRANGED　　PREMIUM AS ARRANGED
经办人 BY _____　核保人 _____　负责人 _____
总公司地址:上海市浦东南路855号　电话:021-58369558
邮政编码:200120　网址:www.ccic-net.com.cn

(2)保险单。

中国大地财产保险股份有限公司

China Contient Property & Casualty Insurance Company Ltd.

货物运输保险单

CARGO TRANSPORTATION INSURANCE POLICY

发票号(INVOICE NO.)　　　　　　保单号次(POLICY NO.)
合同号(CONTRACT NO.)
信用证号(L/C NO.)
被保险人(INSURED)._____.

中国大地财产保险股份有限公司(以下简称本公司)根据被保险人的要求,由被保险人向本公司缴付约定的保险费,按照本保险单承保险别和背面所载条款与下列特款承保下述货物运输保险,特立本保险单。
THIS POLICY OF INSURANCE WITNESSES THAT CHINA CONTINENT PROPERTY & CASUALTY INSURANCE COMPANY LTD. OF CHINA(HEREIN AFTER CALLED "THE COMPANY") AT THE REQUEST OF THE INSURED AND IN CONSIDERATION OF THE AGREED PREMIUM PAID TO THE COMPANY BY THE INSUSRED, UNDERTAKES TO INSURE THE UNDERMENTIONED GOODS IN TRANSPORTATION SUBJECT TO THE CONDITIONS OF THIS POLICY AS PER THE CLAUSES PRINTED OVERLEAF AND OTHER SPECIAL CLAUSES ATTACHED HEREON.

标记 MARKS & NUMBERS	包装及数量 QUANTITY	保险货物项目 DESCRIPTION OF GOODS	保险金额 AMOUNT INSURED
总保险金额 TOTAL AMOUNT INSURED:			

保费： PERMIUM	AS AR-RANGED	起运日期 DATE OF COMMENCE-MENT		装载运输工具 PER CON-VEYANCE	
自 FROM		经 VIA		至 TO	

承保险别 CONDITIONS

所保货物，如发生保险单项下可能引起索赔的损失或损坏，应立即通知本公司下述代理人勘查。如有索赔，应向本公司提交保单正本（本保险单共有 2 份正本）及有关文件。如一份正本已用于索赔，其余正本自动失效。

IN THE EVENT OF LOSS OR DAMAGE WHICH MAY RESULT IN A CLAIM UNDER THIS POLICY, IMMEDIATE NOTICE MUST BE GIVEN TO THE COMPANY'S A-GENT AS MENTIONED HEREUNDER. CLAIMS, IF ANY, ONE OF THE ORIGINAL POLICY WHICH HAS BEEN ISSUED IN TWO ORIGINAL(s) TOGETHER WITH THE RELEVANT DOCUMENTS SHALL BE SURRENDERED TO THE COMPANY. IF ONE OF THE ORIGINAL POLICY HAS BEEN ACCOMPLISHED, THE OTHERS TO BE VOID.

赔款偿付地点 CLAIM PAYABLE AT		中国大地财产保险股份有限公司 ChinaContient Property & Casualty Insurance Company Ltd. 杨菲
日期和地点 DATE AND PLACE		（Authorized Signature）

任务九　制作附属单据

学习目标

能力目标
1. 能根据信用证条款和其他信息，制作受益人证明
2. 能根据信用证条款和其他信息，制作装船通知
3. 能根据信用证条款和其他信息，制作船公司证明

知识目标
1. 熟悉受益人证明的格式和内容
2. 熟悉装船通知的格式和内容
3. 熟悉船公司证明的格式和内容

任务设计

单证员小张在确认好海运提单后，将商业发票、装箱单和海运提单的副本传真给开证申请人，开始制作受益人证明、装运通知及船公司证明。

（1）下面是某信用证中有关随附单证缮制的内容：

……

APPLICANT	50：	VERSIONS LIMITED
		32 COSGROVE WAY LUTON, BEDFORDSHIRE LU1 1XL U.K.
APPLICANT BANK	51A：	HSBC BANK PLC(FORMERLY MIDLAND BANK PLC)LONDON
BENEFICIARY	59：	SHANGHAI JINTAI IMP. AND EXP. CO., LTD.
		300 NANJING ROAD, SHANGHAI CHINA
DOCUMENTS REQUIRED	46A：	

……

+ CERTIFICATE SENT BY BENEFICIARY TO APPLICANT, EVIDENCING THAT COPIES OF INVOICE, BILL OF LADING AND PACKING LIST HAVE BEEN FAXED TO APPLICANT ON FAX NO. 01－5824－3470 WITHIN 3 DAYS OF BILL OF LADING DATE.

……

+ THIS IS TO CERTIFY THAT S. S. HONGJI FLYING THE PEOPLE'S REPUBLIC OF CHINA FLAG, WILL NOT CALL AT ANY ISRAELI PORTS DURING THIS

PRESENT VOYAGE, AND SHE IS NOT BLACK LISTED BY THE ARAB COUNTRIES.

……

ADDITION CONDITION. 47A:

+ APPLICANT'S ORDER NO. 599/2009 MUST BE SHOWN ON ALL DOCUMENTS

……

(2)其他相关资料：
①发票号码：JT09E0718　　　　　发票金额：GBP74 150.00
②提单号码：COSU2381862　　　　提单日期：2009年8月15日
③承运人：中国远洋运输(集团)总公司 CHINA OCEAN SHIPPPING(GROUP)CO.
④提单签署人：上海中远集装箱船务代理有限公司
　 COSCO SHANGHAI CONTAINER SHIPPING AGENCY CO., LTD.
⑤船名航次：HONGJI V.068
⑥启运地：上海　　　　　　　　　目的地：伦敦

任务分解

1. 读懂所给资料
2. 根据所给资料，制作受益人证明、装运通知及船公司证明

任务描述

单证员小张的工作任务是根据信用证的规定及其他相关资料准确制作受益人证明、装运通知及船公司证明。

操作示范

(一)受益人证明的填写

第一栏，根据信用证的内容，填写受益人的英文名称和地址。
第二栏，根据信用证的要求，填写"证明信"和"CERTIFICATE"。
第三栏，填写发票号码。
第四栏，填写发票日期"2009年8月18日"或"8月19日"。
第五栏，根据信用证要求，填写开证申请人的名称与地址。
第六栏，根据信用证要求，填写证明信的内容。
请注意：
(1)根据信用证要求使用动词"EVIDENCE"，而不是"CERTIFY"。
(2)在"… FAXED TO APPLICANT …"的时候，不能机械照抄，而要将"APPLICANT"改为具体开证申请人"VERSIONS LIMITED"。
第七栏，根据信用证的要求，填写"VERSIONS' ORDER NO.599/2009"。
第八栏，盖"金太"公司的条形章和法人代表的签署章。

缮制完毕的受益人证明如下:

上海金太进出口有限公司
SHANGHAI JINTAI IMP. AND EXP. CO., LTD.
300 NANJING ROAD, SHANGAHI CHINA

证明信
CERTIFICATE

No.:JT09E0718
Date: AUG.18, 2009

To:
VERSIONS LIMITED
23 COSGROVE WAY
LUTON, BEDFORDSHIRE
LU1 2SL. U. LK.

WE HEREBY EVIDENCE THAT COPIES OF INVOICE, BILL OF LADING AND PACKING LIST HAVE BEEN FAXED TO VERSIONS LIMITED ON FAX NO. 01-5824-3470 WITHIN 3 DAYS AFTER BILL OF LADING DATE.

VERSION' ORDER NO.599/2009

上海金太进出口有限公司(章)
SHANGHAI JINTAI I/E CO., LTD.

朱倩(章)

(二)装船通知的填制

虽然此装船通知不是该信用证中规定要求出口商提交的单据,但在实际业务中,卖方一般都会发送装船通知给买方,让进口商做好接货、投保(FOB 和 CFR 术语)、赎单的准备。

第一栏,填写上海金太进出口有限公司的中英文名称和地址,写上单据的名称"SHIPPING ADVICE"。

第二栏,填写开证申请人的名称和地址。

第三栏,按惯例填写发票号码。

第四栏,因信用证中对装船通知无要求和规定,日期可以与受益人证明信一样,填写"2009年8月18日"或"2009年8月19日"。

第五栏,根据海运提单上的信息,填写品名、数量、船名航次、开航日期等。

第六栏,盖金太公司的条形章和法人代表的签署章。

因信用证对装船通知不作要求,所以在装船通知中,买方的订单号可以显示,也可以不显示。

缮制完毕的装船通知如下:

```
                    上海金太进出口有限公司
              SHANGHAI JINTAI IMP. AND EXP. CO., LTD.
                 300 NANJING ROAD, SHANGAHI CHINA
                           装船通知
                        SHIPPING ADVICE

To:
    VERSIONS LIMITED                    No: WL 09E0718
    23 COSGROVE WAY                     Date: AUG. 18, 2009
    LUTON, BEDFORDSHIRE
    LU1 2SL. U. LK.

    WE ARE HEREBY PLEASED TO INFORM YOU THAT THE GOODS UNDER L/C NO. DC
LD1300945 HAVE BEEN SHIPPED. THE DETAILS ARE AS FOLLOWS:
    Description of Goods:      CUSHION COVERS AND RUGS
    No. & Kind of Pkgs:        350 CTNS
    Port of Loading:           SHANGHAI
    Port of Discharge:         FELIXSTOWE
    S. S. And Voy. No. :       ANDAMAN SEA V. 707W
    Bill of Lading No. :       COSUSH6311803
    Bill of Lading Date:       AUG. 15, 2009
    Invoice Value:             GBP74 150.00
    Shipping Marks:
    VERSIONS                   VERSIONS
    C COVER                    RUG
    O/NO. 599/2009             O/NO. 599/2009
    FELIXSTOWE                 FELIXSTOWE
    NO. 1—200                  NO. 1—150

    VERSION' ORDER NO. 599/2009

                                   上海金太进出口有限公司(章)
                                   SHANGHAI JINTAI I/E CO., LTD.

                                                        朱倩(章)
```

(三) 船公司证明的填制

可根据信用证的规定,出具相应的船公司证明,下面要缮制的是船籍和航程证明。

第一栏,填写证明内容,即单据的名称即"ITINERARY CERTIFICATE"。

第二栏,填写抬头,即开证申请人的名称。

第三栏,单据的签发地点,即上海。

第四栏,船名,即红旗号。

第五栏,证明内容。

第六栏,签署,即船公司签署。

缮制完毕的船公司证明如下:

ITINERARY CERTIFICATE

TO: VERSIONS LIMITED   PLACE: SHANGHAI
RE: S. S. HONGJI V. 068

THIS IS TO CERTIFY THAT S. S. HONGHJI V. 068 FLYING THE PEOPLE'S REPUBLIC OF CHINA FLAG, WILL NOT CALL AT ANY ISRAELI PORTS DURING THIS PRESENT VOYAGE, AND SHE IS NOT BLACK LISTED BY THE ARAB COUNTRIES.

COSCO SHANGHAI CONTAINER SHIPPING AGENCY CO., LTD.
张进

必备知识

一、受益人证明

受益人证明(beneficiary's certificate)是一种内容多种多样、格式简单的单据。它由受益人自己出具,以证明自己履行了信用证规定的任务或证明自己按信用证的要求办事,证明的内容包括:寄出有关的副本单据、船样、样卡、码样、包装标签,商品已经检验、已发出装船通知等。

受益人证明一般不分正、副本,但若来证要求正本,可以在"beneficiary's certificate"的正下方,打"original"字样。

受益人证明的特点是自己证明履行某项义务。一份受益人证明书一般有几个栏目:

---

1. NAME & ADDRESS OF BENEFICIARY
2. BENEFICIARY'S CERTIFICATE

5. TO: WHOM IT MAY CONCERN   3. DATE:
                                      4. RE: L/C NO.... INVOICE NO....

6. WE HEREBY CERTIFY THAT

                                      7. SIGNATUR

第一栏:填写出口公司名称和地址。

第二栏：填写单据名称，按 L/C 规定填写，如"BENEFICIARY'S CERTIFICATE,BENEFICIARY'S STATFMENT,BENEFICIARY'S DECLARATION"。

第三栏：日期，应与证明的内容符合。例如，提单日期是 4 月 20 日，受益人证明的有关内容是："WE HEREBY CERTIFY THAT ONE SET OF NON-NEGOTIABLE SHIPPING DOCUMENTS HAS BEEN AIRMAILED TO THE APPLICANT WITHIN 2 DAYS AFTER THE SHIPMENT DATE"，受益人证明不能早于 4 月 22 日，当然也不能晚于交单日期。

第四栏：参考号码，填写信用证号码和发票号码。

第五栏：抬头栏，可采用笼统填法，如致有关当事人（TO:WHOM IT MAY CONCERN）。

第六栏：证明内容，根据信用证缮制，但有时应对所用时态作相应变化。例如，信用证条款规定"BENEFICIARY'S CERTIFICATE CERTIFY THAT ALL THE PACKAGES TO BE LINED WITH WATERPROOF PAPER AND BOUND WITH TWO IRON STRAPS OUTSIDE"，则受益人证明应作成："...PACKAGES HAVE BEEN LINED..."。

第七栏：签名。注明出口公司名称并签章。

二、装船通知

装船通知（shipping advice）是出口商根据信用证规定在货物装船并取得提单后，以传真、电报或电传方式将与装船有关的情况及时告知收货人等有关当事人的单据。

在以 FOB 或 CFR 条件下，装船通知是进口商办理进口货物保险的凭证。装船通知也可使在以 CIF 或 CIP 价格成交的买方了解货物装运情况、准备接货或筹措资金。

按惯例，在以 FOB 或 CFR 条件下，卖方未及时通知买方保险，货物在运输途中发生的损失，应由卖方负责。因此，在以 FOB 或 CFR 条件下，卖方是否及时发出装船通知显得尤为重要。买方为了避免卖方因疏忽未及时通知，所以经常在信用证中明确规定，卖方必须按时发出装船通知，并规定通知的内容，而且在议付时必须提供该装船通知的副本，与其他单据一起向银行议付。

若信用证未对装船通知的出单日期作出明确规定，一般要求出口商在货物离开启运地后三个工作日内向进口商发出装船通知。

1. 装船通知的内容

装船通知按内容一般分为两种：一种是通知买方购买保险，其内容主要包括货名、数量、唛头、装运港名称、目的港名称、买方名称或买方指定的保险公司、预约保单号码、装船的具体时间、装载船名、航次和转船及开航时间等；另一种是通知装船，以利买方报关接货或筹措资金，卖方必须把装船情况详细电告买方，如合同号、信用证号、船名、装船日期、装运港、目的港、品名、规格、件数、重量、金额、唛头等，更改船名或开船日期也应通知买方。

2. 装船通知的缮制方法

```
            1. NAME & ADDRESS OF EXPORTER
            2. NAME OF DOCUMETNS
3. TO:      4. DATE:
            5. RE:L/C NO. ...
            INVOICE NO. (OPEN POLICY NO. ...)
```

> 6. WE HEREBY INFORMED YOU THAT THE GOODS UNDER THE ABOVE MENTIONED CREDIT HAVE BEEN SHIPPED. THE DETAILS OF SHIPMENT ARE STATED BELOW.
> COMMODITY:
> QUANTITY:
> INVOICE VALUE:
> OCEAN VESSEL/SHIPPED PER S. S. :
> DATE OF SHIPMENT:
> PORT OF SHIPMETN:
> PORT OF LOADING:
> PORT OF DESTINATION:
> MARKS:
> 7. WE HEREBY CERTIFY THAT THE ABOVE CONTENT IS TRUE AND CORRECT.
> 8. SIGNATURE

装船通知样式如上，具体制作方法如下：

第一栏：填写出口公司名称和地址。

第二栏：填写单据名称，按L/C规定填，如"Shipping Advice, Beneficiary's Certified Copy of Fax"以及"Declaration of Shipment"等。

第三栏：抬头。按L/C规定填写，如买方/保险公司/开证行等。

第四栏：日期。填写制装船通知的日期，一般与提单日期相同。

第五栏：参考号码。填L/C号码、发票号码。若发出装船通知是为了让买方及时投保，参考号码栏中一般还需加预约保单号码(OPEN POLICY NO. /COVER NOTE NO.)。

第六栏：按L/C规定将具体细节一一列明。

第七栏：若信用证规定需有证明副本装船通知真实性的文句，则应加上此句。若无规定，则不必加。

第八栏：签名。由出口公司签署。

三、船公司证明

船公司证明(shipping company's certificate)是信用证受益人应开证申请人的要求，请船公司出具的不同认定内容的证明。常见的船公司证明有以下几种。

1. 船籍和航程证明

(1)船籍和航程证明(itinerary certificate)概述。船籍证明是说明载货船舶国籍的证明。航程证明是说明载货船舶航程中停靠港口的证明。例如，阿拉伯国家开来的信用证通常要求提供非以色列船只，并且不得停靠以色列港口，不是黑名单船只，不得挂以色列国旗等。

如来证要求："SHIPMENT MUST NOT BE EFFECTED ON ISRAELI VESSEL AND NOT CALL AT ANY ISRAELI PORTS, AND NOT BLACK LISTED VESSEL."按此条款，应提供由船方或其代理出具的船籍和航程证明。

(2)船籍和航程证明的缮制。

```
                    1. ITINERARY CERTIFICATE
2. TO:WHOME IT MAY CONCERN      3. PLACE:
                                4. RE:S. S. ...

5. THIS IS TO CERTIFY THAT S. S. ... FLYUING THE PEOPLE'S REPUBLIC OF CHINA
FLAG, WILL NOT CALL AT ANY ISRAELI PORTS DURING THIS PRESENT VOYAGE, AND
SHE IS NOT BLACK LISTED BY THE ARAB COUNTRIES.
                                                        6. SIGNATURE
```

第一栏:单据名称。

第二栏:抬头。

第三栏:签发地点。

第四栏:船名。

第五栏:证明内容。

第六栏:签名。由船公司签署。

2. 船长收据

(1)船长收据(master's/captain's receipt)概述。有些信用证规定货物装运后将有关副本单据交装货船只的船长随船带交收货人。此时,需船长签发收据,收据上必须由船长转递单据的承诺。

如来证要求:"COPIES OF SHIPPING DOCUMENTS MUST BE SENT TO THE MASTER OF THE CARRYING VESSELS, AND THE MASTER'S RECEIPT REQUIRED FOR NEGOTIATION."按此条款,应提供由船长签发的随船单据的收据。

(2)船长收据的缮制。

```
                            1. RECEIPT
2. RE:B/L NO. ... INVOICE NO. ...
3. THE UNDERSIGNED MASTER OF THE CARRYING VESSEL S. S. ... HEREBY CERTIFY
HAVING RECEIVED FROM M/S ... (受益人)THE FOLLOWING SHIPPING DOCUMENTS
WHICH SHALL BE HANDED OVER TO M/S...(收货人).
(1) ONE COPY OF B/L
(2) COPEIS OF INVOICES
(3) COPIES OF PACKING LIST
(4) ...
4. SIGNATURE
```

第一栏:单据名称。

第二栏:提单号码、发票号码。

第三栏:内容。

第四栏:签名。由船公司签署并由船长或其代理签名。

3. 集装箱船只证明

(1)集装箱船只证明概述。如信用证仅规定货物需装载集装箱船只,则只要在提单上注明货物是集装箱运输(THE GOODS HAVE BEEN SHIPPED BY CONTAINER)即可。如信用证不仅规定货物需装载集装箱船只且要求单独递交证明文本,则不仅需在提单上注明货物是集装箱运输,还需提供集装箱船只证明。

如来证要求:"SHIPMENT TO BE MADE BY CONTAINER VESSEL AND BENEFICIARY TO CERTIFY THIS EFFECT."按此条款,不仅需在提单上注明货物是集装箱运输,还需提供集装箱船只证明。

(2)集装箱船只证明的缮制。

---

1. CERTIFICATE
2. TO:WHOM IT MAY CONCERN　　　　3. PLACE
　　　　　　　　　　　　　　　　4. RE:INVOICE NO. ...　　L/C NO. ...
5. THIS IS TO CERTIFY THAT SHIPMENT HAVE BEEN EFFECTED BY THE CONTAINER VESSEL.
　　　　　　　　　　　　　　　　　　　　　　6. SIGNATURE

第一栏:单据名称。

第二栏:抬头。

第三栏:签发地点。

第四栏:发票号码、信用证号码。

第五栏:证明内容。

第六栏:签名。由船公司签署。

4. 船龄证明

船龄证明是说明载货船舶的证明。有时信用证要求提供标明运输船舶的船龄不得超过多少年的证明,格式可参考前面三种。

5. 运费证明

运费证明是承运人签发给托运人的有关货物运费收讫的凭证。在CFR或CIF条件下,如果信用证要求提供船公司运费账单,则船公司必须提供该类证明。单据的名称通常为"FREIGTH INVOICE"、"FREIGHT ACCOUNT"、"FREIGHT VOUCHER",格式可参考前面三种。

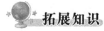 **拓展知识**

除了上述提及的各种证明之外,有时根据进口商的要求,还需出具相关证明,如生产过程证明和价格单等,下面就这两种单据作以说明。

一、生产过程证明

在食品、药品出口时,信用证往往要求出口商提供生产过程证明,目的是了解产品从原材料到成品所经过的一系列生产环节是否符合相应的规范。

生产过程证明一般没有固定统一的格式,只要符合信用证要求即可。如果信用证要求生产过程证明必须经过专门机构的认证,则出口商需要到相应的认证机构对其生产过程证明进行认证盖章。如果信用证未做此要求,只需出口商或生产厂商签字盖章即可。

二、价格单

价格单通常是在进口商希望核实货物价格,或者进口国海关核实货物是否存在倾销情况下提供的,价格单的内容和商业发票一样,但货币是出口国货币而不是进口国或第三国货币。例如,我国企业出具的价格单,一定是采用人民币(CNY)计价的。在实务中,价格单通常采用FOB价格的90%计算。

有时信用证要求价格单必须由商会证实,这就要求出口商将价格单拿到相应的机构去认证。目前我国的贸促会视同商会,可行使此认证职权。

技能训练

训练项目一

(一)训练资料

1. BENEFICIARY: SHANGHAI MACHINERY IMP. & EXP. CO., LTD.
2. L/C NO.: HU65926
3. DOCUMENTS REQUIRED:
BENEFICIARY'S CERTIFICATE CERTIFYING THAT COMMERCIAL INVOICE, PACKING LIST AND ORIGINAL EXPORT LICENCE HAVE BEEN DESPATCHED BY COURIER DIRECTLY TO YOUTA TRADING COMPANY.
4. INVOICE NO.: TB—M85062
5. DATE OF ISSUING THE BENEFICIARY'S CERTIFICATE: AUG. 3, 2010

(二)根据上述资料缮制一份受益人证明

训练项目二

(一)训练资料

1. 信用证部分资料

Credit Number:	LRT9903887
Date of Issue:	030505
Expiry:	Date 030716 PLACE CHINA
Applicant:	ABC CORP. AKEKSANTERINK AUTO P.O. BOX9, FINLAND
Beneficiary:	GUANGDONG RONGHUA TRADE CO., LTD. 168, DEZHENG ROAD SOUTH, GUANGZHOU CHINA
Amount:	CURRENCY USD AMOUNT 36 480.00(SAY US DOLLARS THIRTY SIX THOUSAND FOUR HUNDRED AND EIGHTY ONLY.)
Loading In Charge:	GUANGZHOU
For Transport To:	HELSINKI
Shipment Period:	AT THE LATEST JULY 16, 2003
Descrip. of Goods:	9 600PCS OF WOMEN'S SWEATERS UNIT PRICE: USD3.80/PC, PACKING: 12PCS/CTN OTHER DETAILS AS PER S/C NO. 99SGP468001 CFRHELSINKI

Documents Required: ADVICE OF SHIPMENT MUST BE SENT BY FAX TO MARKE INSURANCE CO. HELSINKI, FINLAND (FAX NO. 33333) WITH DETAILS OF SHIPMENT INCLUDING VALUE, NAME OF VESSEL, DATE OF SHIPMENT, NAME OF COMMODITY, NUMBER OF PACKAGE; TOTAL NET AND GROSS WEIGHT QUOTING THEIR POLICY NO. 3RT20053. COPY OF THIS FAX TO BE PRESENTED WITH DOCUMENTS UPON NEGOTIATION.

Additional Cond.: (1)T.T. REIMBURSEMENT IS PROHIBITED
(2)ALL DOCUMENTS MUST BE MARKED THE S/C NO. AND THE L/C NO.
(3)SHIPPING MARKS:ABC/HELSINKI/NO.1—UP

2. 其他资料
INV. NO. :2003PCI448   DATE OF SHIPMENT:MAY.20,2003
B/L NO. :FKK9078533   MEASUREMENT:(405080)CM/CTN
G. W. :23KGS/CTN   N. W. :18KGS/CTN
NAME OF STEAMER:DONGFRNEG E003
DATE OF ADVICE:MAY.21,2003
S/C NO. :99SGP468001

(二)请根据上述资料缮制一份装船通知

训练项目三

(一)训练资料

(1)商品名称:ALARMING CLOCK WITH CALENDAR
(2)承运人:中国远洋运输(集团)总公司 CHINA OCEAN SHIPPING(GROUP)CO.
(3)提单签署人:上海中远集装箱船务代理有限公司
COSCO SHANGHAI CONTAINER SHIPPING AGENCY CO., LTD
(4)装运日期:2010.10.18   船名航次:HONGJI V.038
(5)起运港:SHANGHAI   目的港:DOHA
(6)开证银行:QATAR NATION BANK 开证日期:2010.8.28
(7)信用证号码:LC/2010/00839
(8)开证申请人:TAMIM AL MARRI(地址略)
(9)受益人:SHANGHAI HUI YUAN TRADE CO., LTD.(地址略)
(10)信用证关于船公司证明的条款:
+A CERTIFICATE FROM SHIPPING COMPANY OR ITS AGENT SHOWING THE NAME,FLAG AND NATIONALITY OF THE CARRYING VESSEL ALSO CONFIRMING THAT THE VESSEL WILL NOT PASS BY AND ISRAELI PORTS THROUGH ITS PRESENT VOYAGE AND THAT IS PERMITTED TO ENTER ARAB PORTS.

(二)请根据上述资料缮制一份船公司证明

任务十　制作汇票

学习目标

能力目标
能够根据信用证和其他相关信息,准确制作汇票

知识目标:
1. 熟悉汇票的分类和票据行为
2. 熟悉 ISBP681 关于汇票的条款

任务设计

2009年8月27日,苏州泰山箱包有限公司外贸单证员李芳制作好附属单据后,准备在信用证交单期要求交单之前,根据任务三中的信用证 N5632405TH11808 和以下相关资料制作汇票。
1. 信用证(见任务三中的信用证 N5632405TH11808)
2. 相关资料
发票号码:TSI0801005

任务分解

制作符合信用证要求的汇票。

任务描述

汇票是国际贸易结算中非常重要的一种票据。它属于资金单据,可以代替货币进行转让或流通。因此,汇票是一种重要的有价证券。在国际贸易结算实务中,汇票在信用证和托收业务中都是重要的支付工具,掌握汇票的缮制方法和要求,是企业顺利结汇的要求,也是单证员的制单技能之一。

操作示范

第一步:读懂信用证条款
认真仔细地阅读信用证条款,弄清信用证条款中对汇票的要求,为准确缮制汇票作好准备。
第二步:制作汇票
严格依据信用证要求,制作汇票。
汇票样式如下:

<div align="center">**BILL OF EXCHANGE**</div>					
凭 Drawn Under			不可撤销信用证 Irrevocable L/C No.	
日期 Date		支 取 Payable with interest	@ ％ 按 息 付款	
号码 No.		汇票金额 Exchange for		苏州 SuZhou	
	见票 at	******		日后（本汇票之副本未付）付交 Sight of this FIRST of Exchange(Second of Exchange being
unpaid)pay to the order of						
金额 the sum of						
此致 to						

1. **出票根据**（drawn under）

这一栏按信用证的规定填写开证行名称与地址。托收汇票在出票条款内加注"FOR COLLECTION"。

本案填写：CITY NATIONAL BANK NEW YORK，U.S.A

2. **信用证号码**（L/C No.）

正确填写信用证号于该栏，但有时也可接受来证不要求填写此栏的要求。

本案填写：N5632405TH11808

3. **开证日期**（date）

正确填写信用证的开证日期。

本案的填写：JUL.15,2009

4. **年息**（payable with interest @…％）

这一栏由结汇银行填写，用以清算企业与银行间利息费用，出口公司不必填写此栏目。

5. **号码**（No.）

汇票号码，一般都以相应的发票号码兼作汇票号码。其用意是核对发票与汇票中相同和相关的内容，例如金额、信用证号码等。一旦出现这一栏内容在一套单据错误或需要修改时，只要看汇票号是否与发票号码相同，就能确定它们是否是同一笔交易的单据，从而为核对和纠正错误带来方便。

本案的填写：TSI0801005

6. **汇票小写金额**（exchange for）

此栏填写汇票小写金额，由货币名称缩写及阿拉伯数字组成。金额数保留两位小数。例如，

USD100.20,HKD345.78。

在填制汇票金额时,应注意以下几点:

(1)除信用证另有规定,汇票金额所使用的货币应与信用证规定和发票上的货币一致。

(2)汇票金额一般不超过信用证规定的金额。如信用证规定汇票金额为发票金额的97%,那么发票金额应为100%,其差额3%一般为应付的佣金。这种做法通常用于中间商代开信用证的场合。

(3)如信用证规定部分信用证付款,部分托收,则分做两套汇票:信用证下支款的汇票按信用证允许的金额填制,其余部分为托收项下汇票的金额,两者之和等于发票金额。

(4)汇票上的金额大、小写必须一致,不得涂改,不允许更改后加盖校对章。

本案的填写:USD 22 422.00

7. 汇票大写金额

由小写金额翻译而成。一般要求顶格填写,以防有人故意在汇票金额上做手脚。货币名称写在数额之前,金额后加"ONLY",也可在货币名称前加"SAY"(计)。

如:USD100.20 大写金额可表述为:

(SAY) UNITED STATES DOLLARS ONE HUNDRED AND CENTS TWENTY ONLY.

本案的填写:(SAY)U.S DOLLARS TWENTY TWO THOUSAND FOUR HUNDRED AND TWENTY TWO ONLY

8. 出票日期和地点(date and place of issue)

地点一般已印好,无需现填。出票地点后的横线填写出票日期,信用证方式下,一般以议付日期作为出票日期。该日期不得早于随附的各种单据的出单日期,同时不能迟于信用证的交单/有效期。该日期一般由银行代填。

本案的填写:AUG.27,2009,SuZhou

9. 付款期限(at...sight)

付款期限是汇票的重要项目,在缮制汇票时,应按信用证规定填写汇票付款期限。汇票付款期限分即期和远期两种。

(1)即期汇票的付款期限这一栏的填法较简单,只需在横线上用"＊＊＊"或"——"或"×××"表示,也可直接打上"AT SIGHT",但不能留空。

(2)远期汇票,按信用证的规定填入相应的付款期限。

例如,来证规定:"drafts at 30 days after sight",这是见票后30天付款的远期汇票,填写时,在此栏打上"30 DAYS AFTER"。

例如,来证规定:"drafts at 45 days after date",这是汇票出票日后45天付款的远期汇票,填写时,在此栏打上"45 DAYS AFTER DATE",并把已印的"sight"划掉。

例如,来证规定:"drafts at 60 days after the B/L date",B/L 日期为 AUG.20,2008,这是提单日后60天付款远期汇票,填写时,在此栏打上"60 DAYS AFTER THE B/L DATE,AUG.20,2008",并把已印的"sight"划掉。

例如,来证规定:"drafts to be drawn as follows:USD29 000.00—drafts to be drawn at sight on National Australia Bank LTD., Brisbane, Queensland, Australia USD21 000.00—drafts to be drawn at 90 days sight on National Australia Bank LTD., Brisbane, Queensland, Australia"。

这是要求一笔交易分两个期限付款的信用证,需要填写两张汇票。一张在付款期限上用"＊＊＊"或"——"或"×××"表示,也可直接打上"AT SIGHT",该汇票金额为USD29 000.00。另一张在付款期限栏目中填"90 DAYS"表示见票后90天付款,该汇票金额为USD21 000.00。

本案的填写：＊＊＊

10. **受款人/收款人**（pay to the order of）

应从信用证的角度来理解这一栏目的要求。在信用证支付的条件下,汇票中受款人这一栏目中填写的应是银行名称和地址,一般都是议付行的名称和地址。究竟要哪家银行作为受款人,这要看信用证中是否有具体的规定。

通常,信用证对受款人的规定是过两种形式表示:一种是限制受款人,即限制议付行;另一种是不限制受款人,即不限制议付行,可自由议付。

例如,来证规定:"by negotiation against the documents detailed herein and beneficiary's drafts at 30 days after sight with BANK OF CHINA, HANGZHOU BRANCH",此证限制在中国银行杭州分行议付,即受款人是中国银行杭州分行。在填写这样要求的汇票时,应在"pay to the order of"之后的栏目中打上"BANK OF CHINA, HANGZHOU BRANCH"。

例如,来证规定:"by negotiation against the documents detailed herein and beneficiary's drafts at 30 days after sight with ABC Banking group LTD. 120 Wall Street, New York, USA",此证限制在美国纽约的ABC银行集团议付,即受款人是美国纽约的ABC银行集团。在填写这样要求的汇票时,应在"pay to the order of"之后的栏目中打上"ABC Banking group LTD. 120 Wall Street, New York, USA"。但是,对限制在国外银行议付的来证,受益人往往要仔细考虑是否办得到,这意味着受益人要把全套制作好的单据交到在美国的一家银行,从那里取得货款。对于这种限制在国外议付的信用证,我方不主张接受。

例如,来证规定:"by negotiation against the documents detailed herein and beneficiary's drafts at 30 days after sight with any bank in beneficiary's country",此证不限制议付行,不限制受款人,可在受益人所在国家的任何银行议付。收款人可以在自己的国家里选择任何一个合适的银行作为受款人或议付行。在填写这样要求的汇票时,应在此栏目中直接填入选择好的银行名称、地址。如选择在中国银行杭州分行议付,则在此栏目中打上"BANK OF CHINA, HANGZHOU BRANCH"。

本案的填写:BANGK OF CHINA, SUZHOU BRANCH,CHINA

11. **付款人**（payer）

在信用证方式下,应按照信用证的规定,以开证行或其指定的付款行为付款人。倘若信用证中未指定付款人,应填写开证行。

本案的填写:CITY NATIONAL BANK, NEW YORK

12. **出票人**（drawer）

虽然汇票上没有出票人栏,但习惯上在右下角空白处盖上出票人全称印章和负责人的手签印章。出票人一般为出口公司。

本案的填写:SUZHOU TAISHAN SUITCASE & BAG CO., LTD.

　　　　　　张奇

汇票在没有特殊规定时,都打两张,一式两份。汇票一般都在醒目的位置上印着"1""2"字样,表示第一联和第二联。汇票的第一联和第二联在法律效力上无区别。第一联生效则第二联自动作废,第二联生效则第一联自动作废,即"付一不付二,付二不付一"。

制作好的汇票如下：

		BILL OF EXCHANGE			
凭 Drawn Under	CITY NATIONAL BANK NEW YORK, U.S.A		不可撤销信用证 Irrevocable L/C No.		N5632405TH11808
日期 Date	JUL. 15,2009	支 取 Payable with interest		@ ％ 按 息 付 款	
号码 No.	TSI0801005	汇票金额 Exchange for	USD 22 422.00	苏州 SuZhou	AUG. 27,2009
	见票 at	＊＊＊＊＊＊	日后（本汇票之副本未付）付交 Sight of this FIRST of Exchange(Second of Exchange being		
	unpaid) pay to the order of		BANK OFCHINA, SUZHOU BRANCH, CHINA		
金额 the sum of		U.S DOLLARS TWENTY TWO THOUSAND FOUR HUNDRED AND TWENTY TWO ONLY			
此致 to		CITY NATIONAL BANK, NEW YORK	SUZHOUTAISHAN SUITCASE & BAG CO., LTD. 张奇		

必备知识

一、汇票的含义

《中华人民共和国票据法》对汇票的定义："汇票是出票人签发的，委托付款人在见票时或在指定日期无条件支付确定的金额给收款人或其指定人或持票人的票据。"

《英国票据法》对汇票的定义："汇票是由一人签发给另一人的无条件书面命令，要求受票人见票时或于未来某一规定的或可以确定的时间，将一定金额的款项支付给某一特定的人或其指定人或持票人。"

二、汇票的种类

1. 按照出票人的不同，汇票可分为银行汇票和商业汇票

银行汇票的出票人是银行，商业汇票的出票人是工商企业或个人。在国际结算中，商业汇票通常是由出口商开立，向国外进口商或银行收取货款时使用的汇票。

2. 按照付款时间的不同，汇票可分为即期汇票和远期汇票

见票即付的是即期汇票，将来某一时间付款的是远期汇票。远期汇票的付款日期有记载方法,主要有:①规定某一个特定日期,即定日付款;②付款人见票后若干天;③出票日后若干天;④运输单据日后若干天,其中,较多用"提单日期后若干天"。

3. 按照承兑人的不同,汇票可分为商业承兑汇票和银行承兑汇票

商业承兑汇票是由工商企业或个人承兑的远期汇票,它是建立在商业信用的基础之上,其出票人也是工商企业或个人。

银行承兑汇票是由银行承兑的远期商业汇票,它通常由出口人签发,银行对汇票承兑后即成为该汇票的主债务人,而出票人则成为次债务人。因此银行承兑汇票是建立在银行信用的基础之上。

4. 按照是否附有货运单据,汇票可分为光票和跟单汇票

光票是指不附带货运单据的汇票。光票的流通全靠出票人、付款人或出让人(背书人)的信用。在国际结算中,光票除少量用于货款结算外,一般仅限于贸易从属费用、货款尾数、佣金等的托收或支付时使用。

跟单汇票是指附有货运单据的汇票。跟单汇票的付款以附交货运单据为条件,付款人要取得货运单据提取货物,必须付清货款或提供一定的担保。跟单汇票体现了钱款与单据对流的原则,对进出口双方提供了一定的安全保证。在国际结算中,大都采用跟单汇票作为结算工具。

三、汇票的使用

汇票的使用随汇票是即期还是远期而有所不同。即期汇票只须经过出票、提示和付款。

远期汇票需经过承兑手续,如需流通转让,通常要经过背书。汇票遭到拒付时,还要涉及作成拒绝证明,依法行使追索权等法律问题。

1. 出票

出票是指出票人签发票据并将其交付给收款人的票据行为。出票由两个动作组成:一是由出票人写成汇票,并在汇票上签字;二是由出票人将汇票交付给收款人。由于出票是设立债权债务的行为,因此,只有经过交付汇票才开始生效。

2. 提示

提示是指收款人或持票人将汇票提交付款人要求付款或承兑的行为。提示可分为提示承兑和提示付款。提示承兑是指远期汇票持票人向付款人出示汇票,并要求付款人承诺付款的行为。提示付款是指汇票的持票人向付款人(或远期汇票的承兑人)出示汇票要求付款人(或承兑人)付款的行为。

3. 承兑

承兑是指汇票付款人承诺在汇票到期日支付汇票金额的票据行为。汇票一经承兑,付款人就成为汇票的承兑人,并成为汇票的主债务人,而出票人便成为汇票的次债务人。

4. 付款

付款是指付款人向持票人支付汇票金额的行为。即期汇票在付款人见票时照付;远期汇票于到期日在持票人作提示付款时由付款人付款。汇票一经付款,汇票上的一切债权债务即告结束。

5. 背书

背书是一种以转让票据权利为目的的行为。背书通常由持票人在汇票的背面或粘单上签上

自己的名字,或者再加上受让人即被背书人的名称,并把汇票交给受让人。汇票经过背书后,收款的权利就转让给了被背书人。

6. 拒付与追索

拒付包括拒绝付款和拒绝承兑两个内容。汇票被拒付,持票人除可向承兑人追索外,还有权向其前手,包括所有的背书人和出票人行使追索权。持票人进行追索时,应将拒付事实书面通知其前手,并提供被拒绝承兑或被拒绝付款的证明或退票理由。持票人不能出示拒绝证明、退票理由书的,丧失对其前手的追索权。追索的金额包括被拒付的汇票金额和自到期日或提示付款日起至清偿日至的利息,以及取得拒绝证书和向前手发出被拒绝通知的费用。

拓展知识

ISBP681关于汇票的条款是第43~56条,主要是关于票期和到期日的计算。

ISBP681第43条规定,汇票票期必须与信用证条款一致。值得注意的是,第43条d款规定:根据UCP600第3条的指引,当使用"从一起"(from)和"在……之后"(after)来确定汇票到期日时,到期日的计算从单据日期、装运日期或其他事件的次日起算,也就是说从3月1日起10日或3月1日后10日均为3月11日。

技能训练

训练项目一

(一)训练资料

任务三中技能训练的资料。

(二)制作汇票

凭
Drawn under _____

号码 汇票金额 上海 20
No. _____ Exchange for _____ SHANGHAI _____ , 20 ____

见票 _____ 日后(本汇票之正本未付)付交 分行
At _____ sight of this FIRST of Exchange (Second of Exchange being unpaid) Pay to the order of _____

金额
the sum of _____

_____

款已收讫
Value received

此致:
　To _____
　　　_____

训练项目二

(一)训练资料

```
L/C NO. 03/1234-B/128 DATED JUN. 2,2010
FROM: COMMERCIAL BANK OF KUWAIT
ADVISING BANK: BANK OFCHINA, HANGZHOU
APPLICANT: NEAMAGENRAL TRADING & CONTRACTING EST. KUWAIT
AMOUNT: USD 20 060.00
BENEFICIARY: ZHEJIANG CHEMICALS IMPORT & EXPORT CORPORATION
WE OPEN THIS IRREVOCABLE DOCUMENTARY CREDIT FAVOURING
YOURSELVES FOR 97% OF THE INVOICE VALUE AVAILABLE AGAINST
YOUR DRAFT AT SIGHT BY NEGOTIATION WITH ADVISING BANK ON US.
QUANTITY OF GOODS: 1 000KGS NET
UNIT PRICE: USD 20.00 PER KGS CIFC3KUWAIT
INVOICE NO. : 12469
```

(二)根据以上资料制作汇票

凭
Drawn under _____

号码   汇票金额   上海   20
No. _____ Exchange for _____ SHANGHAI _____ , 20 ____

见票 _____ 日后(本汇票之正本未付)付交   分行
At _____ sight of this FIRST of Exchange (Second of Exchange being unpaid) Pay to the order of _____

金额
the sum of _____
_____

款已收讫
Value received
此致:
　　To _____

任务十一　审核出口单据

学习目标

能力目标

能够根据信用证和信用证项下的单据，准确快速地找出单据中存在的不符点

知识目标

掌握审单原则，熟悉审单方法，熟悉常见的单据不符点

任务设计

以下是信用证以及根据信用证制作的全套单据。

1. 信用证

APPLICATION HEADER 0 700 1546 080404BOTKJPJTCXXX 0135 526592 080404 1447N

       ＊BANK OF TOKYO－MITSUBISHI UFJ，LTD.，
       ＊THE
       ＊TOKYO
       ＊（HEAD OFFICE）

SEQUENCE OF TOTAL	27：	1/1
FORM OF DOC CREDIT	40A：	IRREVOCABLE
DOC. CREDIT NUMBER	20：	41－3894858－150
DATE OF ISSUE	31C：	080404
APPLICABLE RULES	40E：	UCP URR LATEST VERSION
EXPIRY	31D：	080505 CHINA
APPLICANT	50：	RIO YOKOYAMA CO.，LTD.
		15－27，HEIWA 1－CHOME，NAKA－KU，
		NAGOYA，JAPAN
BENEFICIARY	59：	QINGDAO XINDONG INT'L TRADING
		CO.，LTD. 604，GUANGDONG DEVELOPMENT
		BANK BLDG NO. 40 SHANDONG ROAD，
		QINGDAO，CHINA
AMOUNT	32B：	USD16 904.00
POS/NEG. TOL（％）	39A：	5/5
AVAILABLE WITH/BY	41D：	ANY BANK ON SIGHT BASIS
		BY NEGOTIATION
DRAFTS AT	42C：	AT SIGHT
DRAWEE	42D：	BANK OF TOKYO－MITSUBISHI UFJ，LTD.，
		NEW YORK 1251 AVENUE OF THE AMERICAS
		NEW YORK，NY 10020－1104 USA
PARTIAL SHIPMENTS	43P：	NOT ALLOWED

TRANSHIPMENT	43T:	PROHIBITED
AIRPORT OF DEPARTURE	44E:	CHINA
AIRPORT OF DESTINATION	44F:	NEGOYA
SHIPMENT PERIOD	44D:	080420

DESCRIP. OF GOODS 45A:
```
075120-87    PARKA       1 520PCS
075121-87    TANK TOP    2 000PCS
075122-87    TANK TOP    1 600PCS
```
CPT NAGOYA, TOLERANCE MINUS 5% OF QUANTITYACCEPTABLE

DOCUMENTS REQUIRED 46A:
+ SIGNED COMMERCIAL INVOICE IN 4 COPIES INDICATING CREDIT NO.
+ AIRWAY BILL MADE OUT TO ORDER OF APPLICANT MARKED FREIGHT PREPAID, NOTIFY APPLICANT.
+ PRESHIPMENT INSPECTION CERTIFICATE ISSUED BY APPLICANT IN ONE ORIGINAL.
+ PACKING LIST IN ONE ORIGINAL CERTIFYING PACKING IN EXPORT STANDARD SEA WORTHY.
+ WEIGHT LIST IN ONE ORIGINAL.
+ BENEFICIARY'S CERTIFICATE CERTIFYING THAT EACH ONE COPY OF AIRWAY BILL, INVOICE AND PRESHIPMENT INSPECTION CERTIFICATE HAVE BEEN SENT TO THE APPLICANT DIRECTLY WITHIN 2 DAYS AFTER SHIPMENT DATE BY DHL.

ADDITIONAL CONDITION 47A:
+ T/T REIMBURSEMENT IS NOT ACCEPTABLE.
+ THIS L/C IS NOT TRANSFERABLE.
+ INSURANCE TO BE EFFECTED BY APPLICANT.
+ DOCUMENTS ISSUEDPRIOR TO THE L/C ISSUING DATE ARE NOT ACCEPTABLE.
+ DETAILS OF SHIPMENT UNDER THIS L/C MUST BE ADVISED TO APPLICANT BY FAX WITHIN 2 DAYS AFTER SHIPMENT DATE. A COPY OF SUCH ADVICE MUST ACCOMPANY THE ORIGINAL DOCUMENTS.
+ BENEFICIARY'S CERTIFICATE CONFIRMING THEIR ACCEPTANCE OR NON-ACCEPTANCE OF THE AMENDMENT(S)ISSUED UNDER THIS CREDIT QUOTING THE RELAVANT AMENDMENT NUMBER, SUCH CERTIFICATE IS NOT REQUIRED IF NO AMENDMENT HAS BEEN ISSUED UNDER THIS CREDIT.

DATAILS OF CHARGES 71B: ALL BANKING CHARGES OUTSIDE JAPAN ARE FOR ACCOUNT OF BENEFICIARY.

PRESENTATION PERIOD 48: DOCUMENTS MUST BE PRESENTED WITHIN

		15 DAYS AFTER THE DATE OF SHIPMENT BUT WITHIN THE CREDIT EXPIRY.
CONFIRMATION	49:	WITHOUT
REIMBURSING BANK	53D:	BANK OF TOKYO-MITSUBISHI UFJ, LTD. , NEW YORK 1251 AVENUE OF THE AMERICAS NEW YORK, NY 10020—1104 USA.
INSTRUCTIONS	78:	FORWARD RELATIVE SHIPPING DOCUMENTS TO US, OUR ADDRESS: 21－24, NISHIKI 3-CHOME, NAKA-KU, NAGOYA 460－8660, JAPAN, IN ONE LOT BY COURIER SERVICE.
		THE NEGOTIATING BANK IS AUTHORIZED TO CLAIM REIMBURSEMENT FROM THE ABOVE REIMBURSING BANK.
		PLEASE CLAIM REIMBURSEMENT DEDUCTING A DISCREPANCY FEE OF USD45.00 IF DOCUMENTS CONTAINING DISCREPANCIES ARE PRESENTED TO YOU UNDER THIS CEEDIT.
ADVISE THROUGH	57D:	BANK OF CHINA SHANDONG BRANCH NO.37 HONGKONG MIDDLE ROAD, QINGDAO, CHINA

2. 信用证项下的单据
(1)汇票。

DRAFT

DRAWN UNDER BANK OF TOKYO—MITSUBISHI UFJ, LTD. , TOKYO, JAPAN

L/C NO.: 41－3894858－150   DATED APR.4,2008   PAYABLE WITH INTEREST
_____% PER ANNUM

NO.: PJL080426 EXCHANGE FOR USD16 575.00 QINGDAO CHINA MAY. 4, 2008

AT SIGHT OF THIS FIRST OF EXCHANGE(SECOND OF THE SAME TENOR AND DATE UNPAID) PAY TO THE ORDER OF OURSELVES THE SUM OF U.S DOLLARS SIXTEEN

THOUSAND FIVE HUNDRED AND SEVENTY FIVE ONLY.

TO: BANK OF TOKYO—MITSUBISHI JUF, LTD.
NEW YORK 1251 AVENUE OF THE AMERICAS
NEW YORK, NY 10020－1104 USA

　　　　　　　　　　　QINGDAO XINGDONG INT'L TRADING CO. , LTD.

　　　　　　　　　　　　　　　　　　　金永男

(2) 发票。

EXPORTER(NAME,ADDRESS) QINGDAO XINDONG INT'L TRADING CO., LTD. 604,GUANGDONG DEVELOPMENT BANK BLDG NO.40. SHANDONG ROAD, QINGDAO CHINA	青岛新东国际贸易有限公司 QINGDAO XINDONG INT'L TRADING CO., LTD. 发 票	
TO:RIO YOKOYAMA CO.,LTD. 15—27,HEIWA 1—CHOME, NAKA—KU, NAGOYA,JAPAN		
ISSUED BY(BANK AND BRANCH)	INVOICE NO.:PJL080426	DATE:APR. 3,2008
	YOUR ORDER NO.	OUR ORDER NO.
	DOCUMENTARY CREDIT NO. 41—3894858—150	
VESSEL/AIRCRAFT:MU743	COUNTRY OF ORIGIN OF GOODS CHINA	
FROM QINGDAO CHINA TO NAGO-YA JAPAN	TERMS OF DELIVERY AND PAYMENT CPT NAGOYA	
MARKS AND NUMBERS	NO. AND KIND OF PKGS QUANTITY UNIT PRICE AMOUNT DESCRIPTION OF GOODS	
N/M	075120—87 PARKA 1 500PCS 5.20 7 800.00 075121—87 TANK TOP 2 010PCS 2.50 5 025.00 075122—87 TANK TOP 1 500PCS 2.50 3 750.00 INCLUDING A SET OF FREE ADVERTISINA TOTAL: 5 010PCS 16 575.00 AND PROMOTION MATERIAL

QINGDAO XINDONG INT'L TRADING CO., LTD. 金永男 | |

(3)装箱单和重量单。

PACKING LIST AND WEIGHT LIST
INVOICE NO. PJL080426

DOCUMENTARY CREDIT NO. 41-3894858-150

MARKS	ART NO. AND QUNATITY OF THE GOODS	N.W. (TOTAL)	G.W. (TOTAL)
N/M	075120-87 PARKA 26CTNS 075121-87 TANK TOP 1CTNS 075122-87 TANK TOP 4CTNS WE CERTIFY THAT GOODS PACKING IN EXPORT STANDARD SEA WORTHY.	497KGS 10KGS 40KGS	529KGS 11KGS 44KGS
	TOTAL PACKEDIN 31CTNS	547KGS	584KGS

(4)装船前检验证明。

RIO YOKOYAMA CO., LTD.
15-27, HEIWA 1-CHOME, NAKA-KU

OSKAK, JAPAN

TO: QINGDAO XINDONG INT'L TRADING CO., LTD.　　　　DATE: APR. 22,2008

GOODS UNER LC NO. 41-3894858-150

WE HEREBY CERTIFY THAT INSPECTION TOOK PLACE ON APR. 22,2008 AND GOODS MEET OUR REQUIREMENT IN PERFECT CONDITION.

YOURS FAITHFULLY,
SIGNED BY
MR. *JOHNSON SUKI*

(5)空运单。

AIRWAY BILL

AIRPORT OF DEPARTURE QINGDAO,CHINA	AIRPORT OF DESTINATION NAGOYA,JAPAN	MASTER AIR WAYBILL NUMBER 781-5562-7924	AIR WAYBILL NUMBER QDXD28042492
FLIGHT/DATE (FOR CARRIER USE ONLY) MU743 / APR. 20, 2008.			

ROUTING AND DESTINATION						NOT NEGOTIABLE AIRWAYBILL (AIR CONSIGNMENT NOTE) ***XINDONG AIR-FREIGHT CO., LTD.*** MEMBER OF FIATA
TO 1ST	BY FIRST CARRIER	TO	BY	TO	BY	COPIES 1, 2 AND 3 OF THIS AIR WAY-BILL ARE ORIGINALS AND HAVE THE SAME VALIDITY.

CONSIGNEE'S A/C NUMBER. 00001	CONSIGNEE'S NAME	THIS AIRWAY BILL IS SUBJECT TO THE CONDITIONS OF CONTRACT ON THE REVERSE HEREOF THE SHIPPER'S ATTENTION IS DRAWN TO THE NOTICE CONCERNING CARRIERS' LIMITATION OF LIABILIY. SHIPPER MAY INCREASE SUCH LIMITATION OF LIABILITY BY DECLARING A HIGHER VALUE FOR CARRIAGE AND PAYING A SUPPLEMENTAL CHARGE IF REQUIRED GOODS HAVE BEEN ACCEPTED FOR CARRIAGE.
TO RIO YOKOYAMA CO., LTD.		
NOTIFY PARTY: RIO YOKOYAMA CO., LTD. 15-27,HEIWA 1-CHOME NAKA-KU NAGOYA,JAPAN		
SHIPPER'S A/C NUMBER 0002	SHIPPER'S NAME AND ADDRESS	
QINGDAO XINDONGINT'L TRADING CO., LTD. 604,GUANGDONG DEVELOPMENT BANK BLDG NO. 40 SHANDONG ROAD, QINGDAO,CHINA		

CURRENCY USD	WT/VL		OTHER		DECLARED VALUE NVD	DECLARED VALUE FOR CUSTOMS	AMT OF INSURENCE	INSURANCE= IF CARRIER OFFERS INSURANCE & SUCH INSURANCE IS REQUESTED IN ACCORDANCE WITH CONDITIONS ON REVERSE HEREOF.
	PD	CL	PD	CL				
NO. OF PKGS	ACTUAL G. W.				CHARGE-ABLE WEIGHT	RATE	WEIGHT CHARGE	NATURE AND QUANTITY OF GOODS INCLUDING DIMENSIONS OR VOLUME

31CTNS (584KGS)		584KGS	KQ	AS ARRANGED	3.18CBM 075120-87 PARKA 075121-87 TANK TOP 075122-87 TANK TOP LC NO. 41-3894858-150 FREIGHT PREPAID GOODS DESPATCHED ON APR 21, 2008 ON FLIGHT NO. MU743
SPECIAL HANDLING INFORMATION INSURANCE: IF CARRIER OFFERS INSURANCE, AND SUCH INSURANCE IS REQUESTED IN ACCORDANCE WITH THE CONDITIONS THEREOF, INDICATE AMOUNT TO BE INSURED IN FIGURES IN BOX MARKED AMOUNT OF INSURANCE. PACKAGING IS NOT SUFFICIENT FOR THE AIR JOURNEY.					
P R E P A I D	WEIGHT CHGS	OTHER CHARGES		TOTAL CHARGES COLLECT:	SIGNATURE OF SHIPPER OR HIS AGENT **WILLIAM WANG** SIGNED FOR THE CARRIER EXECUTED ON APR. 20, 2008 QINGDAO,CHINA
	TAX			TOTAL CHARGES PREPAID:	

ORIGINAL 2 (FOR CONSIGNEE)

（6）受益人证明。

青岛新东国际贸易有限公司

QINGDAO XINDONG INT'L TRADING CO., LTD.

DATE: APR. 23, 2008

INVOCIE NO.: PJL080426
L/C NO.: 41-3894858-150

TO: RIO YOKOYAMA CO., LTD.
15-27, HEIWA1-CHOME,
NAKA-KU, NAGOYA, JAPAN

WE HEREBY CERTIFY THAT EACH COPY OF AIRWAY BILL, INVOCIE AND PRESHIPMENT INSPECTION CERTIFICATE HAVE BEEN SENT TO THE APPLICANT DIRECTLY WITHIN 2 DAYS AFTER SHIPMENT DATE BY DHL.

QINGDAO XINDONG INT'L TRADING CO., LTD.
金永男

(7)装船通知。

青岛新东国际贸易有限公司
QINGDAO XINDONG INT'L TRADING CO. , LTD.

SHIPMENT ADVICE

DATE:APR. 23,2008
INVOCIE NO. :PJL080426
L/C NO. :41－3894858－150

TO:RIO YOKOYAMA CO. , LTD.
15－27,HEIWA1－CHOME,
NAKA－KU,NAGOYA,JAPAN

SHIPMENT DTAILS:

GOODS:	QUANTITY:
075120－87 PARKA	26CTNS
075121－87 TANK TOP	1CTNS
075122－87 TANK TOP	4CTNS

SHIPMENT FROM QINGDAO,CHINA TO NAGOYA JAPAN
FLIGHT NO. AND DATE:ON FLIGHT NO. MU747,APR. 21,2008
VALUE OF DOCUMENTS:USD16 575.00

QINGDAO XINDONG INT'L TRADING CO. , LTD.
金永男

任务分解

1. 读懂以上信用证和所提供的单据
2. 根据以上信用证和所提供的单据,找出单据中的不符点

任务描述

审核信用证审核单据中存在的不符点即审单,是单证员必须具备的一项基本岗位技能。从技术层面看,对单证人员的专业素质要求,审单比制单更为严格。它要求单证员完全看懂信用证内容,熟悉 UCP600、ISB681 的相关条款和各种单据的制作要点,在此基础上,找出单据中同信用证、UCP600 和 ISBP681 相关条款不相符的地方。

操作示范

第一步:根据信用证条款审核商业发票

通过审核,发现商业发票中存在以下不符点:

(1)发票的出票日"APR. 3,2008"早于信用证的开证日"APR. 4,2008"。
(2)漏了开证行名称。
(3)075121－87 TANK TOP 溢装。

(4)075122-87 TANK TOP 短装。

(5)货物描述部分显示了"INCLUDING A SET OF FREE ADVERTISING AND PROMOTION MATERIAL"。

第二步：根据信用证条款、发票审核装箱单和重量单

将装箱单和重量单做成联合单据是错误的，应分开制作。

第三步：根据信用证条款、发票、装箱单、重量单审核空运单

空运单上显示的装运时间"APR.21,2008"迟于信用证规定的最迟装运期"APR.20,2008"。

第四步：根据信用证条款、发票、装箱单、重量单和空运单审核装船前检验证明

(1)申请人地址"OSAKA"错，应为"NAGOYA"。

(2)正文内容显示检验发生在"APR.22,2008"错，应发生在"APR.21,2008"或之前。

第五步：根据信用证条款、发票、装箱单、空运单审核装船通知

正文中航班号"MU747"错，应为"MU743"。

综上所述，全套结汇单据存在以下不符点：

(1)发票的出票日"APR.3,2008"早于信用证的开证日"APR.4,2008"。

(2)发票漏了开证行名称。

(3)发票上的 075121-87 TANK TOP 溢装；075122-87 TANK TOP 短装。

(4)货物描述部分显示了"INCLUDING A SET OF FREE ADVERTISING AND PROMOTION MATERIAL"，应删除。

(5)装箱单和重量单做成联合单据错误，应分开制作。

(6)空运单上显示的装运时间"APR.21,2008"迟于信用证规定的最迟装运期"APR.20,2008"。

(7)装船强检验证明中申请人地址"OSAKA"错，应为"NAGOYA"。

(8)装船强检验证明正文内容显示检验发生在"APR.22,2008"错，应发生在"APR.21,2008"或之前。

(9)装船通知正文中航班号"MU747"错，应为"MU743"。

必备知识

一、审单原则

广义的审单包括银行审单和外贸企业单证员审单。

对银行而言，在信用证结算方式下，审单的原则是单证一致和单单一致；在托收方式下，审单的原则是审核出口方提交的托收单据的种类、份数是否与托收申请书一致；在付汇结算方式下，由于单据由出口商自寄，无需银行审单。

对外贸企业单证员而言，在信用证结算方式下，审单的原则是单货一致、单证一致和单单一致；在托收方式和付汇结算方式下，审单的原则是单货一致、单同一致和单单一致。

单货一致，即单据上对货物的相关描述要同实际装运货物一致；单同一致，即各种单据要与合同条款一致；单单一致，即各种单据描述同一事项的内容要一致；单证一致，即指所提交的单据在种类、份数和内容上都要与信用证、UCP600 和 ISBP681 的相关条款相符。

二、常用单据的审核要点

1. 汇票的审核要点

(1)应有"汇票"字样。

(2)信用证规定需记载出票条款时,内容应与信用证规定相符。

(3)出票日不能迟于信用证的效期和交单期。

(4)付款人和付款地必须与信用证规定相符。

(5)开立的金额应与发票金额一致,且未超过信用证可以利用的余额。

(6)金额大小写必须一致,货币必须与信用证的币别相符。

(7)注有信用证规定的付款期限。

(8)准确计算到期日。

(9)收款人名称确定无误。

(10)载有信用证要求的条款。

(11)应由受益人出票并签字。

(12)票面不应有涂改。

2. 商业发票的审核要点

(1)必须由信用证中指定的受益人出具。

(2)除非另有规定,以申请人(买方)为抬头。

(3)标题不可以是"预开发票"、"临时发票"或类似的发票。

(4)货物描述应与信用证中引述的货物描述一致。

(5)数量应与信用证规定相符,与其他单据不矛盾。

(6)单价和总金额满足信用证的要求。

(7)唛头、运输信息、运输费用等内容与运输单据显示的不矛盾。

(8)加注的相关内容必须符合情理。

(9)信用证要求需签字、公证、认证等,应予以照办。

(10)如数提交信用证要求的正本和副本。

3. 运输单据的审核要点

(1)运输单据的种类必须与信用证规定相符。

(2)托运人、收货人和到货被通知人、装货港(地)、卸货港(地)、装运日期应符合信用证规定。

(3)货物描述符合信用证,货名可以用统称,唛头、数量、重量、规格等(如有)与其他单据所显示的一致。

(4)提单上有关运费的记载与发票和信用证的相关记载一致。

(5)除非信用证另有规定,必须提交全套正本提单。

(6)表面注明承运人的名称,由承运人、船长或其具名代理签署或以其他方式证实。

(7)装运日期不得迟于最后装运期并符合 UCP600 的规定。

(8)符合 UCP600 关于分批/分期装运和转运的规定。

(9)除非信用证另有规定,可接受简式/背面空白的提单、表明货物可能装于舱面的提单、据托运人报称的提单和发货人为第三方的提单。

(10)在其他方面符合国际惯例和信用证规定。

4. 保险单据的审核要点

(1)根据信用证的要求提交相应的保险单据。

(2)由保险公司、承保人或其代理出具和签发。除非信用证另有规定,银行不接受由保险经纪人签发的暂保单。
(3)提交所出具的全套正本。
(4)被保险人符合按信用证的规定。
(5)保险日期或保险生效日期最迟为货物装船、发运或接受监管的日期。
(6)承保金额按信用证规定。
(7)除非信用证允许,应使用与信用证相同的货币开立。
(8)承保信用证规定的险别。
(9)信用证要求保险单时,不得以保险凭证代替,反之则可以。

5. 包装单据的审核要点
(1)应单独出具,不可与其他单据联合。
(2)内容应符合信用证的要求,并与其他相关单据不矛盾。
(3)出具日期与其他单据不抵触。
(4)通常无需签字。

6. 产地证的审核要点
(1)应由信用证中指定的机构出具。
(2)内容必须与信用证及其他单据的相关内容一致。
(3)应注明货物的原产地。
(4)需注明日期。
(5)根据信用证的要求签字、公证、认证或签证。

7. 检验证书的审核要点
(1)应由信用证规定的检验机构出具并签发。
(2)内容必须与发票或其他单据的记载保持一致,并符合信用证的规定。
(3)检验证书上的发货人和收货人应正确填写。
(4)签发日期最好不迟于提单日期。
(5)需签字。

8. 证明书的审核要点
(1)证明书内容要符合信用证的要求。
(2)要表明是信用证下的单据,并且与其他单据相关联。
(3)一般情况下应注明出具日期。
(4)由出具人签字。

拓展知识

UCP600 第 14 条"单据审核标准"对相符单据的确定原则、银行的审单期限、受益人递交单据的期限等均有明确的规定,具体内容可以参考 UCP600。

 技能训练

(一)训练资料
1. 信用证
MT 700　　　　　　　　ISSUE OF A DOCUMENTARY CREDIT
SENDER　　　　　　　 HSBC BANK PLC,DUBAI,U. A. E.
RECEIVER　　　　　　 NANTNG CITY COMM2ERCIAL BANK, NANTONG, CHINA

SEQUENCE OF TOTAL	27: 1/1
FORM OF DOC. CREDIT	40A: IRREVOCABLE
DOC. CREDIT NUMBER	20: NNN07699
DATE OF ISSUE	31C: 080225
APPLICABLE RUELE	40E: UCP LATEST VERSION
DATE AND PALCE OF EXPIRY	31D: DATE 080510 PLACE IN CHINA
APPLICANT	50: SIK TRADING CO. ,LTD. 16 TOM STREET, DUBAI, U. A. E.
BENEFICIARY	59: NANTONG JINYUAN IMPORT & EXPORT CO. , LTD. 118XUEYAN STREET, NANTONG, JIANGSU CHINA
AMOUNT	32B: CURRENCY USD AMOUNT 54 000.00
AVAILABLE WITH/BY	41D: ANY BANK IN CHINA BY NEGOTIATION
DRAFTS AT	42C: 30 DAYS AFTER SIGHT
DRAWEE	42A: HSBC BANK PLC, NEW YORK
PARTIAL SHIPMENT	43P: PROHIBITED
TRANSSHIPMENT	43T: ALLOWED
PORT OF LOADING/ AIRPORT OF DEPARTURE	44E: CHINESE MAIN PORT
PORT OF DISCHARGE	44F: DUBAI, U. A. E.
LATEST DATE OF SHIPMENT	44C: 080425
DESCRIP OF GOODS AND /OR SERVICES	45A: 4500 PIECES OF LADIES JACKET, SHELL: WOVEN TWILL 100% COTTON, LINING: WOVEN 100% POLYESTER, ORDER NO. SIK768, AS PEER S/C NO. NTJY0739

STYLE NO.	QUANTITY	UNIT PRICE	AMOUNT
L357	2 250PCS	USD12.00/PCS	USD27 000.00
L358	2 250PCS	USD12.00/PCS	USD27 000.00

AT CIFDUBAI, U. A. E.

DOCUMENTS REQUIRED	46A: + SIGNED COMMERCIAL INVOICE IN TRIPLICATE. +PACKING LIST IN TRIPLICATE. +CERTIFICATE OF CHINESE ORIGIN CERTIFIED BY CHAMBER OF COMMERCE OR CCPIT. +FULL SET (3/3) OF CLEAN "ON BOARD" OCEAN BILLS OF LADING MADE OUT TO ORDER MARKED FREIGHT PREPAID AND NOTIFY APPLICANT. +ISURANCE POLICY/CERTIFICATE IN DUPLICATE

	ENDORSED IN BLANK FOR 110% INVOICE VALUE, COVERING ALL RISKS OF CIC OF PICC(1/1/1981)INCL WAREHOUSE AND I.O.P. AND SHOWING THE CLAIMING CURRENCY IS THE SAME AS THE CURRENCY OF CREDIT.
	+ SHIPPING ADVICE SHOWING THE NAME OF THE CARRYING VESSEL, DATE OF SHIPMENT, MARKS, QUANTITY, NET WEIGHT AND GROSS WEIGHT OF THE SHIPMENT TO APPLICANT WITHIN 3 DAYS AFTER THE DATE OF BILL OF LADING.
ADDITIONAL CONDITION	47A:
	+ DOCUMENTS DATED PRIOR TO THE DATE OF THIS CREDIT ARE NOT ACCEPTABLE.
	+ THE NUMBER AND THE DATE OF THIS CREDIT AND THE NAME OF ISSUING BANK MUST BE QUOTED ON ALL DOCUMENTS.
	+ MORE OR LESS 5 PCT OF QUANTITY OF GOODS IS ALLOWED.
	+ TRANSSHIPMENT ALLOWED AT HONGKONG ONLY.
	+ SHORT FORM / CHARTER PARTY / THIRD PARTY BILL OF LADING ARE NOT ACCEPTABLE.
	+ SHIPMENT MUST BE EFFECTED BY 1×40' FULL CONTAINER LOAD. B/L TO SHOW EVIDENCER OF THIS EFFECT IS REQUIRED.
	+ THE GOODS SHIPPED ARE NEITHER ISRAELI ORIGIN NOR DO THEY CONTAIN ISRAELI MATERIALS NOR ARE THEY EXPORTED FROM ISRAEL, BENEFICIARY'S CERTIFICATE TO THIS EFFECT IS REQUIRED.
	+ ALL PRESENTATIONS CONTAINING DISCREPANCIES WILL ATTRACT A DISCREPANCY FEE OF USD60.00 PLUS TELEX COSTS OR OTHER CURRENCY EQUIVALENT. THIS CHARGE WILL BE DEDUCTED FROM THE BILL AMOUNT WHETHER OR NOT WE ELECT TO CONSULT THE APPLICANT FOR A WAIVER.
CHARGES	71B: ALL CHARGES AND COMMISSIONS OUTSIDE U.A.E. ARE FOR ACCOUNT OF BENEFICIARY EXCLUDING REIMBURSING FEE.
PERIOD FOR	48: WITHIN 15 DAYS AFTER THE DATE OF SHIP-

	MENT, BUT WITHIN THE VALIDITY OF THIS CREDIT.
CONFIRMATION INSTRUCTION	49: WITHOUT
REIMBURSING BANK	53A: HSBC BANK PLC, NEW YORK
INFORMATION TO PRESENTING BANK	78: ALL DOCUMENTS ARE TO BE REMITTED IN ONELOT BY COURIER TO HSBC BANK PLC, TRADE SERVICES, DUBAI BRANCH, P O BOX 66, HSBC BANK BULIDING 312/45 A1 SUQARE ROAD, DUBAI, U.A.E.

2. 信用证项下的单据

(1) 商业发票。

NANTONG JINYUAN IMPORT & EXPORT CO., LTD.
118 XUEYAN STREET, NANTONG, JIANGSU CHINA
COMMERCIAL INVOCIE

To:	SIL TRADING CO., LTD. 16 TOM STREET, DUBAI, U.A.E.		Invoice No.	NT08018
			Invoice Date	APR. 11, 2008
			S/C No.	NTJY0739
			S/C Date	FEB. 15, 2008
From	SHANGHAI, CHINA	To	DUBAI, U.A.E.	
L/C No.	NNN07699	Issued By	HSBC BANK PLC, DUBAI, U.A.E.	
Date of Issue	FEB. 25, 2008			
Marks and Numbers	Number and Kind of Pkgs Description of Goods	Qty (PCS)	Unit Price	Amount
SIK NTJY0739 L357/L358 DUBAI, U.A.E. C/NO.:1-502	LADIES JACKET SHELL: WOVEN TWILL 100% COTTON, LINING: WOVEN 100% POLYESTER, ORDER NO. SIK768 STYLE NO. L357 STYLE NO. L358 PACKED IN 9 PCS/CTN. TOTALLY FIVE HUNDRED AND TWO CARTONS ONLY.	2 250 2 268	CIF DUBAI, U.A.E. USD12.00 USD12.00	USD 27 000.00 USD 27 216.00
	TOTAL:	4 518		USD54 216.00

SAY TOTAL	U. S DOLLARS FIFTY FOUR THOUSAND TWO HUNDRED AND SIXTY ONLY.
	NANTONG JINYUAN IMPORT & EXPORT CO. ,LTD. 王立

(2)装箱单。

NANTONG JINYUAN IMPORT & EXPORT CO., LTD.
118 XUEYAN STREET, NANTONG, JIANGSU CHINA
PACKING LIST

To:	SIL TRADING CO. , LTD. 16 TOM STREET, DUBAI, U. A. E.	Invoice No.	NT08018
		Invocie Date	APR. 11,2008
		S/C No.	NTJY0739
		S/C Date	FEB. 15,2008

From	SHANGHAI,CHINA	To	DUBAI,U. A. E.			
Marks and Numbers	Number and Kind of Pkg Description of Goods	Quantity (PCS)	Package CTNS	G. W KGS	N. W KGS	MEAS. M3
SIK NTJY0739 L357/L358 DUBAI, U. A. E. C/NO. :1—502	LADIES JACKET STYLE NO. L357 STYLE NO. L358 PACKED IN 9 PCS/CTN. SHIPPED IN 1×40'FCL	2 250 2 268	250 252	2 500 2 520	2 250 2 268	29.363 29.597
	TOTAL:	4 518	502	5 020	4 518	58.96
SAY TOTAL	SAY FIVE HUNDRED AND TWO CARTONS ONLY.					

(3)一般原产地证。

ORIGINAL	
1. Exporter	Cerfiticate No. CCPIT051921964

NANTONG JINYUAN IMPORT & EXPORT CO., LTD. 118 XUEYAN STREET, NANTONG, JIANGSU CHINA 2. Consignee SIK TRADINGCO., LTD. 16 TOM STREET, DUBAI, U. A. E.	CERTIFICATE OF ORIGIN OF THE PEOPLE'S REPUBILC OF CHINA
3. Means of transport and route SHIPPED FROMSHANGHAI TO DUBAI, U. A. E. BY SEA 4. Country/ region of destination U. A. E.	5. For certifying authority use only

6. Marks and Numbers	7. Number and Kind of Pkgs Description of Goods	8. H. S. Code	9. Quantity	10. Number and Date of Invoice
SIK NTJY0739 L357/L358 DUBAI, U. A. E. C/NO.:1—502	FIVE HUNDRED AND TWO (502) CARTONS OF LADIES JACKETS AS PER L/C NO. NNN07699 L/C DATE: FEB. 25, 2008 NAME OF ISSUINGBANK: HSBC BANK PLC, DUBAI, U. A. E.	6204320090	4 518PCS	NT08018 APR. 11, 2008

11. Declaration by the exporter	12. Certification
The undersigned hereby declares that the above details and statements are correct, that all the goods were produced in China and that they comply with the Rules of Origin of the People's Republic of China. NANTONG JINYUAN IMPORT & EXPORT CO., LTD. 李 立	It is certified that the declaration by the exporter is correct. CHINA COUNTIL FOR THE PROMOTION OF INTERNATIONAL TRADE (NANTONG) 江通海
NANTONG APR. 11, 2008	NANTONG, APR. 11, 2008
Place and date, signature and stamp of authorized signature	Place and date, signature and stamp of certifying authority

(4) 海运提单。

Shipper Insert Name, Address and Phone			B/L NO. 2651 中远集装箱运输 有限公司 COSCO CONTAINER LINES TLX:33057 COSCO CN FAX:0086(021)6545 8984 **ORIGINAL** Port-to-Port **BILL OF LADING** Shipped on board and condition except as other...	
NANTONG JINYUAN IMPORT&EXPORT, CO.,LTD. 118 XUEYAN STREET, NANTONG, JIANGSU CHINA				
Consignee Insert Name, Address and Phone				
TO ORDER				
Notify Party Insert Name, Address and Phone				
SIK TRADINGCO.,LTD. 16 TOM STREET, DUBAI, U.A.E.				
Ocean Vessel Voy, No.		Port of Loading		
QING YUN HE, VOY. NO.1325		SHANGHAI		
Port of Discharge		Port of Destination		
DUBAI, U.A.E				
Marks & Numbers. Container/ Seal No.	No. of Containers or Package	Description of Goods	G.W	Means.
SIK NTJY0739 L357/L358 DUBAI,U.A.E. C/NO.:1—502	502CARONGS 1×40'FCL	LADIES JACKET L/C NO. NNN07699 DATE:FEB.28,2008 NAME OF ISSUING BANK HSBC BANK PLC,DUBAI U.A.E	4 518KGS FREIGHT COLLECT	58.96M3
Description of contents for shipper's use only(Not Part of This B/L Contract)				
Total Number of containers and /or packages(in words): FIVE HUNDRED AND TWO CARTONS ONLY.				
Ex Rate:	Prepaid at	Payable at	Place and date of issue	
	SHANGHAI		SHANGHAI APR.17,2008	
	Total Prepaid	No. of original B/L	Signed for the carrier	
		THREE(3)	COSCO CONTAINER LINES 张一	

(5)保险单。

中国大地财产保险股份有限公司
China Contient Property & Casualty Insurance Company Ltd.

货物运输保险单
CARGO TRANSPORTATION INSURANCE POLICY

发票号(INVOICE NO.) NT08018　　　保单号次(POLICY NO.) BJ123456
合同号(CONTRACT NO.) NTJY0739
信用证号(L/C NO.) NNN07699
被保险人(INSURED) NANTONG JINYUAN IMPORT & EXPORT CO., LTD.

中国大地财产保险股份有限公司(以下简称本公司)根据被保险人的要求,由被保险人向本公司缴付约定的保险费,按照本保险单承保险别和背面所载条款与下列特款承保下述货物运输保险,特立本保险单。
THIS POLICY OF INSURANCE WITNESSES THAT CHINA CONTINENT PROPERTY & CASUALTY INSURANCE COMPANY LTD. OF CHINA (HEREIN AFTER CALLED "THE COMPANY") AT THE REQUEST OF THE INSURED AND IN CONSIDERATION OF THE AGREED PREMIUM PAID TO THE COMPANY BY THE INSUSRED, UNDERTAKES TO INSURE THE UNDERMENTIONED GOODS IN TRANSPORTATION SUBJECT TO THE CONDITIONS OF THIS POLICY AS PER THE CLAUSES PRINTED OVERLEAF AND OTHER SPECIAL CLAUSES ATTACHED HEREON.

标记 MARKS AND NUMBERS	包装及数量 QUANTITY	保险货物项目 DESCRIPTION OF GOODS	保险金额 AMOUNT INSURED
AS PER INVOCIE NO. NT08018 502CTNS		LADIES JACKET THE DATE OF L/C: FEB. 25, 2008 THE NAME OF ISSUING BANK: HSBC BANK PLC, DUBAI, U. A. E.	USD54 216.00
总保险金额 TOTAL AMOUNT INSURED:		SAY U. S. DOLLARS FIFTY FOUR THOUSAND TWO HUNDRED AND SIXTEEN ONLY.	

保费：PER-MIUM	AS ARRANGED	起运日期 DATE OF COMMENCEMENT	APR. 17, 2008	装载运输工具 PER CONVEYANCE	QING YUN HE, VOY. NO. 132S
自 FROM	SHANGHAI	经 VIA	* * *	至 TO	DUBAI, U. A. E.

承保险别 CONDITIONS
COVERING ALL RISKS OF CIC OF PICC(1/1/1981) INCL. WAREHOUSE TO WAREHOUSE AND I. O. P

所保货物，如发生保险单项下可能引起索赔的损失或损坏，应立即通知本公司下述代理人勘查。如有索赔，应向本公司提交保单正本(本保险单共有2份正本)及有关文件。如一份正本已用于索赔，其余正本自动失效。
IN THE EVENT OF LOSS OR DAMAGE WHICH MAY RESULT IN A CLAIM UNDER THIS POLICY, IMMEDIATE NOTICE MUST BE GIVEN TO THE COMPANY'S AGENT AS MENTIONED HEREUNDER. CLAIMS, IF ANY, ONE OF THE ORIGINAL POLICY WHICH HAS BEEN ISSUED IN TWO ORIGINAL(s) TOGETHER WITH THE RELEVANT DOCUMENTS SHALL BE SURRENDERED TO THE COMPANY. IF ONE OF THE ORIGINAL POLICY HAS BEEN ACCOMPLISHED, THE OTHERS TO BE VOID.

赔款偿付地点 CLAIM PAYABLE AT	DUBAI IN USD	中国大地财产保险股份有限公司 ChinaContient Property&Casualty Insurance Company Ltd. 杨菲
出单日期 ISSUE OF DATE	APR. 18, 2008	(Authorized Signature)

(6) 装运通知。

<table>
<tr><td colspan="4" align="center">NANTONG JINYUAN IMPORT & EXPORT CO., LTD.
118 XUEYAN STREET, NANTONG, JIANGSU CHINA</td></tr>
<tr><td colspan="4" align="center">SHIPPING ADVICE</td></tr>
<tr><td rowspan="5">TO:</td><td rowspan="5">SIK TRADINGCO., LTD.
16 TOM STREET,
LONDON, U.K.</td><td>ISSUE DATE:</td><td>APR. 18, 2008</td></tr>
<tr><td>S/C NO.</td><td>NTJY0739</td></tr>
<tr><td>L/C NO.</td><td>NNN07699</td></tr>
<tr><td>L/C DATE</td><td>FEB. 25, 2008</td></tr>
<tr><td>NAME OF ISSUING BANK</td><td>HSBC BANK PLC, DUBAI, U.A.E.</td></tr>
</table>

Dears Sir or Madam:

We are glad to advice you that the following mentioned goods has been shipped out, full details were shown as follows:

Invocie Number:	NT08018
Bill of Lading Number:	2651
Ocean Vessel:	QING YUN HE. VOY. NO. 132
Port of Loading:	SHANGHAI
Date of Shipment:	APR. 17, 2008
Port of Destination:	DUBAI, U.A.E.
Estimated Date of Arrival:	MAY. 4, 2008
Containers/Seals Number:	GATU8585677/3320999
Description of Goods:	LADIES JACKET
SHIPPING MARKS:	SIK NTJY0739 L357/L358 DUBAI, U.A.E. C/NO.: 1—502
QUANTITY	4 518PCS
GROSS WEIGHT:	5 020KGS
NET WEIGHT:	4 515KGS
TOTAL VALUE:	USD54 216.00

Thanks you for patronage. We look forward to the pleasure of receiving your valuable repeat orders.

Sincerely yours,

NANTONG JINYUAN IMPORT & EXPORT CO., LTD.

王立

(7)受益人证明。

NANTONG JINYUAN IMPORT & EXPORT CO., LTD.				
118 XUEYAN STREET, NANTONG, JIANGSU CHINA				
BENEFICIARY'S CERTIFICATE				
To:	WHOM IT MAY CONCERN		Invoice No.	NT08018
				Date:	APR. 17, 2008
WE HEREBY CERTIFY THAT THE GOODS SHIPPED ARE NEITHER ISRAELI ORIGIN NOR DO THEY CONTAIN ISRAELI MATERALS NOR THEY EXPORTED FROM ISRAEL. L/C NO.: NNN07699 L/C DATE: FEB. 25, 2008 NAME OF ISSUING BANK: HSBC BANKPLC, DUBAI, U. A. E. NANTONG JINYUAN IMPORT & EXPORT CO., LTD. 王立				

(8)汇票。

BILL OF EXCHANGE				
凭 Drawn Under	HSBC BANK PLC, DUBAI, U. A. E.	不可撤销信用证 Irrevocable L/C No.		NNN07699
日期 Date	FEB. 25, 2008	支取 Payable with interest	@ % 按 息 付款	
号码 No.	NT08018	汇票金额 Exchange for	USD54 216.00	南通 Nantong	APR. 21, 2008
	见票 AT	* * *	日后(本汇票之副本未付)付交 sight of this FIRST of exchange (Second of exchange		
	being unpaid) Pay to the order of		BANK OF CHINA NANTONG BRANCH	
金额 the sum of	SAY U. S. DOLLARS FIFTY FOUR THOUSAND TWO HUNDRED AND SIXTEEN ONLY.			
此致 TO	HSBC BANK PLC, NEW YORK	NANTONG JINYUAN IMPORT & EXPORT CO., LTD. 王立		

(二)请根据上述信用证和 UCP600 审核上述出口单据,找出不符点

经审核,单据中存在如下不符点:

1.
2.
3.
4.
5.

第三篇
国际贸易单证制作综合实训篇

综合实训一 汇付（电汇）方式下单据制作

一、训练资料

（一）以下是一份售货确认书及该笔业务的有关交易条件

合同号为2010LT－016项下的有关交易条件：

(1) 发票号：VVA2010－016

(2) 货物明细单：

货号	数量(PCS)	毛重(KGS)	净重(KGS)	尺码
AEJ21	9 900	28	26	37*29*46cm
AEJ31	10 800	29	27	42.5*32*40cm

(3) 提单号：DONGFENG88565609

(4) 运输工具名称：HONGXIANG

(5) 保单号：166088

(6) 装运日期：SEP. 7,2010

(7) 商品编码(H. S. CODE)：8534.1600

(8) 允许转船：不允许分批装运

(9) SHIPMENT FROM SHANGHAI TO LONDON

(10) TOTAL G. W. ：20 173KGS；TOTAL N. W. ：18 763KGS

(11) TOTAL CARTONS：725CTNS

　　 TOTAL MEASUREMENT：36.98CBM

(12) 汇入行：BANK OFCHINA，NANJING BRANCH

　　 账号：280000000000000

(13) 保险公司在伦敦的代理：

　　 The Ming An Insurance Co. ，(LONDON)LTD.

　　 International Building 10th　Floor

　　 Tel：5－87652342　　Fax：029－5－87642568

(二)销货确认书

江苏彩亮进出口公司
JIANGSU CAILIANG IMPORT & EXPORT CORPORATION
FOREIGNTRADE BUILDING, NANJING, CHINA

销货确认书　　　　　　　编号：
SALES CONFIRMATION　　NO. 2010LT-016
　　　　　　　　　　　　日期：
　　　　　　　　　　　　Date: APR. 28, 2010

买方
Buyers: EFD OF LONDON
地址
Address: 48/48A COMMERCIAL STR, LONDON

兹经买卖双方同意按下列条款成交
The undersigned Sellers and Buyers have agreed to close the following transaction according to the terms and conditions stipulated below:

货号 ART. NO.	品名及规格 Description	数量 Quantity	单价 Unit Price	金额 Amount
AEJ11 AEJ11	GOODS: POLYSTER SCHOOL BAG SIZE: 14 * 10.5 * 4 PACK: 36PCS/CTN(37 * 29 * 46mm) TOTAL: 275CTNS GOODS: POLYSTER SCHOOL BAG SIZE: 16 * 2 * 7 PACK: 24PCS/CTN(42 * 32 * 40mm) TOTAL: 450CTNS	9 900PCS 10 800PCS	CIF LONDON USD 1.10/PC USD1.10/PC ------------ TOTAL:	USD10 890.00 USD11 800.00 ------------ USD22 770.00

1. 数量及总值 5% 的增减由卖方决定
With 5% more or less both in amount and quantity allowed at the seller's option

2. 总值
Total Value: SAY US DOLLARS TWENTY-TWO THOUSAND SEVEN HUNDRED SEVENTY ONLY

3. 包装
Packing: AT SELLER'S OPTION

4. 装运期
Time of shipment: SEPTEMBER/OCTOBER, 2010

5. 装运口岸和目的地
Loading port & Destination: FROM ANY CHINESE PORT TO LONDON
Maritime transport or combined transport by land and sea will be at the seller's option

6. 保险由卖方按发票全部金额110％投保至____为止的____险

Insuance：TO BE COVERED BY THE SELLER COVERING ALL RISKS AND WAR RISK FOR 110％ OF THE INVOICE VALUE AS PER CIC.

7. 付款条件

Teams of Payment：BY T/T

8. 装运标记

Shipping Mark：EFD LTD.
     LONDON
     C/NO. 1－725
     MADE IN CHINA

9. 备注

Remarks：

    卖方   买方
   THE SELLERS   THE BUYERS
    张红   TOM

二、根据以上信息，制作下列单据

1. 发票

江苏彩亮进出口公司

JIANGSU CAILIANG IMPORT & EXPORT CORPORATION

5TH FLOOR FOREIGN TRADE BUILDING ZHANQIAN ROAD, NANJING, CHINA

INVOICE

TO：   Invoice No.：_____

             Date：_____

             S/C No.：_____

From	To		
L/C No.	Issued by		
Marks & Numbers	Quantities & Description	Unit Price	Amount

JIANGSU CAILIANG IMPORT & EXPORT CORPORATION

2. 装箱单

江苏彩亮进出口公司
JIANGSU CAILIANG IMPORT & EXPORT CORPORATION
5TH FLOOR FOREIGN TRADE BUILDING ZHANQIAN ROAD, NANJING CHINA

PACKING LIST

Number: _____

Date: _____

Total N. W. : _____

Total G. W. : _____

Total No. of Package: _____

TO:

NAME OF ARTICLE:

ARTICLE NO.	DESCRIPTION	QUANTITY	WEIGHT IN KILOS		MEASURE-MENT (CBM)
			NET@	GROSS@	

JIANGSU CAILIANG IMPORT & EXPORT CORPORATION

_____

3. 一般原产地证书

1. Goods Consigned from (Exporter's full name address and country)	CERTIICATE No. :
2. Goods Consigned to (Consignee's full name, address and country)	**CERTIFICATE OF ORIGIN OF THE PEOPLE'S REPUBLIC OF CHINA**
3. Means of Transport and Route (as far as known)	5. For Certifying Authority Use Only
4. Country/ Region of Destination	

6. Marks and Numbers of Packages	7. Number and Kind of Pkgs; Description of Goods	8. H. S. Code	9. Quantity or Weight	10. Number and Date of Invoice
11. Declaration by the exporter The undersigned hereby declares that the above details and statements are correct; that all the goods were produced in China and that they comply with the Rules of Origin of the People's Republic of China. ————————— Place and date, signature and stamp of certifying authority		12. Certification It is hereby certified that the declaration by the exporter is correct ————————— Place and date, signature and stamp of certifying authority		

4. 保险单

中 国 人 民 保 险 公 司

THE PEOPLE'S INSURANCE COMPANY OF CHINA

总公司设于北京　　　一九四九年创立

Head Office: BEIJING　　　Established in 1949

保　险　单　　　号次

INSURANCE POLICY　　　No.

中 国 人 民 保 险 公 司 （ 以 下 简 称 本 公 司 ）

This Policy of Insurance witnesses that The People's Insurance Company of China (Herein after called

根据

"the Company"), at the request of—————————————————

（以下简称被保险人） 的 要 求, 由 被 保 险 人 向 本 公 司 缴 付 约 定

(herein after called "the Insured") and in consideration of the agreed premium paid to the Company by the

的 保 险 费, 按 照 本 保 险 单 承 保 险 别 和 背 面 所 载 条 款 与 下 列

Insured, undertakes to insure theundermentioned goods in transportation subject to the conditions of this Policy

条 款 承 保 下 述 货 物 运 输 保 险, 特 立 本 保 险 单。

as per the clause printed overleaf and other special clauses attached hereon.

标　记 Marks & NoS.	包装及数量 Quantity	保险货物项目 Description of Goods	保险金额 Amount Insured
As per Invoice No.			

总保险金额：

Total Amount Insured:—————————————————

保　费　　　　　费率　　　　　装载运输工具

Premium: as arranged　　Rate　as arranged　　Per conveyance S. S.———　————

开行日期　　　　　自　　　　　至

Slg. on or abt.————————　From—————————　to—————————

承保险别

Conditions

所保货物，如遇出险，本公司凭本保险单及其他有关证件给付赔款。
Claims, if any, payable on surrender of this Policy together with other relevant documents.
所保货物，如发生本保险单项下负责赔偿的损失或事故，
In the event of accident whereby loss or damage may result in a claim under this Policy immediate notice
应立即通知本公司下述代理人查勘。
Applying for survey must be given to the Company's Agent as mentioned hereunder：

赔款偿付地点
Claim payable at ………………………

日期　　　　　　　　　　　　　　　　　　　　中国人民保险公司上海分公司
Date—————————————————— THE PEOPLE'S INSURANCE CO. OF CHINA
　　　　　　　　　　　　　　　　　　　　　　　　　　　　SHANGHAI BRANCH
地址：中国上海中山东一路23号。
Address：23Zhongshan Dong Yi Lu Shanghai, China.
Cables：42001Shanghai. ——————————————
Telex：33128 PICCS CN　　　　　　　　　　　　　　　　　　　*General Manager*

5. 提单

Shipper			B/L No.
Consignee or order			中国对外贸易运输总公司 上海　SHANGHAI 联　运　提　单 COMBINED TRANSPORT BILL OF LADING
Notify address			RECEIVER the foods in apparent good order and condition as specified below unless otherwise stated herein. THE Carrier, in accordance with the provisions contained in this document, (1) undertakes to perform or to procure the performance of the entire transport from the place at which the goods are taken in charge to the place designated for delivery in this document, and (2) assumes liability as prescribed in this document for such transport one of the bills of lading must be surrendered duty indorsed in exchange for the goods or delivery order.
Pre-carriage by	Place of receipt		
Ocean vessel	Port of loading		
Port of discharge	Place of delivery	Freight payable at	Number of original Bs/L
Marks and Numbers. Measurement(m³)	Number and kind of packages	Description of goods	Gross weight(kgs.)
Freight and charges		IN WITNESS whereof the number of original bills of lading stated above have been signed, one of which being accomplished, the other(s) to be void.	
		Place and date of issue	
		Signed for or on behalf of the carrier	

综合实训二　托收方式下单据制作

一、训练资料

(1) EXPORTER：ZHEJIANG KANGDAIMPORT & EXPORT CORPORATION
　　　　180 BAOSHAN ROAD, HANGZHOU CHINA

(2) IMPORTER：Buyers：POURQUOI M. P. S INC
　　　　　　28EI MANSHIA SQUARE P. O. BOX
　　　　　　999 PORT SAID – EGYPT

(3) S/C NO. ：2008 – JX0314；DATE：JUN. 21, 2008

(4) INVOICE NO. ：PGK2008－031　DATE：AUG. 25, 2008

(5) INVOICE AMOUNT：USD 119 700.00

(6) B/L DATE：OCT. 15, 2008

(7) REMITTING BANK：BANK OFCHINA ZHEJIANG BRANCH

二、根据以上信息，制作汇票

Drawn under
L/C No. _____ Dated _____
号码　　　　汇票金额　　　　　　　　杭州
NO. _____　Exchange for _____　　Hangzhou _____
见票_____日后(本汇票之正本未付)付交中国银行浙江省分行
At _____ sight of this FIRST of Exchange (Second of Exchange being unpaid) Pay to the order of _____
金额
the sum of _____

_____

款已收讫
Value received
此致：
　To _____
　　　_____

综合实训三 信用证方式下单据制作

一、训练资料

(一)信用证

BASIC HEADER F 01 BK CHCNBJA5×× 9828 70783
APPL: HEADER O 700 1630000731 CATHUS6LA×××1809 042841 0008010730N
　　　　　　　　　　　　　　+ CATHAY BANK, LOS ANGELES, CA, USA
(BANK NO:2504000)　　　　+LOS ANGELES, USA
MT:700ISSUE OF DOCUMENTARY CREDIT

SEQUENCE OF TOTAL	27:	1/1
FROM OF DOCUMENTARY CREDIT	40A:	IRREVOCABLE
DOCUMENTARY CREDIT NUMBER	20:	001M01413
DATE OF ISSUE	31C:	080731
APPLICANT RULE	40E:	LATEST VERSION
DATE AND PLACE OF EXPIRY	31D:	090112 CHINA
APPLICANT	50:	NEW WORLD INTERNATIONAL INC. NWIC AND A CO. 129 HAY WARD WAY SO. ELMONTE, CA 91733
BENEFICIARY	59:	SHANGHAI IMPORT & EXPORT TRADE CORPORATION PINGDU BRANCH SHANGHAI,CHINA
CURRENCYCODE, AMOUNT	32B:	USD12 500.00
AVAILABLE WITH…BY…	41D:	ANY BANK IN CHINA BY ENGOTIATION
DRAFTS AT	42C:	AT SIGHT FOR 100PCT OF INVOICE VALUE
DRAWEE	42D:	CATHAY BANK LOS ANGELES, CA.
PARTIAL SHIPMENT	43P:	NOT ALLOWED
TRANSHIPMENT	43T:	NOT ALLOWED
LOADING/DISPATCH/TAKING/FROM	44F:	SHANGHAI PORT, CHINA
FOR TRANSPORTATION TO	44F:	LOS ANGELES PORT, CA,USA
LATEST DATE OF SHIPMENT	44C:	090316
DESCRPT OF GOODS/SERVICES	45A:	COTTON BLANKT ART NO. H666 500　PCS USD 5.50/PC ART NO. HX88 500　PCS USD 4.50/PC ART NO. HE21 500　PCS USD 4.80/PC ART NO. HA56 500　PCS USD 5.20/PC

	ART NO. HH46 500 PCS USD 5.00/PC CIF MONTE
DOCUMENTS REQUIRED	46A: +COMMERCIAL INVOICE IN TRIPLICATE +PACKING LIST INTRIPLICATE + CERTIFICATE OF ORIGIN GSPCHINA FORM A, ISSUED BY THE CHAMBER OF COMMERCE OR OTHER AUTHORITY DULY ENTITLED FOR THIS PURPOSE. +2/3 SET OF CLEAN ON BOARD OCEAN BILLS OF LADING CONSIGNED TO ORDER OF SHIPPER. AND BLANK ENDORSED AND MARKED "FREIGHT PREPAID" AND NOTIFY APPLICANT. + FULL SET OF NEGOTIABLE INSURANCE POLICY OR CERTIFICATE BLANK ENDORSED FOR 110 PCT OF INVOICE VALUE COVERING ALL RISKS AND WAR RISK.
ADDITIONAL CONDITIONS	47A: + A DISCREPANCY FEE OF USD50.00 WILL BE DEDUCTED FROM PROCEEDS ON EACH SET OF DISCREPANT DOCUMENTS PRESENTED. + THE REQUIRED DOCUMENTS MUST BE SENT TO CATHAY BANK, 777 NORTH BROADWAY, LOS ANGELES, CALIFORNIA 90012, USA ATTN. INTERNATIONAL DEPT. IN ONE LOT BY EXPRESS AIRMAIL.
CHARGES	71B: +ALL BANKING CHARGES OUTSIDE OF OUR COUNTER ARE FOR ACCOUNT OF THE BENEFICIARY.
PERIOD FOR PRESENTATIONS	48: + DOCUMENTS MUST BE PRESENTED TO PAY/NEGO. BANK WITHIN 15 DAYS AFTER DATE OF SHIPMENT BUT WITHIN VALIDITY OF THE L/C.
CONFIRMATION INSTRUCTION	49: WITHOUT
ADVICE THROUGH BANK	57D: YOUR PINGDU SUB-BRANCH 98 ZHENG YANGROAD SHANGHAI CHINA
SENDER TO RECEIVER INFO	72: THIS CREDIT IS SUBJECT TO THE UNI-

FORM CUSTOMS AND QRACTICE FOR DOCUMENTARY CREDIT, 2007 REVISION, ICC PUBLICATION NO. 600

TRAILER　　MAC A 758689 CHK：39D0ADB5BC9A

(二)其他参考资料

(1) INVOICE NO.：XH056671

(2) INVOICE DATE：FEB. 1,2009

(2) S/C NO. HX090264

(3) PACKING

　　G. W.：20.5KGS/CTN

　　N. W.：20KGS/CTM

　　MEANS：0.2CBM/CN

　　PACKED IN 250 CARTONS OF 10 PCS EACH

　　PACKED IN TWO 20'CONTAINER（集装箱号：TEXU2263999；TEXU2264000）

(4) H. S. CODE：5802.3090

(5) VESSEL：NANGXING V. 086

(6) B/L NO.：COCS0511861

(7) B/L DATE：FEB. 26,2009

(8) POLICY NO. SH058812

(9) REFERENCE NO.：20090819

(10) FREIGHT FEE：USD1 100.00

(11) INSURANCE FEE：USD1 000.00

(12) 注册号：7895478966

(13) 证书号：580511478

(14) 报检单编号：896541231

(15) 报检单位登记号：1254789479

(16) 生产单位注册号：12345Q

(17) 投保单编号：TB0562311

(18) 金发编号：JF0387124

(19) 人民币账号：RMB061222

(20) 外币账号：wb68432144

(21) 海关编号：78968664423

(22) 境内货源地：上海

(23) 生产厂家：上海毛巾厂

(24) 上海进出口贸易公司海关注册号：0387124666

二、根据上述信用证、其他补充资料，制作下列有关单据

1. 商业发票

上海进出口贸易公司
SHANGHAI IMPORT & EXPORT CORPORATION
PINGDU BRANCH
INVOICE

TO：　　　　　　　　　　　　　　　　　　　　Invoice No.：_____
　　　　　　　　　　　　　　　　　　　　　　　Date：_____
　　　　　　　　　　　　　　　　　　　　　　　S/C No.：_____

From		To		
L/C No.	Issued by			
Marks & Numbers	Description of Goods	Quantities	Unit Price	Amount

TOTAL AMOUNT：

QINGDAO IMPORT & EXPORT CORPORATION
PINGDU BRANCH
_____

2. 装箱单

上海进出口贸易公司
SHANGHAI IMPORT & EXPORT CORPORATION
PINGDU BRANCH

PACKING LIST

　　　　　　　　　　　　　　　　　　　　　　　INV NO.：_____
　　　　　　　　　　　　　　　　　　　　　　　DATE：_____
　　　　　　　　　　　　　　　　　　　　　　　S/C NO.：_____

TO：　　　　　　　　　　　　　　　　　　　　　MARKS & NOS.

DESCRIPTION OF GOODS & PACKING	QTY (PCS)	CTNS	WEIGHT (KGS)		MEAS (CBM)
			G. W	N. W	
TOTAL					

SHANGHAI IMPORT & EXPORT CORPORATION
PINGDU BRANCH
_____

3. 普惠制产地证明书申请书和普惠制产地证书

(1) 普惠制产地证明书申请书。

普惠制产地证明申请书

申请单位盖章(加盖公章): 　　　　　　　　　证书号:_____

　　　　　　　　　　　　　　　　　　　　　　注册号:_____

申请人郑重声明:

　　本人是被正式授权代表出口单位办理和签署本申请书的。

　　本申请书及普惠制产地证格式 A 所列内容正确无误,如发现弄虚作假,冒充格式 A 所列货物,擅改证书,自愿接受签证机关的处罚并负法律责任。现将有关情况申报如下:

生产单位		生产单位联系人电话	
商品名称 (中英文)		H.S.税目号 (以六位数码计)	
商品 FOB 总值(以美元计)		发票号	
最终销售国		证书种类"√"	加急证书　　　普通证书
货物拟出运日期			

贸易方式和企业性质(请在适用处画"√")						
一般贸易 C	来进料加工 L	补偿贸易 B	中外合资 H	中外合作 Z	外商独资 D	零售 Y	展卖 M

包装数量或毛重或其他数量

原产地标准:

　　本项商品系在中国生产,完全符合该给惠国给惠方案规定,其原产地情况符合以下第____
　　(1)"P"(完全国产,未使用任何进口原材料);
　　(2)"W"其 H.S.税目号为_____(含进口成份);
　　(3)"F"(对加拿大出口产品,其进口成份不超过产品出厂价值的40%)。

本批产品系:

　　1.直接运输从_____到_____。
　　2.转口运输从_____中转国(地区)_____到_____。

申请人说明: 　　　　　　　　　　　　领证人(签名)
　　　　　　　　　　　　　　　　　　电话:
　　　　　　　　　　　　　　　　　　日期:　　年　　月　　日

　　现提交中国出口商业发票副本一份,普惠制产地证明书格式 A(FORM A)一正二副,以及其他附件(　)份,请予审核签证。

　　注:凡含有进口成份的商品,必须接受要求提交《含进口成份受惠商品成本明细单》。

商检局联系记录

(2)普惠制产地证书。

1. Goods Consigned from (Exporter's full name, address and country)	Reference No.:
	GENERALIZED SYSTEM OF PREFERENCES CERTIFICATE OF ORIGIN (Combined declaration and certificate) **FORM A** Issued in _____ (Country) See Notes. Overleaf
2. Goods Consigned to (Consignee's full name, address and country)	
3. Means of Transport and Route (as far as known)	4. For Certifying Authority Use Only

5. Item Number	6. Marks and Numbers of Packages	7. Number and Kind of Pkgs; Description of Goods	8. Origin Criterion (see notes overleaf)	9. Gross Weight or other Quantity	10. Number and Date of Invoice

11. Certification It is hereby certified that the declaration by the exporter is correct. ———————————————— Place and date, signature and stamp of certifying authority	12. Declaration by the Exporter The undersigned hereby declares that the above details and statements are correct, that all the goods were produced in _____ (country) and that they comply with the origin requirements specified for those goods in the generalized system of preferences for goods exported to _____ _____ (importing country) ———————————————— Place and date, signature and stamp of certifying authority

4. 出境货物报检单

中华人民共和国出入境检验检疫
出境货物报检单

报检单位(加盖公章)   *编 号：

报检单位登记号： 联系人： 电话： 报检日期： 年 月 日

发货人	（中文）				
	（外文）				
收货人	（中文）				
	（外文）				

货物名称（中/外文）	H.S.编码	产地	数/重量	货物总值	包装种类及数量

运输工具名称号码		贸易方式		货物存放地点	
合同号		信用证号		用途	
发货日期		输往国家（地区）		许可证/审批号	
启运地		到达口岸		生产单位注册号	
集装箱规格、数量及号码					

合同、信用证订立的检验检疫条款或特殊要求	标记及号码	随附单据(划"√"或补填)	
		□合同 □信用证 □发票 □换证凭单 □装箱单 □厂检单	包装性能结果单 □许可/审批文件 □ □ □

需要证单名称(划"√"或补填)		检验检疫费
□品质证书 正 副 □重量证书 正 副 □数量证书 正 副 □兽医卫生证书 正 副 □健康证书 正 副 □卫生证书 正 副 □动物卫生证书 正 副	□植物检疫证书 正 副 □熏蒸/消毒证书 正 副 □出境货物换证凭单	总金额（人民币元） 计费人 （签署） 收费人 （签署）

报检人郑重声明: 1.本人被授权报检。 2.上列填写内容正确属实,货物无伪造或冒用他人的厂名、标志、认证标志,并承担货物质量责任。 签名:_____	领取证单	
	日 期	
	签 名	

注:有"＊"号栏由出入境检验检疫机关填写　　◆国家出入境检验检疫局制

5. 投保单和保险单

(1)投保单。

中 国 人 民 保 险 公 司　青 岛 分 公 司

出口运输险投保单

编号:_____

兹将我处出口货物依照信用证规定拟向你处投保国外运输险计开:

被保险人(中文) （英文）			
标记及发票号码	件数	货物名称	保险金额
运输工具及转载工具		约 于　年　月　日启运	赔款偿付地点
运输路程	自____经____到____		转载地点
投保险别: 投保单位签章 年　月　日			

(2)保险单。

中国人民保险公司
THE PEOPLE'S INSURANCE COMPANY OF CHINA

总公司设于北京	一九四九年创立
Head Office: BEIJING	Established in 1949
保 险 单	保险单号次
INSURANCE POLICY	POLICY No.

中 国 人 民 保 险 公 司（以 下 简 称 本 公 司）
This Policy of Insurance witnesses that The People's Insurance Company of China (Herein after called 根据
"the Company"), at the request of ————————————————————————————
（以下简称被保险人）的 要 求，由 被 保 险 人 向 本 公 司 缴 付 约 定
(herein after called "the Insured") and in consideration of the agreed premium paid to the company by the
的 保 险 费，按 照 本 保 险 单 承 保 险 别 和 背 面 所 载 条 款 与 下 列
Insured, undertakes to insure the undermentioned goods in transportation subject to the conditions of this policy
条 款 承 保 下 述 货 物 运 输 保 险，特 立 本 保 险 单。
as per the clause printed overleaf and other special clauses attached hereon.

标　记 Marks & Numbers	包装及数量 Quantity	保险货物项目 Description of Goods	保险金额 Amount Insured

总保险金额：
Total Amount Insured: ————————————————————————————

保　费	费　率	装载运输工具
Premium: as arranged	Rate　as arranged	Per conveyance S.S. ———　———
开行日期	自	至
Slg. on or abt. _____	From _____	to _____

承保险别
Conditions: ————————————————————————————
所保货物，如遇出险，本公司凭本保险单及其他有关证件给付赔款。
Claims, if any, payable on surrender of this Policy together with other relevant documents.
所保货物，如发生本保险单项下负责赔偿的损失或事故，
In the event of accident whereby loss or damage may result in a claim under this Policy immediate notice
应立即通知本公司下述代理人查勘。
applying For survey must be given to the Company's Agent as mentioned hereunder:
赔款偿付地点
Claim payable at _____

日期
Date————————————————
地址：中国上海中山东一路23号。
Address: 23Zhongshan Dong Yi Lu Shanghai, China.
Cables: 42001Shanghai. ————————————
Telex: 33128 PICCS CN

中国人民保险公司上海分公司
THE PEOPLE'S INSURANCE CO. OF CHINA
SHANGHAI BRANCH

General Manager

6.海运货物委托书和海运提单
(1)海运货物委托书。

海 运 货 运 委 托 书

经营单位（托运人）				编号	
提单B/L项目要求	发货人 Shipper：				
	收货人 Consignee：				
	通知人 Notify Party：				
海运费（ ） Sea Freight	预付（ ）或到付（ ） Prepaid or Collect		提单份数	提单寄送地址	
启运港		目的港		可否转船	可否分批
集装箱预配数				装运期限	有效期限
标记唛码	包装件数	中英文货号 Description of Goods	毛重（公斤）	尺码（立方米）	成交条件（总价）
内装箱(CFS)地址			特种货物冷藏货危险品	重件：每件重量	
				大件（长×宽×高）	
门对门装箱地址			特种集装箱：（ ）		
			货物备妥日期	年 月 日	
外币结算账号			货物进栈：自送（ ）或派送（ ）		
声明事项			人民币结算账号		
			托运人签章		
			电话		
			传真		
			联系人		
			地址		
			制单日期		

(2)海运提单。

Shipper		B/L No.
Consignee or order		中国对外贸易运输总公司 上海 SHANGHAI 联 运 提 单 COMBINED TRANSPORT BILL OF LADING
Notify address		RECEIVER the foods in apparent good order and condition as specified below unless otherwise stated herein. THE Carrier, in accordance with the provisions contained in this document, (1) undertakes to perform or to procure the performance of the entire transport from the place at which the goods are taken in charge to the place designated for delivery in this document, and (2) assumes liability as prescribed in this document for such transport one of the bills of lading must be surrendered duty indorsed in exchange for the goods or delivery order.
Pre-carriage by	Place of receipt	
Ocean vessel	Port of loading	
Port of discharge	Place of delivery	Freight payable at	Number of original Bs/L
Container seal No. or marks and numbers.	Number and kind of packages Description of goods	Gross weight(kgs.)	Measurement(m^3)
REGARDING TRANSHIPMENT INFORMATION PLEASE CONTACT		IN WITNESS whereof the number of original bills of lading stated above have been signed, one of which being accomplished, the other(s) to be void.
Freight and charges		Place and date of issue
Freight payable at		
		Signed for or on behalf of the carrier

7. 出口货物报关单

中华人民共和国海关出口货物报关单

预录入编号：　　　　　　　　　　　　海关编号：

出口口岸		备案号		出口日期		申报日期	
经营单位		运输方式		运输工具名称		提运单号	
发货单位		贸易方式		征免性质		结汇方式	
许可证号		运抵国（地区）		指运港		境内货源地	
批准文号		成交方式		运费		保费	杂费
合同协议号		件数		包装种类		毛重（公斤）	净重（公斤）
集装箱号		随附单据				生产厂家	
标记唛码及备注							

项号	商品编号	商品名称、规格号	数量及单位	最终目的国（地区）	单价	总价	币制	征免

税费征收情况			
录入员 录入单位	兹声明以上申报无讹并承担法律责任	海关审单批注及放行日期（签章）	
		审单　　　　审价	
报关员 单位地址 邮编　　电话	申报单位（签章） 填制日期	征税　　　　统计	
		查验　　　　放行	

8. 装运通知

SHANGHAIIMPORT & EXPORT CORPORATION

SHIPPING ADVICE

                   INV No：_____
                   S/C No.：_____
                   L/C No.：_____

TO MESSRS：

WE HEREBY INFORM YOU THAT THE GOODS UNDER THE ABOVE MENTIONED CREDIT HAVE BEEN SHIPPED. THE DETAILS OF THE SHIPMENT ARE AS FOLLOWS：

COMMODITY：_____
NUMBER OF CTNS：_____
TOTA G. W.：_____
OCEAN VESSEL：_____
DATE OF DEPARTURE：_____
B/L NO.：_____
PORT OF LOADING：_____
DESTINATION：_____
SHIPPING MARKS

9. 汇票

凭
Drawn under _____
号码   汇票金额   上海   20
No. _____ Exchange for _____ SHANGHAI _____, 20 ___
见票_____日后（本汇票之正本未付）付交   分行
At _____ sight of this FIRST of Exchange (Second of Exchange being Unpaid) Pay to the order of _____
金额
the sum of

款已收讫
Value received
此致：
 To _____
   _____

参考文献

[1] 李元旭,吴国新.国际贸易单证实务[M].北京:清华大学出版社,2008.

[2] 黄飞雪,李志洁.UCP600与ISBP681述评及案例[M].厦门:厦门大学出版社,2009.

[3] 中国国际贸易学会商务专业培训考试办公室.外贸业务理论与实务[M].北京:中国商务出版社,2007

[4] 舒兵.国际商务单证教程[M].北京:化学工业出版社,2007.

[5] 全国国际商务单证专业培训考试办公室.国际商务单证理论与实务[M].北京:中国商务出版社,2010.

[6] 俞涔,朱春兰.外贸单证实务[M].杭州:浙江大学出版社,2004.

[7] 广银芳.外贸单证制作实务[M].北京:清华大学出版社,2009.

[8] 王莉等.进出口业务单证操作手册[M].广州:广东经济出版社,2005.

[10] 全国国际商务单证专业培训考试办公室.国际商务单证专业培训及复习指南[M].北京:中国商务出版社,2009.

[11] 全国国际商务单证专业培训考试办公室.国际商务单证基础理论知识[M].北京:中国商务出版社,2009.

[12] 海关总署报关员资格考试教材编写委员会.2010年版报关员资格全国统一考试教材[M].北京:中国海关出版社,2007.

[13] 姚大伟.国际贸易单证实务[M].北京:中国商务出版社,2007.

[14] 杨立平.进出口单证实务[M].北京:中国对外经济贸易出版社,2001.

[15] 中国国际货运代理协会.国际货运代理基础知识[M].北京:中国对外经济贸易出版社,2009.

[16] 张建华.国际贸易实务模拟[M].北京:高等教育出版社,2009.

[17] 姚大伟.国际贸易单证实务[M].北京:中国商贸出版社,2009.

[18] 海关总署报关员资格考试教材编委会.报关员资格全国统一考试指定教材[M].北京:中国海关出版社,2010年.

[19] 海关总署监管司.中国海关通关指南[M].北京:中国海关出版社,2005.

[20] 章安.外贸单证操作[M].北京:高等教育出版社,2008.

[21] 汪圣佑.国际商务单证[M].北京:北京交通大学出版社,2010.

[22] 马朝阳,丛凤英.外贸单证实务[M].北京:科学出版社,2007.

图书在版编目(CIP)数据

国际贸易单证制作/陈卫华,王红梅主编.—西安:
西安交通大学出版社,2011.8(2020.1重印)
ISBN 978-7-5605-3945-4

Ⅰ.①国… Ⅱ.①陈… ②王… Ⅲ.①国际贸易-原始凭证
Ⅳ.①F740.44

中国版本图书馆 CIP 数据核字(2011)第 101058 号

书　　名	国际贸易单证制作
主　　编	陈卫华　　王红梅
责任编辑	赵怀瀛
出版发行	西安交通大学出版社
	(西安市兴庆南路1号　邮政编码 710048)
网　　址	http://www.xjtupress.com
电　　话	(029)82668357　82667874(发行中心)
	(029)82668315(总编办)
传　　真	(029)82668280
印　　刷	西安日报社印务中心
开　　本	787mm×1092mm　1/16　印张 14.375　字数 348 千字
版次印次	2011 年 8 月第 1 版　　2020 年 1 月第 5 次印刷
书　　号	ISBN 978-7-5605-3945-4
定　　价	36.80 元

读者购书、书店添货,如发现印装质量问题,请与本社发行中心联系、调换。
订购热线:(029)82665248　(029)82665249
投稿热线:(029)82668133
读者信箱:xj_rwjg@126.com

版权所有　侵权必究